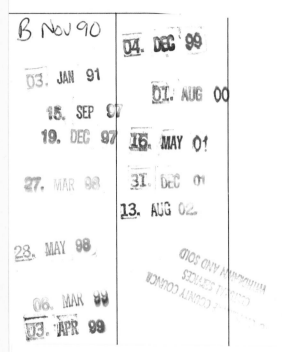

BAREKNUCKLES

A Social History of Prize-Fighting

6 (

BAREKNUCKLES

A Social History of Prize-Fighting

Dennis Brailsford

Lutterworth Press
Cambridge

Lutterworth Press
PO Box 60
Cambridge
CB1 2NT

British Library Cataloguing in Publication Data
Brailsford, Dennis, 1925-
    Bareknuckles: A social history of prize-fighting.
    1. England. Prizefighting, 1720-1910
    I. Title
    796.8'3'0942

ISBN 0-7188-2676-0

First published in 1988 by Lutterworth Press

Printed in the United Kingdom

To the memory of

Philip Juchau *Moorfields 1765*

Ben Curtis *Molesey Hurst 1821*

John Wilson *Millbank 1821*

Frederick Winkworth *Hampstead 1829*

Sandy M'Kay *No Man's Land 1833*

'Brighton Bill' *Royston 1838*

John Foster *Banwell Marsh 1843*

Rory Gill *Formby, Lancs 1853*

Thomas Callis *Long Reach 1872*

Alex Agar *Sydney 1884*

and the many other pugilists who met their deaths in the prize ring

Contents

Plates

Maps

Foreword

The History of Prize Fighting

As leisure in general and sport in particular became matters of sustained social and political interest, the first individual sports to win serious attention were inevitably those which still absorb us today. They were taken up virtually in rank order of their present acceptability, cricket and horse-racing leading the way, and the several codes of football following close at their heels. Understandably, the fighting sports of the eighteenth- and nineteenth-centuries did not immediately offer themselves as sources for enlightenment to the twentieth. The practices of the bull ring, the cock pit, the dog pit, and the prize-ring were roundly enough condemned by many in their own day as callous and degrading, and any gratuitous raking over the ashes of their past cruelties could apparently claim little merit. The passions aroused and fed by these spectacles were none the less real and widespread at the time. Their importance as social phenomena is unquestionable. There can be no understanding of the leisure life of the age, let alone a whole gamut of its attitudes towards, for instance, human and animal life, the law, social order, health and fitness, peace and war, without taking its darker sporting pleasures into account. Even within the narrow field of sports history, neglect of the fighting sports has left gaps in our appreciation of the common competitive core which runs through the whole modern sporting tradition. County cricket is the less comprehensible without an awareness of county cock-fighting, which had a long-established pattern of three-day matches, played out between about 11 a.m. and 6.30 p.m. The *Articles of Agreement* governing important cricket matches are given a new dimension if they are compared with similar compacts for fist-fights or dog-fights, while it was not by chance that the *Rules for Matching and Fighting of Cocks* appeared regularly in the *Racing Calendar*. When boxing itself at last found a measure of respectability through the Queensberry Rules, it looked back to the time-honoured practice of the cock-pit for its count of ten for a knock-out.

No youngster brought up in pre-Victorian England, whatever his social class or geographical region, could avoid contact with the fighting sports. In the common experience they left the still maturing modern spectator sports far behind. Certainly large crowds could turn out for race meetings, culminating in the 100,000 or more who flocked to Epsom Downs on Derby Day, but even if he were prepared to walk twenty miles for his sport - and he might well be - the pre-Victorian worker would be lucky to find himself within reach of more than four or five days' racing a year. His football would either be a half organised scramble after a makeshift missile, or possibly one of the great annual swarming communal mauls which still managed to survive, often at Shrovetide. His chance of either playing or watching any organised cricket would be slim, outside the game's south eastern heartland, and large crowds only gathered at a few centres such as Lord's, Nottingham, Sheffield and (briefly, towards the end of the eighteenth century) Hambledon. By contrast, he would find cock-fighting everywhere, dog-fighting commonplace, bull-baiting widespread before the 1820s, and bareknuckle fighting a part of his growing up, as well as a frequent public event of greater or less formality. Only in the distant reaches of Devon and Cornwall, Cumberland and Westmoreland, did wrestling offer serious rivalry, and only in parts of Lancashire did the rough and ready fighting manners of the pre-prize ring days survive with any force. The conventions of organised prize-fighting filtered down into street fighting, and here - where it was more a matter of living than playing - he stood a more than even chance of direct involvement. He might aspire, though more rarely with each generation, to breeding and training his own gamecock, and taking it along to the local tavern for the regular shake-bag matches, open to all and sundry. The racing pigeon and the canary were still several decades away from supplanting the fighting cock in the working man's affections.

The arguments for searching enquiry into any fighting sport have much in common with those for enquiry into any other sport. The fighting sports offer a perspective on the lives of our predecessors that may at first appear either irrelevant or repugnant, or both, but it is one which reveals more about the lives of more people than any deriving from the up and coming spectator sports. If, as this present survey suggests, the fighting sports constituted a cultural dead end, a narrowing and fading pathway to nowhere, especially when contrasted with horse-racing, cricket, and, eventually, football, they were also, in their own day, a focus for major issues of social policy, public and private morality, and law and order. They embodied, too, motives and emotions which our own age does well to remember were once acknowledged as firmly within the ambit of sport. Is there perhaps a stream here that has not wholly dissipated itself into the dry sands of time, but found other and less candid sporting expression?

Of all the fighting sports, pugilism may appear the least alien, at least distantly recognisable through its modern derivative of boxing. It remained, though, a bruising, bloody and sometimes murderous business, riddled with fraud and deception. A historian cannot stand aside from today's world, today's morality, and the story of fist-fighting would hardly be worth resurrecting but for the many wider issues which it raises, and the light that these may throw on the broad development of organised sport, on the historical uses of leisure, and the forces making for social and ethical change. The history of pugilism is, for example, about the establishment and application of agreed sporting rules, about match-making and gambling, about training and technique, about patronage, management and promotion, about sporting economics, about spectators and critics. As the first sport of modern times to match contestants from different racial and religious groups, its history is also about nationalism and prejudice. As an illegal sport, it has much to suggest on policing and law enforcement, and as a sport increasingly rejected by growing sections of contemporary society, it has much to say about how sports can, or cannot, adapt themselves to changing social expectations.

These and others like them are the threads that have to be untangled. This might invite the thematic approach successfully adopted by John Ford in his pioneering study, *Prizefighting: The Age of Regency Boximania* (Newton Abbot, 1971), but what was appropriate for thirty years of comparative stability will not serve for a century and a half of change. Time and mutation become important elements in the account, and the most promising prospect lies in a central narrative, picking up from it, at each stage of the sport's history, some dominant theme or significant individual pugilist for particular attention. If this compromise can sustain, over the longer period, the level of critical analysis undertaken by Ford (and, from a different standpoint, by J.C. Reid in *Bucks and Bruisers: Pierce Egan and Regency England* (London, 1971), it will have served its purpose. Advances in social history, and in the study of sport and leisure, have inevitably invited some changes in stress from theirs - formal organisations tend to lose ground to underlying changes in attitude, while cataclysm theories of sudden transformation suffer some levelling out in the face of fuller awareness of contemporary events. Thus, the Pugilistic Club seems less influential than it did, and Gentleman John Jackson's departure from the management of the Prize Ring is now shown to have been gradual, and only one aspect of the ten-year long decline and transmutation of Regency pugilism.

Such new emphases have already marked several rewarding studies of the American Ring, most notably, Elliott Gorn's *The Manly Art: Bareknuckle Prize Fighting in America* (Ithaca, 1986). They have enlarged and deepened the vision of American pugilism, and set the sport comprehensively within a wider conceptual framework. British prize-fighting, though, ranged over twice the duration of the sport across the Atlantic, where, as Gorn allows, it had no deep roots, and this alone rules out a similar discursive approach in a comparatively brief account of a century and a half of organised sporting activity. The British prize ring is, in any event, barely ready for such confident analysis. As the bibliographical appendix makes clear, much of the extensive available evidence on *all* British popular sports through the nineteenth century is still undigested. This applies forcibly to post-Regency prize-fighting, where it would be premature to reach too far beyond establishing significance and order in hitherto unassimilated material. Excursions into sociological hypotheses on modernity in sport would be as out of place as discussions of expansive issues of working class culture. Preference is given to empirical and provisional notions of what constitutes modern sport, rather than to all-embracing models which can only leave pugilism where it has always obviously belonged, struggling in the broad no man's land between the primitive and the contemporary. Nor does this account see in pugilism the rise of any new popular culture in Victorian Britain. The ring appears, throughout most of its history, as yoked to ageing and dying social forces, and never, so long as it remained an unlimited bareknuckle sport, part of any new birth. Similarly, glove boxing, for all its possible fascinations, appears as a new phenomenon, structurally and socially apart from its fist-fighting ancestry, and with no role in this survey.

So this history seeks to stay close to the brave and bloody realities of the ring itself. It is plain tale from one who, so far as British pugilism is concerned, can do no better than echo the words of a far more astute historian of half a century ago - H.A.L. Fisher, who prefaced his *History of Europe* (London, 1936) with the comment that 'Men wiser and more learned than I have discerned in history a plot, a rhythm, a predetermined pattern. These harmonies are concealed from me.'

The most accessible social historians, from G. M. Trevelyan onwards, have been aware that their subject is *people*, that the serious consideration of the everyday human past does not have to be desiccated and sterilised by obtrusive theory. Notions of social control, concepts of hegemony, and the polemics of class conflict, may provide useful aids to definition and discrimination, so long as they arise justifiably from historical evidence. This caution is particularly applicable to sports history, where twenty five years of eminently valuable scholarship still leaves much of the evidence relatively unsystematised, and too easily moulded into pre-determined shape. Certainly, to derive some wider understanding from any aspect of leisure life, to generalise, to conceptualise, to probe critically beneath the surface, to question conventional categorisations - these must be prime aims of any sports history. We must begin, though, firmly on the boards and the turf of the prize-ring, all the more so because the sport in its original homeland has been subject to limited historical attention. It is about *us*, as we were a century or more ago, but it can only be about us if we can bring the ring briefly back to life, if we can recreate a sense of its noise, its bustle, tensions, excitements and dangers, its dust and mud, its frantic scrambles from place to place, the suffocating crush of its crowds, the lashing threat of the beaters' whips, the pick-pockets, sharpers, the peers and the bully-boys. We have to breathe again the all-pervading smells of sweat, embrocation and brandy, the smoke of cigars and pipes, the horse droppings, the mown hay and pollen of the summer fields, the sharp tang of December hail and snow, the stale breath of man and beast, and the lurking awareness of blood and death. To know, to sense, to feel, is not to forgive. It is to realise what we were, and to make us always more wary of what we might become.

Acknowledgements

This book began when Allen Guttman of Amherst College introduced me to William Rose of the Community Film Unit, Cambridge, Massachusetts, to help with historical aspects of his documentary *The Combat Sport: Boxing Today and Yesterday*. The experience confirmed what all students of eighteenth- and nineteenth-century sport were already aware of, namely the inadequacy of existing historical enquiry into prize-fighting.

That deficiency has already been considerably remedied in North America by Elliott Gorn and others, while in Britain papers by Peter Radford of the University of Glasgow have now indicated several helpful lines of thought. Nerida Clarke of the Australian Institute of Sport has given valuable bibliographical information, and I am grateful also for help from Brian Stoddart of the Canberra College of Advanced Education.

My long-standing debts, however, are to the University of Birmingham - to Charles Jenkins of the Department of Sports Sciences and Physical Education for his unfailing encouragement over the many years of our friendship, and to the University Library staff, particularly Michelle Shoebridge of the Sports Documentation Centre, and the photographic section for help with illustrations.

In its production, the book owes much to my wife for proof reading, research assistance, and boundless patience, to Sheena Pearce for typing the manuscript, and to David Game for being an understanding and helpful editor. But with all this support, any shortcomings the book may reveal are all my own.

Preston
Weymouth
Dorset

May 1988

Note : To avoid repetition, references have been kept to a minimum. The sources used are indicated in the bibliography and in the notes at the end of the book.

1. Jack Broughton (from the painting by Frank Hayman, R.A.)

1

Jack Broughton's Rules

On any bright London morning in the late 1780s, the crowd at the Walworth Road market was more than likely to include an elderly gentleman, notable at first glance only for the old-fashioned cut of his clothes. As he moved among the curio stalls, examining here a Roman coin, there a heavy Bible or an Elizabethan miniature, his slow walk was still certain and deliberate, his appreciation of articles that caught his eye still quick and positive. This was no broken old man, nor a destitute one either. His tricorn hat and his full coat might be fifty years behind the times and faded with the years, but they showed their quality, and if some trinket took his fancy there was a well-filled purse in his large hand. Only the thickened fingers and the swollen knuckles looked out of place as he handed over his sovereign or two in exchange for some delicate piece of glassware.

In the nearby tavern he stayed only a little while and drank sparingly. The talk there might be about Mr Warren Hastings's trial or that new-fangled constitution those rebellious American colonists had just come up with. It was more likely, though, to be about old John Wilkes turning up at the Westminster cockpit, creaking with rheumatism and his arm in a sling; about the new Equestrian Emporium at Whitechapel; about Captain O'Kelly's removal of his horses, including the famous Eclipse, from Epsom; and about the new big sweepstake called the St Leger to be run at Doncaster. The old man's attention became keener when the talk turned to pugilism and the new names that were on everybody's lips, Richard Humphries and Daniel Mendoza. He remained silent, though. His own departure from the ring many years ago could still rankle if he let his mind dwell on the injustice of it. Yet the aged Mr Broughton of today was still the Jack Broughton whose crown these youngsters were challenging for, and it was his rules they would be fighting under. His fighting days were long past. His old adversaries were all gone - George Stevenson, the coachman; Jack James; George Taylor, his rival in both fisticuffs and business; and even Jack Slack who took the championship from him and had outlived the others, quietly prospering in his butcher's shop in Covent Garden until ten or so years back. They said that his daughter, Mrs Belcher, had a son who looked like developing into a lively lad.

Mr Broughton finished off the little ale that was left in his tankard. It was nearly time for him also to be going.

And so - quietly, unobtrusively - Jack Broughton slipped from the scene, with no one to pronounce the obituary he deserved as the begetter of one of the first modern sports. Indeed, it was hardly a claim which he would have made himself. Pugilism had slumped since his own active days and he just failed to see its rebirth.

Sophisticated modern sports are the work of many hands and minds. Personalised myths such as Abner Doubleday's invention of baseball and William Webb Ellis's creation of Rugby football collapse sooner or later. Perhaps Broughton was no lone founding father, but no one sport owed more for its beginnings to one man than boxing owed to him.

Three recognisably modern sports were firmly established in Britain before the eighteenth century was out: horse-racing, cricket and pugilism. What made them modern was a whole complex of features, shared unevenly between the three but with each having enough of the elements there to distinguish them quite sharply from the old traditional folk play. Modern sport must first of all have rules and the means of arbitration to determine whether the rules have been broken. It must have a more-or-less regular programe of events and be able to match the best competitors against one another. It has specialised venues for play and is essentially commercial, paying the performers, charging people to watch and giving the chance of profits to promoters and backers. It seeks publicity before its events and creates a thirst for accounts of play immediately afterwards. In short, a modern sport develops both an economic and literary life of its own, and its transactions are important to significant sections of the community.

Individual sports acquire these characteristics at different rates. In some, not all of them emerge. British golf still has no formal national ruling body even though the Royal and Ancient Golf Club does carry out many of such a body's functions. Most of the modern features were discernible, though, in horse-racing, cricket and pugilism by the second half of the eighteenth century. Racing and cricket have had a continuous history since, finding just enough resilience to adapt themselves later to the demands of Victorian morality. The changing social and ethical expectations that the first two sports were gradually able to meet did in the end defeat bareknuckle prize-fighting.

The pugs had slipped too far away from the new respectability ever to be able to scramble back into its scheme of things. Only through rebirth, in a totally new form, could boxing emerge as a more-or-less acceptable twentieth-century sport. Although it could not change its nature enough to meet the new expectations for order, honesty and decorum, pugilism was far from being a static sport over the 150 years of its history, before its re-creation in a totally new form. Most of its aspects changed over the years - its organisation, managers and patrons; its locations and geographical distribution; its commercial base; and the styles of fighting, the rules and the fighters themselves. The central and unchanging feature of the sport, though, was that two human beings - usually, but not invariably, male - faced up to each other with bare fists, exchanging blows and throws until one of them could take punishment no longer. It began when pugilism became distinguishable from cudgel-fighting and wrestling, and when the combatants fought in a stand-up posture - as against the Lancashire style of fighting or American gouging contests, where the real fighting only began when the two men had pulled each other to the ground. It ended when the boxers put on padded gloves and fought time-limited bouts which did not depend on a knock-out for a result.

Jack Broughton's long life saw pugilism's emergence out of the welter of other combat sports with which it was associated and its development from a fairground knock-about into an organised affair of national interest, followed by prince and peer, ploughman and potboy alike. There had been earlier glimmerings of what was to come. A well-known report in the *Protestant Mercury* of 1681 told of a prize-fight between the Duke of Albemarle's footman and 'a butler'; the latter proved to be the hero of the day and, in spite of his anonymity, was described as 'the best in that exercise in England'. The implication that there was already a national sport in which country-wide reputations could be made has little other evidence to support it. More typical of the times was the 'fray' at Westminster Stairs which Pepys watched with enthusiasm on a Sunday morning in August 1660.[1] He found that the fight 'made good sport'. The combatants were a Dutchman and, significantly, a waterman - the first trade that Jack Broughton followed was that of waterman.

It was a tough life, that of a Thames waterman; it was hard on the muscles to pull the heavy oars of the wherries upstream, against the tide or from one bank to the other. The Thames was London's main highway, constantly busy with the comings and goings of boat-loads of passengers or cargo ranging from the coal barges at the Savoy quay to the fast cutters by the hundred which the city apprentices took to at weekends. For the professional boatmen it was a fiercely competitive business, with much jostling for the most lucrative fares. There were attempts to regulate the traffic, particularly over Sunday hiring, which persisted in spite of its illegality. When Jack Broughton began his working life, the Sunday trade was governed by a novel exercise in industrial insurance. Under the 1698 River Thames Act, forty watermen were allowed to operate on the Sabbath, but for a fixed wage only. All receipts above that were paid into a fund for sick or injured fellow workers and for the relief of their widows and children.

Competition on the river was not always, or not solely, a business matter. Young watermen in particular were always racing each other, whether as an incidental part of the day's work or for wagers and prizes. It was competition that the keen and powerful young Broughton took to with zest. He was lucky in his timing. He began work just as the Dublin-born actor, Thomas Doggett, founded his annual race to discover the fastest man on the river. By its fourth year, 1720 (the last race which Doggett himself lived to see), it was already attracting many entrants and drawing large crowds to the riverside on its appointed date of 1 August. The winner's uniform, Doggett's Coat and Badge, was resplendent and victory meant public fame. Broughton entered the 1720 race and won.[2] From the obscurity of the waterfront, he now became a well-known London figure, impressive in stature and bearing, and popular because of his easy manner. Given his physique, his poise and mobility, his keen competitiveness and his tough schooling on the river, he gravitated naturally into the other new athletic venture of the day, boxing.

A few months before Jack's victory in Doggett's race, James Figg had opened the first indoor boxing arena on the Oxford Road (now Oxford Street). Hitherto, pugilism had been an occasional entertainment of fairs and a few outdoor 'rings'. The Puritans had clamped down on fairs, as on most other public amusements, but since the Restoration fairs and markets had come into their own again, multiplied and soon established themselves as 'traditional', whether or not they had the history to support the claim. Hogarth's well-known print of Southwark Fair shows a boxing-booth in prime position and while fairs might be transient some of the booths, like this one of Figg's at Southwark, had an air of permanence about them. His advertisements claimed that it was 'fitted up in a most commodious manner for the better reception of gentlemen, etc., etc.'. Another booth at Smithfield was said to have been owned and run by Andrew Johnson, uncle of Samuel, and it certainly is not hard to believe that the pugnacious doctor came from fighting stock. As well as booths, there were actual rings, which were circular, as their name originally indicated, the most notable being that at Hyde Park, laid out in 1720 on the instructions of George I. Hyde Park was to see many minor skirmishes over the next hundred years, though rarely any major ones - it was much too public once the sport was outlawed. Booths and rings were not sharply distinguished. The site at Moorfields was referred to as both. Nor were they confined to London. The region around Bristol, for instance, from the start one of the main cradles of English prize-fighters, had boxing contests as one of the unfailing attractions at its local fairs.

The support of wealthy backers enabled James Figg to set up the first indoor boxing arena. The court of George I - 'that honest blockhead', as Lady Mary Wortley Montagu described him - was not noted for its subtlety or refinement and there were influential men enough to help the infant sport into more convenient settings. Figg's amphitheatre was a hybrid structure, a cross between a large fairground booth and a theatre, similar to Astley's riding theatres in London and Birmingham. It was meant for instruction as well as exhibition, and its prices kept it exclusive. When the young Mancunian, John Byrom, went to see a contest between Figg himself and Sutton, the admission charge was 2s 6d. - virtually a day's wage for most workers and very expensive when compared with the usual 2d. or 3d. to watch a day's cricket. A well-known figure like Broughton, though, was a welcome adornment to the proceedings as he quickly began to pick up the skills of his new profession.

From the start, Jack's interest was in fist-fighting alone and not in the mix of cudgelling and quarterstaff play that went with it in the amphitheatre's early days. Indeed, as far as the teaching side went, Figg's main emphasis was on the backsword and the staff, only a little removed from the familiar provision of the fencing schools. The public contests themselves were as likely to be between swordsmen or quarterstaff specialists as between boxers.[3]

Broughton's own interest and involvement in the amphitheatre's affairs grew much stronger in the 1730s as fist-fighting came to predominate. Individual contests, often with newcomers to the ring, provided more variety and sharper competition than the repetitive bouts between the amphitheatre's familiar retainers. As a fellow water-man, he felt a certain sympathy with the hefty Venetian gondolier who was beaten by the lumbering Bob Whittaker, whose crude speciality was to bore an opponent to the floor and throw his own bulk painfully upon him. It was a short but celebrated encounter. The Venetian's straight right hand to the head caught Whittaker so much by surprise that he was knocked out of the ring by the first blow. As the stage had been raised to 5 ft to give more of the big-spending patrons a better view, this might have been the end of the afternoon's entertainment. However, Whittaker scrambled back, rushed in under his opponent's raised fists and dealt a heavy blow to the solar plexus, flooring the winded Venetian. A few more minutes of mauling at close quarters and Whittaker forced his opponent to quit.

A straight blow could clearly be delivered from a much safer distance than the usual swinging hits, as long as the fighter was also ready to drop his arms to defend his

2 James Figg's business card with fisticuffs still very subsidiary to quarterstaff and swordplay (reproduced in Miles's *Pugilistica*)

body. There was soon to be another lesson for Broughton to note, one in selective punching. Even as Whittaker was enjoying the plaudits of the crowd, Thomas Figg promised them that, if they would return at the same time the next week, he would produce a man fit to take on Whittaker and capable of beating him in ten minutes. He proved as good as his word. His new man was Nathaniel Peartree, reputed less for his strength than for his courage and cunning. Peartree very deliberately aimed all his blows around Whittaker's eyes. He did this to such effect that within six minutes Bob, whose defence was not his strong point, was so cut and swollen that he was blinded into surrender.[4]

By the time that Jack Broughton became a regular exhibition in the amphitheatre, the bouts there - and in at least three other indoor booths - were regular, well advertised and well supported. In addition to growing in style and skill, pugilism was offering the possibility of good cash returns. The takings often amounted to £150, implying audiences of 1200 or so, at 2s 6d. a head. The proprietor kept one-third of this himself, the rest being split between the day's two main fighters, two parts to the winner and one to the loser. Supporting bouts had to rely on money thrown on the stage in appreciation at the end of the fight, but the leading boxers - and Broughton was soon one of them - stood to take home the equivalent of a working craftsman's annual wage for one afternoon's work, and this was irrespective of any side-betting or gratitude from patrons. The new sport flourished, and Broughton joined a coterie of boxers whose public renown was quickly growing. There were the gypsy, 'Prince' Boswell; George Stevenson the coachman; Tom Smallwood; Jack James; Field; John Smith, known as 'Buckhorse', and Tom Pipes and George Gretting, the two leading figures in the amphitheatre in the mid-1730s. Above all, there was young George Taylor, who took over its management in 1734.

Broughton, some ten years older than Taylor, had already beaten him in the ring and George had the sound sense never to seek another encounter, happy to have him as the established star of his hall. Taylor was an able enough boxer, strong, shifty, with a strong wrestling throw. There was some suspicion that he did not like to take too much punishment. He still had sword-play in his repertoire, had an eye to business and seized an early opportunity to take over the amphitheatre soon after Figg's death. Broughton was prepared to work for him as he saw profit for the sport in Taylor's managerial skills and repeated victories were lining his own pocket well enough. Taylor's advertisements were lurid with the promise of combat, mayhem and gore. He used the press to put out the heated challenges and counter-challenges which heralded forthcoming contests and set the style of much in later boxing journalism. William Willis reminded Tom Smallwood that he had already 'bruised and battered him more than anyone he had ever encountered' and at their next encounter he would overwhelm him 'by pegs, hard blows, falls, and crossed buttocks'. Nothing daunted, Smallwood replied modestly that he was 'known for my intrepid manhood and bravery', which was just as well! Patrick Henry threatened John Francis with 'one of my bothering blows, which will convince him of his ignorance in the art of boxing', this in reply to Francis's threat to 'give him the truth of a good beating'. Taylor always made sure that the business details were there - the time when his doors would be opened and the times when the fighters would make their appearance, usually in mid-afternoon.

With his record and reputation, Jack Broughton had little need of such braggadocio. He began, though, to find his supporting role more and more frustrating. George's boasts extended to calling himself 'champion', an impertinence when everyone knew that he, Jack Broughton, had never been beaten by anybody. He had to acknowledge, at least for the time being, that the proprietor, with a monopoly control over the major pugilistic venues, did have certain privileges. Meanwhile, his own fights attracted more and more attention and defeated opponents such as Tom Pipes and George Gretting showed, like Taylor, no inclination to try their strength against him a second time. The one challenger who held out against him for any length was George Stevenson, and this was in a hastily arranged match when Broughton was far from well. After half an hour's hard fighting Broughton was near to exhaustion and only his wrestling skills saved him. He put a lock on Stevenson, prevented him from falling and gained enough of a breathing space to be able to take the fight a few minutes later. He was always to acknowledge that this was his hardest victory and that Stevenson was a first-rate fighter.

By now Broughton was eager for independence. He was a popular man with a growing circle of influential contacts. His ideas for a new amphitheatre devoted wholly to fisticuffs fell on receptive ears, particularly as he promised much better facilities for spectators than Taylor's Spartan emporium offered. Subscriptions were readily forthcoming once it was evident that Broughton's scheme had royal backing in the already not inconsiderable shape of the young Duke of Cumberland. The new amphitheatre opened with a flourish on 13 March 1743, just a few weeks before the soldier duke rode alongside his father, George II, at the Battle of Dettingen. The last appearance of a British monarch on the field of battle thus coincided with the first steps towards formalising a new style of combat. Everyone, apart from George Taylor, was happy with Broughton's new theatre, with its boxes and gallery for those seeking space and comfort and its pit for those who crowded round the raised stage. Taylor had good cause for alarm. The rival emporium was immediately on his own back doorstep and Broughton timed his opening event to clash with a contest between Taylor and Field at the old amphitheatre, undercutting Taylor's prices by charging a maximum entrance fee of 1s 0d. He offered an extensive bill of fare for the grand commencement, a large number of exhibitors and a 'battle royal' with 'the noted Buckhorse'. Buckhorse's fame sprang not from his boxing abilities alone but also from both his grotesque features - 'as ugly as Buckhorse' was a common saying for a long time after his death - and his remarkable reputation with the ladies. He was just the man to help draw the crowds. 'His ruling passions were LOVE and BOXING, in both of which', according to an early writer, 'he was equally formidable, ... neither nymph nor bruiser could withstand the violence of his attack, for it was generally allowed he conquered both by the strength of his members, and the rigour of his parts'.[5]

Broughton's venture was an immediate success. Taylor protested loudly through the press, and there was a bitter war of words. Taylor accused Broughton of keeping too much of the gate money for his own pocket, a rash charge since Broughton was never known to be other than straightforward in his dealings and was able to show that he only took the proprietor's usual one-third share of the takings. Honesty apart, his high-ranking patronage was bound to win the day for Broughton. There was an empty challenge from Taylor, who offered to fight his rival, but it was a half-hearted and unconvincing gesture and he soon had the sense to succumb, close his own theatre and cross to Broughton's, taking his troop of fighters with him. It was a setback from which George Taylor never fully recovered. After a few years he left the ring to become landlord of the Fountain Inn at Deptford, but, like too many others after him, he tried to come back, taking up the challenge of Tom Faulkner, the Kent cricketer, who saw a chance of revenging two earlier defeats. They fought for 200 guineas and the gate money. Taylor was beaten and, his pride shattered, he died a few months later.

Tom Faulkner, on the other hand, flourished into a ripe old age, teasing out batsmen with his underarm twisters and even returning to the ring at the age of 53 to knock out Thornhill in a fight in Warwickshire in 1791 after 'an extremely severe' contest. This brought him two-thirds of the £80 gate money and the tribute of being 'one of those lucky men who closed a career of exceptional length with the garland of victory on his grey head'.[6]

For Broughton, the opening of his new amphitheatre heralded seven years of prosperity and prestige. He provided comfortable accommodation for the gentry, cheaper entrance for the generality and, above all, more ordered competition than the ring had seen before. This was greatly aided by his codification of rules for boxing, giving the sport the framework within which it was to operate, with little change, for nearly a century.

It was the great age of English jurisprudence, soon to culminate in Blackstone's definitive *Commentaries on the Laws of England*, and sport was sharing in the move towards greater regulation. Horse-racing was already well ordered, particularly at Newmarket where, within the next decade, the Jockey Club would be gradually tightening its control over arrangements. Articles governing cricket matches were set out in 1727 and would be revised within a few months of the formulation of Broughton's rules for pugilism. It was more than coincidence. In all three sports the motives for codification were the same; the concern was for fair gaming than for fair play. As wagers on sport increased, so did demands to make the gambling more reliable, the play more regular and the conditions of the contest more predictable. The rules for pugilism were concerned with defining victory and defeat, the maintenance of order within the ring and the division of the takings, with only one short reference to the fighting itself. They were Jack Broughton's summary of the best practice that he had noted in the ring over the years, they were clear-cut as far as they went and were readily agreed to by his patrons. The rules 'produced by Mr Broughton, for the better regulation of Amphi-theatre, and approved of by the gentlemen, and agreed by the pugilists, August 18th, 1743' laid the foundations for the sport. They were simple, direct, forcefully stated and easily understood. They constitute the basic text in any history of bareknuckle fighting:

1. That a square of a yard be chalked in the middle of the stage; and on every fresh set-to after a fall, or being parted from the rails, each second is to bring his man to the side of the square, and place him opposite to the other; and till they are fairly set to at the lines, it shall not be lawful for the one to strike the other.

2. That, in order to prevent any disputes as to the time a man lies after a fall, if the second does not bring his man to the side of the square within the space of half a minute, he shall be deemed a beaten man.

3. That, in every main battle, no person whatever shall be upon the stage, except the principals and the second. The same rule to be observed in bye-battles, except that in the latter, Mr Broughton is allowed to be upon the stage to keep decorum, and to assist gentlemen to get their places; provided always, he does not interfere in the battle; and whoever pretends to infringe these rules, to be turned immediately out of the house. Everybody is to quit the stage as soon as the champions are stripped, before they set-to.

4. That no champion be deemed beaten, unless he fails coming up to the line within the limited time, or that his own second declares him beaten. No second is to be allowed to ask his man's adversary any questions, or advise him to give out.

5. That in bye-battles the winning man to have two-thirds of the money given which shall be publicly divided upon the stage, notwithstanding any private agreement to the contrary.

6. That to prevent disputes in every main battle, the principals shall, on the coming on the stage, choose from among the gentlemen present, two umpires, who shall absolutely decide all disputes that may arise about the battle; and if the two umpires cannot agree, the said umpires to choose a third, who is to determine it.

7. That no person is to hit his adversary when down or seize him by the hair, the breeches, or any part below the waist; a man on his knees to be reckoned down.[7]

For Broughton, the rules were solely for the better management of his own amphitheatre, just as the Jockey Club saw itself as regulating Newmarket racing only. They were not formulated as national rules for pugilism - such an idea would not have entered Broughton's head, or anyone else's at the time. If, as it happened, they were almost universally adopted, it was because they codified the best existing practice and were seen to be effective. In his later years, when he had lost all influence on the ring, old Jack himself could probably see where they fell short. When was a man 'down'? Could he go down of his own volition, without taking a blow, to earn a half minute's rest? Was the whole body a legitimate target for blows, as distinct from grapples? By then he was powerless to propose answers, and there was no Jockey Club to amplify the rules of pugilism. In his own day, though, and in his own amphitheatre, the rules were such an advance on the casual arrangements that had gone before that they became the model for the sport.

Broughton was riding high by the time his royal patron was pursuing the beaten army of Bonnie Prince Charlie to its bloody end on Culloden Moor to draw down the curtain on the 1745 rebellion. There were warnings for Broughton's future in the Duke of Cumberland's ruthlessness on that campaign, though for the time being all was well. His patron's influence brought him an appointment as one of the King's Yeomen of the Guard - he had always cut an impressive figure in livery since his Doggett's Coat and Badge days, and in later years he would be glad of the steady income from the pension - and he even accompanied the Duke to the court of Frederick the Great on one of his visits to the Continent.

At home, he remained mindful of the training traditions within which the combat sports had developed. The fencing schools had a long history, and he himself had come to maturity as a pugilist in the 'academies' of Figg and Taylor, with their lessons for the gentry in sword- and staff-play and their rather less successful provision for boxing training. It became clear to Broughton that the reason pugilistic training was not widely taken up was that few gentlemen were prepared to pay the price of pain to face, hands and body that even the most cautious instruction could entail. His answer was to introduce padded gloves, or mufflers, which enabled him to announce that he could offer instruction in 'the mystery of boxing', explaining 'the whole theory and practice of that truly British art, with all the stops, blows, cross-buttocks, etc.' and all done 'with the utmost tenderness and regard to the delicacy of the frame and constitution of the pupil'. The mufflers provided would, be assured the public, 'effectually secure them from the inconveniency of black eyes, broken jaws, and bloody noses'.[8]

Thus, Broughton, as well as being the founding father of organised pugilism, also became the grandfather of later glove-boxing. His training venture at his rooms in the Haymarket was well supported as long as the sport remained in vogue, and his mufflers not only widened the participation in fisticuffs, they also advanced the training opportunities for the fighters themselves. With their hands protected, the fighters could take a serious practice much more frequently. His own skills remained apparently undiminished for, like the great actor-managers of the theatre, he expected to play the leading roles himself. His confidence was supreme; understandably so since no opponent had done anything to diminish it for nearly twenty years. He was still fit, powerful and quick. His great superiority lay in the speed, strength and variety of his punching, matched by a much more careful defence then the ring had seen before. Broughton's style still showed pugilism's descent from sword play - his stance was essentially that of the fencer, right foot forward, with the sword arm used as the principal means of attack and the left used mainly to parry the opponent's blows - but he had all the pugilistic skills, an intense concentration on his opponent's strengths and weaknesses, and an indomitable will to win.

Disaster struck on 10 April 1750, in what seemed a routine contest with Jack Slack. Broughton's main anxiety as the fight approached was that his opponent would not turn up, an outcome he insured against by sending him a present of 10 guineas on the eve of the fight. In spite of a long lay-off from serious competition, Broughton was as confident as everyone else that he would win. His overwhelming ascendancy was reflected in the extraordinary odds offered and taken - after a few minutes of battling Broughton was so clearly ahead that the bets were at 10 to 1 on him. The Duke of Cumberland was said to have laid out £10,000 on his man. It was when the fight was five minutes old that Slack made a despairing assault on Broughton and landed a blow between his eyes. It was a punch which not only ended Broughton's career but also altered the whole course of pugilism's history.

Slack's blow blinded Broughton for all practical purposes. Cumberland fumed. Broughton attempted to fight on, virtually sightless, fumbling after his opponent. His inevitable defeat came after nearly ten further minutes of pathetic fighting. Cumberland accused Broughton of throwing the fight, a charge without substance; such action was alien to all Jack's previous doings. The Duke could be as harsh and unforgiving at some times as he was generous at others, and his was undoubtedly the influence behind the closing of the amphitheatre within weeks of the fatal fight. How it was done remains something of a puzzle. Historians have followed the early commentators, who put the closure down to 'interference by the legislature'. There is no record, in fact, of any such action in the journals or proceedings of either House of Parliament, but a royal duke had many means at his disposal, including pressure on magistrates to use their considerable and ill-defined powers. Whatever the means, the result was that Broughton's amphitheatre was closed down.

It was the end of Broughton's thirty years of successful and highly esteemed public life. While he deeply resented the manner of his going, he had been let off without any permanent physical damage, and he retained his reputation with the people. With his property, savings and pension, he was able to live in reasonable comfort, applying his wits to buying and selling, becoming grumpy and taciturn at times in his old age; a private man, but never forgotten by the devotees of the sport he embellished. When he was laid finally to rest in Lambeth church, on 21 January 1789, his funeral procession 'was adorned with the presence of several capital professors of boxing'. He left £7000, well over a half million pounds in late-twentieth century values. The 'capital professors of boxing' could have no more substantial proof that their sport could bring fame and profit. Jack Broughton had given the ring its rules and embryonic organisation. He had given it also skill, style and repute. Straightness and strength were the hallmarks of both his life and his career. At its spasmodic best, they would also be the characteristics of the sport which he founded.

2

Illegal, Immoral and Injurious

The closing of Broughton's amphitheatre could well have strangled the infant sport at birth. It did survive, but for much of the next half century its existence was precarious and its growth stunted. Broughton's expulsion saw the end of the specialised indoor boxing arena. Pugilism's opportunity to develop, alongside the theatre, as a legitimate public entertainment was lost. Until then, the two could readily be thought of together, enjoying much of their support in common and linked together in the minds of that considerable body of people whose puritan inheritance made them equally suspicious of both. The theatre gradually managed to assert its respectability, aided by such middle-class morality plays as George Lillo's popular *The London Merchant*, with its tale of virtue rewarded. Prize-fighting, though, could propound no such moral lessons, and so it stayed out in the cold.

It was left with few friends. The claims it could muster, as a means of uplift and character training, were slow to find voice. Its apologists would, in time, find pugilism to be the epitome of manliness, honesty, fairness and strength - but not yet. And pugilism itself, where it did remain visible - on the streets, in the fields and on the fairgrounds - was not only rough and brutal, which was not enough to condemn it in a rough and brutal age, but also attracted the idle, the criminal and the cheat, which was much more significant. It interfered with regular labour, produced dangerous public rowdiness and disturbed the public order. It became exposed to the laws on breaches of the peace, creating an affray and, by the 1760s, on duelling; while a death in the ring could bring a manslaughter charge against fighter and seconds alike. Certainly, from the start, the application of the law was highly unpredictable and prevention was much more common than prosecution, but henceforth pugilism had to operate as an illegal sport, with all the inconvenience (and, admittedly, the added spice for some) that illegality entailed.

The progress enjoyed by cricket and horse-racing over the second half of the eighteenth century show how much was denied to pugilism, a denial which was permanently to affect the whole nature of the sport and eventually to condemn it to lose the battle for acceptability. The other two sports could build publicly on their existing foundations. They could establish more-or-less permanent venues, with facilities for players and spectators; they could advertise their events in the press and charge for admission, for grandstand views or for both. They could provide a full and varied day's entertainment, with smock races for girls at cricket matches, and foot races or cocking matches at race meetings. They could produce a steady if unspectacular income for reliable performers and they could sow the seeds that were eventually to produce some national control, through the Jockey Club and the Marylebone Cricket Club.

None of this was possible for pugilism, except in the most erratic fashion. At a time when all popular sports and recreations were coming under growing pressure in the interests of regular patterns of labour, public order and enlightened behaviour, pugilism had to face the added obstacle of illegality. Even cock-fighting could advertise itself widely in the newspapers and was on its way to setting up a more-or-less regular pattern of annual county matches, often three-day events, and every town and many an inn had its own cockpit - which could serve, too, for dog-fighting, badger-baiting or rat-killing. For pugilism, by contrast, there could now be no open advertising of fight venues, though dates were usually known. There could be no settled sites for contests; which came to depend on the sufferance or ignorance of local justices of the peace. The scope for improvement and the opportunities for exercising some beneficial control of the sport were lost to pugilism by its illegality, and the justices' concern for law and order meant a particular discouragement for big fights, likely to attract large crowds of spectators and heighten the sport's attraction.

That pugilism managed to survive at all as a spectator sport was due to its inherent appeal to an age adept at supporting cruelty and refinement alike, to the uncertain application of the law and to a continuing inheritance from the Broughton era. The amphitheatres had fostered a body of professional pugilists, most of whom wanted to continue their careers. The upper-class support did not disappear overnight because the Duke of Cumberland had lost a bet, although enthusiasm certainly waned when there was no physical centre on which to focus. There was, too, Broughton's code for the conduct of fights. Now that pugilism was outside the pale, it was particularly important that such rules existed and, what is more, noteworthy that they were more widely accepted than most sporting rules of the time. Furthermore, there had always been an informal and scarcely acknowledged humble manifestation of the sport in the local fighting that took place around the towns and villages across the land. Local competition continued to produce its own heroes whose reputation might spread abroad, and this local competition, as long as it was on the small scale, was little affected by bans on London amphitheatres. There might no longer be the schools of a Taylor or a Broughton to which aspiring provincial pugilists could attach themselves, but London remained the centre of such loose and spasmodic organisation as the sport could muster and communication between the sporting gentry was effective enough to bring forward those who had made their name in the regions.

Even the disappearance of boxing from enclosed arenas in London was not entirely complete. The Duke of Cumberland himself took a leading role in the setting up of contests at the Tennis Court, Haymarket, in 1760, thereby confirming that his influence on closing down Broughton had arisen from pique rather than principle. As a backer, he continued to pick the wrong man. Jack Slack, who had been expensive to him ten years earlier when he beat Broughton, now lost more of Cumberland's money when, fighting now under His Grace's colours, he was beaten by the Duke of York's Bill Stephens. It was the end of Cumberland's active involvement with the ring. The higher the social status of its supporters, the less regard a contest need have for legal prohibitions, and this second waning of royal patronage was soon aggravated by one of the ring's more blatant instances of dishonesty. Slack, now turned promoter and second to his recent opponent, persuaded Meggs, with a £50 bribe, to let Stephens win when the two met at the Tennis Court in July 1761. It was a singularly unconvincing performance. Meggs took a knock-down from a blow that was far from lethal and then spent twenty minutes offering no more than token resistance before finally surrendering. Not surprisingly, no more was heard of pugilism in so favoured a setting - if it couldn't offer honesty, it would not win protection. There were some other attempts to establish the sport in enclosed arenas but they lacked the support they needed. The most notable was at Sampson's Riding School at the Three Hats, Islington, which managed to mount relatively minor contests for several months until the high constable mounted the stage during the £10-a-side fight between John Pearce and John White on 11 May 1773 and put an end to all proceedings.[1]

Pugilism was now, firmly driven out into the cold. In London it was pushed into those rough areas of open land on the edge of the city which had become notorious for what respectable citizens saw as degrading and disorderly sports. The Long Fields behind Montague House, to the east of Tottenham Court Road and near the present site of London University, was particularly given over to pursuits such as animal-baiting and duck-hunting (carried out with terriers on its ponds). Among the others were Tothill Fields, Moorfields, and Stepney Fields, and a high proportion of the fights recorded from the 1760s onwards took place in such unsalubrious settings as these, close to a large urban population. They still managed to attract some of the more raffish sporting gentry as well as the workers and idlers of the city. Provincial cities like Bristol and Birmingham fell into the same pattern, their fights often anonymous encounters only recorded on account of some sensational detail, usually the death of one of the contestants. A typical report,from Birmingham in 1787 was of:

two pitched battles fought in a field near this town, which, we are sorry to say, were fatally attended. The first, between Pitchfork, a collier, and Smith, a carter, was won by the latter but he died of his wounds the next day. In the second the defeated expired soon after the contest.[2]

The names of fighters that have come down from these years are of little distinction, understandably so given their restricted opportunities in a struggling sport - Bill Stephens, the nailer; Jack Lamb; Abraham da Costa; and Jack Warren, who was responsible for the death of Philip Juchau in a fight on the paved road opposite the Bethlem Gates, Moorfields. Not surprisingly, when Warren attacked him with a cross-buttock, his leg thrust forward to throw him over the hip, Juchau's skull was smashed as he hit the ground. What is surprising is that fights continued to take place there from time to time.

Such venues may have been the only ones which pugilism could find for itself, but they held little promise. As London grew rapidly, the crowds of seekers after dubious pleasure in such sports gave greater and greater offence. Already Lincoln's Inn Fields had been enclosed in the interest of public order and decorum, and the magistrates and their constables began in the 1760s to make determined efforts to clear other open spaces of their more offensive activities. For instance, raids were mounted on Tothill

Fields, Millbank, and the Long Fields on Shrove Tuesday 1768, particularly in this instance to ensure that one of the day's traditional working-class pursuits - cock-throwing, that is hurling missiles at a tethered cock - was not taking place. It was not a setting in which pugilistic matches of any consequence could prosper and from the early 1770s until the revival of pugilism nearly twenty years later fights tended to move further out, beyond the built-up areas of the metropolis. Attempts to mount fights in naturally enclosed arenas were also soon frustrated. Marylebone Basin was said to have taken 3000 spectators for the Stephens v. Taplin fight in 1760, and The Hollow at Islington saw Jack Lamb beat Payne against the odds for a £20 stake in March 1768, but both sites were too close to town to offer any permanent security. It became necessary to take a brisk walk to Hounslow, Mill Hill, Kennington Common or Blackheath to view the occasional fist-fight. The battle would be fought in the open, on the turf, with the ring made of stakes or even formed by the spectators themselves.

Another false start was the attempt to attach contests to inns in the neighbour-hood of the capital. The Crown Inn at Staines became a popular boxing centre in the late 1770s and a number of significant contests were staged there. They hinted strongly at a revival. Harry Sellars, a west countryman, beat Peter Corcoran for a stake of 100 guineas in October 1776, and he had a dubious victory over Duggan Fearns in less than two minutes in September 1780. £500 to £600 was said to have been wagered on the first fight, a clear indication that the gentry enthusiasts were returning with their support and financial backing. The second, however, demonstrated that strain of self-destruc-tion which was never far below pugilism's surface and many left it in disgust, feeling that they had been, in the blunt word of contemporary report, 'swindled'. The same outcome had clouded an earlier venture at the White Lion Inn at Putney. Here, in 1759, Tom Faulkner, fresh from his win over Slack, had a highly suspicious victory over Joe James for a £100 stake. After Faulkner had appeared to be losing the fight convincingly, James was suddenly brought down by a blow of little apparent force and soon gave in. 'The indignation of the spectators', said the report, 'was very highly expressed by their hissing him off the ground.'[3] The inn was central to much early spectator sport, and pugilism had already become enmeshed with the tavern life. It was here that matches were made and where that fighters sometimes based their training. The publicans themselves were increasingly likely to have been boxers. The influence of the tavern was, though, not always wholesome and this early experience taught the gentry the need to divorce fights from the immediate physical presence of the inn. It seems certain that they would have withdrawn their backing, irrespective of magisterial intervention, had taverns continued to be boxing centres.

Eventually it was the racecourse which proved a much happier venue for them. Here the gentry were used to having charge of the day's proceedings, and the advantages of the racecourse soon became apparent. Race meetings guaranteed crowds. Local meetings had by now become annual social events, usually over two or three days, and were the occasion for dinners, balls and general merrymaking as well as for sport. There was already a tradition of spicing the horse-racing with other sporting competition - cock-fighting, often on a large scale, with £200 staked on the overall result and £20 on individual fights; the occasional cricket match; and a whole pot-pourri of athletic contests, races or (more often) challenges against the clock. It was a setting into which pugilism could fit with some hope of success. Bouts at racecourses were not, of course, immune from interference by the law; but courses were, by their nature, outside towns, the race meeting was a relaxed occasion and local justices were themselves as likely as not to be involved in its management. The racecourse, too, usually had at least some rudimentary structure which served as a grandstand and for which admission fees could be charged, so the pugilists themselves stood to gain. It was natural enough that the turf and the ring should find each other and begin their long association at this early stage in pugilism's history. The same sporting gentry who ran and backed their horses, who trained and bred their fighting cocks and who wagered heavily on every conceivable event were, after all, the ones readiest to lend succour to boxing. On the racecourse, where their authority was firmly established, they could exert considerable influence and might even be able to ensure fair competition.

This hope had some early disappointments. In one of the first major racecourse contests, the matchmaker - no less a racing man than Captain O'Kelly, the owner of Eclipse - himself gave a £100 bribe to Bill Darts to throw his fight against Peter Corcoran at the Epsom meeting in May 1771. Darts duly collapsed after a light blow to the side of the head after some ten minutes of gentle sparring, and so brought to an inglorious end a career which had proved him to be one of the period's few fighters of any distinction. His match against Tom Juchau at Guildford in May 1766 (possibly a racecourse meeting as it was close to the usual time of the town races) was said to have been for 1000 guineas, a sum so exceptional that its reliability is questionable. More typically, he fought and beat Doggett, a west-country bargeman, for 100 guineas, and Swansey, in 1767, for 50 guineas. He had declared himself champion and challenged all comers. Lyons and the morbidly nicknamed 'Death' (Stephen Oliver) came forward and were defeated, the latter contest affording contemporary journalists endless opportunities for punning on the 'Darts of Death' and the like. Even after the Corcoran fight and his relegation to supporting roles, Darts found it hard to play straight; Sam Peters withdrew from his fight against Gregory in 1771 because of Bill's constant interference as second on his man's behalf.[4]

The early racecourse experience of pugilism was flawed, but within a few years it was to return there with success. In fact, the next boxing venue of any note achieved its prime fame as a cricket ground. This was the White Conduit Field, the distant ancestor of Lord's, the scene of a fight between Jem Parrott and Joe Hood in 1773. The conjunction of the two sports was not as surprising as it might have been later in their histories. They did, at the time, have certain elements in common. Cricket attracted a similar clientele to pugilism, though cricket's noble support was more consistent and prepared to finance the game more liberally. Cricket crowds had a reputation for disorder, idleness and petty crime little better than that enjoyed by disciples of the ring. Cricket's aristocratic leadership - players as well as patrons - was not, however, prepared to have the game held back by any close association with an illegal sport. In any event, cricket pitches tended to be too public and too adjacent to towns and villages for them to be tolerated for long as pugilistic venues.

And so it was back to the racecourses. Joe Hood met Harry Sellars for £50 a side at Ascot Heath races in June 1777. In September the following year Hood was in action again, against Peter Bath, at Maidenhead races. By May 1786, a stage was being erected for the Humphries v. Martin fight at the very centre of English racing, Newmarket, and a new era for pugilism was about to begin.

Racecourses provided frequent opportunities for fights over the next fifty years. Some were grand affairs, arranged in advance, like the Spring v. Langan fight which packed Worcester racecourse in January 1824. Many more were impromptu bouts, financed by a collection for a purse at the end of day's racing - there were usually aspiring fighters on hand, and sometimes there were even established ones who were having difficulty in finding opponents or backers. The convenience of the racecourse, irrespective of whether there was a race meeting, soon became apparent. A 30 ft stage (as against the more usual 24 ft) was put up at Barnet raceground in November 1784, well after the end of the racing season, for the bout between Bill Day and William Towers, and there were fights there even in years such as 1787, when apparently no race meeting at all was held.

With the exception of Newmarket - and Newmarket always was an exception where horse-racing was concerned - all the boxing racecourses were, at first, within easy travelling distance of London. Newmarket itself, where many of the wealthy stabled their horses, became effectively the sportsman's capital during the six weeks or more when there was racing there. Otherwise London remained the focus of the pugilistic world, even during these struggling years, and no fighter could hope for national fame without first catching the eye of the metropolitan fancy. There was though, also an important provincial aspect of the ring which helped it to survive. Notable fights took place in Norfolk, which was always a popular outpost; the first contest of any importance after the closing of Broughton's amphitheatre was held there. Slack defeated Pettit at Harlston in 1754, before a large crowd. Bristol, Slack's home town, was soon to be recognised as the most illustrious of all pugilistic nurseries. Wiltshire sites became popular, as a reasonable geographical compromise, for contests between west-country pugilists and Londoners. George Megson, for instance, beat the Bath baker, Milsom, at Calne in 1786. By this time provincial backers were sometimes raising considerable sums in support of their heroes; witness the 200 guineas a side fought for between the Derby and Leicester champions, Blunt and Godfrey, in 1788.

Sums of this size were only just coming into the sport, and then only very occasionally. Pugilism had not, so far, brought much material reward to its performers outside the commercially successful amphitheatres. The comfortable old age enjoyed by Broughton and Slack was unusual. Peter Corcoran was among the first to beat the trail followed by many later pugilists when he became landlord of the Blakeney's Head, St Giles, for which, given his loquacity, he was rather better suited than he had been for the ring. The later lives of most of the other early fighters are unremarkable. They would take little capital with them from their ring careers, in which the rewards were patchy and unreliable. The gate money, which had been a reliable source of income for those appearing in the leading fights at the amphitheatre, became very chancy when contests were forced into the open air. Some entrance fees might be collected from grandstand spectators, but how much the boxers received was speculative. En-trance would seldom be fully controlled, entrance money could rarely be secured from all the spectators, nor could there be any guarantee that the gatekeepers were 'official', or would pass on any or all of their takings. They did not usually have much direct interest in the money staked on their behalf either, although a pugilist could expect a share of any winnings and would usually also bet on himself if he had the funds available. It was little wonder that boxers could readily be bought. Both Slack and Darts revealed that they earned more by losing fights than they would have done by winning. As seconds to other boxers, pugilists, even before their own ring days were over, could also increase their returns by influencing the outcome of a fight, particularly if it involved helping their own man to lose.

The inn door and the publican's cloak were beginning to beckon pugilists because they offered both security and a means of maintaining an involvement in their sport. The background and experience of most pugilists was not usually the best preparation for tavern-keeping, but where they did show some business ability there was every likelihood that their houses would become centres for pugilistic affairs. The inn was already the focus of most of the eighteenth century's sporting life. The race meeting in the country town would have its headquarters at a local inn, where entries had to be made and stakes submitted. Cricket clubs were often set up in taverns, which served as their base and often provided their grounds. It was the inns, too, which provided facilities for bowls, skittles and cock-fighting. Some landlords on the edge of cities had adjoining fields where there could be rough-and-ready horse-racing, and others provided ducks on their ponds for hunters. Hard sport and hard drinking went readily together, and the inn was the natural meeting place for arranging fights, handing over the stake money and celebrating or mourning the result. The illegality of pugilism denied it the opportunity of developing any formal organisation or openly avowed headquarters, but by the end of the century there would be several London hostelries clearly identifiable as meeting places for the sport's promoters and enthusiasts.

The outlawing of pugilism also meant that it could only achieve a new prosperity if it enjoyed powerful patronage. Royal interest had proved almost fatal in 1750, but thereafter it was virtually essential if the sport was ever to attain any status. Only backing from the very highest in the land could guarantee immunity from interference, as was evident in the early 1760s when the revival of indoor fighting in London seemed a brief possibility. The real rebirth of pugilism in the late 1780s, when it came, once more owed much to the interest of royal princes; they put the final seal of approval on the rising popularity of the sport, already evident in racecourse contests and increased stake money.

These early symptoms of revival owed little to any advances in pugilism itself. For nearly thirty years after Broughton's retirement, both standards of performance and levels of honesty deteriorated, not surprisingly in view of the uncertain conditions under which the sport had to operate. Jack Slack was a slow-moving fighter, heavy on his feet, a hard hitter and exceptionally durable so far as taking punishment went. His own defensive skills, however, were rudimentary and, since one of his favourite forms of attack was a backhanded blow, so must those of his opponents have been. Bill Darts was another courageous hard striker, until he found losing fights more profitable than winning them. The most skilled and innovative boxer of the 1750s was the lightweight, Edward Hunt, who had learned his trade with Broughton in the amphitheatres and continued to do battle for a further ten years after the closure. He was a small man, only about 9 st., and he nearly always found himself matched against heavier opponents. He became adept at moving around the ring and dodging attacks, being one of the first exponents of the 'shifting' style, which was not much admired unless executed by someone as obviously disadvantaged as Hunt. The approved model was the stand-up slogging match, with the boxers facing each other toe-to-toe, exchanging blows, but Hunt owed his success to his skill in keeping out of his man's reach and using pummelling blows in sudden attacks of his own, sometimes slipping under punches to deliver them. Of necessity, Hunt usually had to fight on the defensive, yet his career was a relatively successful one until he was beaten by Richard Mills 'The Onion Boy' at Islington in May 1758. Stephen 'Death' Oliver was another light fighter who had to rely on agility as much as on strength and he won a high reputation in the 1770s as a scientific boxer, but those who saw both him and the celebrated pugilists of next generation acknowledged that there was a wide gulf between the two.[5]

One of the sports's few advantages was that Broughton's rules had regularised the fighting itself. If they could not ensure straight dealing, they did set some limits on nefarious practice in the ring itself. Instances of foul play are rare, although reports of contests are themselves usually sketchy, a symptom that pugilism had not yet caught the public imagination. Certainly Pettit siezed Jack Slack by the throat, pressed him against the rails and hammered his face severely with his free hand in their Norfolk fight in 1754, but then Pettit was a Frenchman and could hardly be expected to know what was acceptable.[6] Wrestling throws were, of course, still allowed, although they were less the stock in trade of fighting than they became a few years later, which perhaps accounts for the comparative success enjoyed by some of the lighter boxers of the day. Contests took place, wherever possible, on a raised stage with a hard and unforgiving plank floor (as against the turf bed which became popular later), but it would be dangerous to see this as the reason for fewer wrestling throws. The need to avoid pain did not have a high priority among the promoters and followers of eighteenth-century sport.

It was, after all, a callous, hard and cruel age, riddled with paradox, when the fine sensitivity for form and grace in the arts could coexist with a bloody disregard for all life and all feelings, both animal and human. Sport, by its combative nature, could be expected to show more of the time's barbarity than its refinement, especially as much of it appealed primarily to those whose lives offered little opportunity to share in the more polished achievements of the age. So it was that bulls and badgers were torn alive by dogs, the bull, on occasions, having its hooves hacked off to give its attackers more scope. Geese were hung upside down, alive, from the branch of a tree, while contestants tried to pull their heads off. Fighting cocks were armed with vicious metal spurs so that they could inflict even bloodier wounds on each other. Horses were ridden to destruction in coach and chariot races, and John Wesley had no hesitation in ranking horse-racing itself among the cruel sports - with some justification when a horse might well have to run three four-mile heats in a day. Dogs invading cricket pitches were threatened with shooting; unruly crowds of spectators would be beaten back by whips; and mass communal football matches were often marked by a death or two. Life itself was precarious and harsh, and sport could hardly be expected to be less so. Accidental death was commonplace, with endless accidents from road traffic, bolting horses and overturning wagons. Precautions against fire and scalding were rudimentary and early mass-manufacturing processes were developing with little regard for safety. Many illnesses and most major surgery carried the risk of death, and if natural mortality was not sufficient reminder of the fragility of life there were always the public hangings to drive the lesson home, with the quarterly execution days at Tyburn among the most popular London holiday spectacles.

The coarseness and brutality of the age was a virtual guarantee for the survival, in one form or another, of the most elemental form of human competition. Its survival and development as an organised sport was another matter, with all the forces of law and order, at least nominally, ranged against it and most enlightened opinion wholesale in its condemnation. Illegal, immoral and injurious as pugilism was held to be by many - and there were certainly occasions when it was indisputably all of these - pugilism continued to be a part of popular life and it needed only the revived interest of a leisured class to give it new vitality.

3
A Fashionable Sport

In the summer of 1787, George III was being persuaded by William Wilberforce, the great campaigner against the slave trade, to issue his proclamation 'For the Encouragement of Piety and Virtue, and for the preventing and punishing of Vice, Profaneness and Immorality'. At the very same time, his sons were taking up the sport for which none claimed piety, few virtue and many vice, profaneness and immorality. Pugilism, unlike horse-racing, never quite became the sport of kings - each of the royal trio in turn distanced himself from the ring as he drew nearer the crown. What it did become was the sport of princes and peers during its prosperous heyday when, for over thirty years, the association of the palace with the prize-ring was the guarantee of its good standing.

Although there were underlying forces working to the advantage of the spectator sports at the time, the immediate rush of popularity enjoyed by the prize-ring was largely fortuitous. A new fighter had come forward, Richard Humphries, who seemed presentable and reliable enough for a gentleman to have faith in. There was a promising opponent from the West Country in Sam 'The Bath Butcher' Martin. The two were matched at Newmarket during the Second Spring Meeting of 1786. The Prince of Wales, as a keen racing man, was there, so was his brother, the Duke of York, as well as a handful of leading French aristocrats who were already finding England more comfortable than their own seething country. It all amounted to a recipe for success. A stage was set up before the grandstand, the arena was roped off, a guinea was charged for admission and a 'crowd of the best and bravest in the land' turned out for the battle. It was an impressive contest with Humphries showing skill, quick movement and dexterity and Martin showing great gameness in holding out against him for over an hour and a half. What had started as a novel social occasion ended as an advertisement for the prize-ring as the coming sporting attraction.

In January of the next year, the new pugilistic age was confirmed at the contest between Tom Johnson, the undisputed champion of the day, and Will Ward, another west-country challenger. It was away from Newmarket - nobody would venture on to a racecourse, let alone that barren heath, in the depth of winter - but the country venue, at Oakingham in Berkshire, was well organised. The match had been carefully arranged, Ward being brought in from Bristol because the London ring could not find anyone ready to face the champion. The stakes were rising (200 guineas for this fight), the gambling was heavy and again it cost a guinea to get into the galleries around the stage. Enthusiasm ran high and a procession of modish carriages made its way up the Thames valley, heading a motley throng of followers. The new passion even proved strong enough to survive the let-down of the fight itself; it was reduced to near comedy by Ward's crouching stance, his legs bent so that whenever Johnson tried to land a punch he could drop a knee on to the floor and claim to be 'down'. Discretion proved the better part of Ward's valour when Johnson did at last get at him. His loud claims of 'foul!' were ignored, and he fled the field to cheers, jeers and laughter.[1]

The significance of the social change which pugilism was undergoing was illustrated a few months later when Tom Johnson took on another fight without the new upper-class support. He met the ponderous slogger, Fry, at Kingston upon Thames in July. The pair were ill matched, only 50 guineas were at stake, and there was little betting and equally little interest. The contest was badly timed, poorly located and virtually ignored by the quality. Most of them were out of town, preoccupied with their estates and their horse-racing, and in any event Kingston upon Thames was uncomfortably close to London for a championship fight. Johnson was astute enough in the ring, weighing up each opponent's strengths and weaknesses, but he was not very clever outside it. He did not appreciate that the riches and fame of the Ward fight could come his way again, and he did what he had always done in his considerable boxing past - took what was on offer. This bout with Fry, which Johnson won easily, sits so awkwardly in boxing's history that it has always been conveniently displaced into the previous year! *The Daily Register* of 7 July 1787 leaves no doubt about the true date.

Tom Johnson, the rough-and-ready northerner, was essentially the product of an earlier boxing age. He found himself carried along by the new wave of wealthy support only at the peak of his career, when he was well into his thirties. He was inherited by the new social order of the sport rather than being one of its products, but his superiority was so pronounced that he now had no difficulty in finding backers, men who made sure that he didn't waste himself on minor skirmishes again. The stake money that he could attract rose impressively. The 200 guineas for the Ward match grew to 300 for the two fights against the Irish challenger, Michael Ryan, and to 500 for the fights against Isaac Perrins and Ben Bryan. The latter took the title from him in 1791, when he was over forty. The rewards that came Johnson's own way were late and unexpected, and he had neither the experience nor the temperament to manage them. Bryan died within three years, before defending the title, and the new men, Humphries and Mendoza, were by contrast pugilists of the coming generation who rose with quick assurance to fame and fortune. Each enhanced the spectacle and appeal of the prize-ring by the novelty and distinction he brought. Humphries was soon known as 'the Gentleman Boxer', and though his origins were obscure, he was certainly a self-possessed young man, quiet and well-mannered enough outside the ring to seem at ease with his patrons and their circle, and with sufficient acumen to become a successful businessman when he retired. Stripped for action, he had a fine physique, adopted a much-admired upright stance, and had great contemporary appeal as the clean-cut athlete, the epitome of English manliness. Daniel Mendoza, whose rise to fame went step by step with Humphries', was his perfect foil, flamboyant in his boxing style, a strikingly handsome Jew and very proud of his Jewishness.

They were an ideal pair for the times. The composure and classical posture of the one and the colourful skills of the other made them perfect actors in a scene which no dramatist could have improved upon. Between them, they dominated the prize-ring in the early 1790s, until Humphries retired to become a coal factor and Mendoza was beaten by John Jackson, that other 'gentleman' of the ring. Humphries and Mendoza had both made their reputations on a single major fight, each of them beating the luckless Sam Martin in racecourse contests at Newmarket and Barnet respectively. The Prince of Wales led the company at both. The question of who should challenge Johnson then cried out for an answer, and there were three memorable combats between the two, out of which Mendoza eventually emerged victorious, though by then Johnson had retired. They were all well-supported matches, confirming the reluctant verdict of the newspaper that was shortly to become *The Times* that 'this amusement is not of the most humane kind; yet, as a fashionable sport it demands our notice'. Learning the arts of fisticuffs became the vogue, and both Mendoza and Humphries soon opened their own boxing schools, Mendoza in the City and Humphries catering particularly for the boys from Westminster School.

The new patronage was impressive, rivalling that of the turf, with which it had much in common. For the thirty or so of pugilism's greatest years, it included, apart from the Prince Regent (as he became), two royal princes, visiting foreign royalty, the Duke of Hamilton (who put up Ben Bryan's 500-guinea stake against Johnson), sundry lordships of other rank and a host of baronets, knights and esquires. Less remarked upon by historians, but almost as important in bringing some stability to the prize-ring, was the backing of a solid body of middle-class citizens who had made their money in manufacture and trade. They ranged from the wealthy brewer, long-time Member of Parliament and Lord Mayor of London, Harvey Coombe; through the corn factor, Mr Holingsworth, who once employed Tom Johnson; to Mr Rolfe the baker, who was Ryan's second in one of his championship challenges. The view that the prize-ring was the preserve of the aristocracy and the roughest of the lowest classes alone is far from the truth of the matter. There were sporting publicans such as Mr Cullington, of the Black Bull, Tottenham Court Road, and one of Jem Belcher's early backers, who was well enough thought of to be agreed upon as the neutral umpire and stakeholder for one of his boy's later fights. Later there was Mr Franklin of the Lion and Goat, Lower Grosvenor Street, who promoted Jack Randall. Support at this social level could be all important when pugilists faced the crunch of court proceedings, as they did from time to time. Their gentry patrons might exert influence behind the scenes, moving Jem Belcher's Berkshire prosecution, for instance, to the sympathetic King's Bench in London, but they were not prepared to come forward to give evidence or be named as sureties - that was tradesman's business. For Belcher, in that case, bail was secured through Mr Brown, a publican, and Mr Evans, an oyster merchant in Hungerford Market.[2]

Undoubtedly, though, it was the aristocracy and gentry who led the sport into fashion and the Prince of Wales who set the mode. The future Prince Regent had been given his own household in 1783, together with an income of £50,000 a year, which he found no difficulty in overspending. Once released from the domestic sobriety of his upbringing, his racy habits and extravagant tastes blossomed forth and he was game for any new sport or amusement, though he never lost a certain sensitivity which held him back from the wilder excesses of some of his courtiers. The one trait led him into pugilism; the other at length caused him to withdraw from immediate involvement. He led the company at the first fights of both Humphries and

Mendoza, and he was present at the fight between Crabb and Oliver in April 1788 (fought on the turf at Blackheath) and also at Jackson's first contest at Smitham Bottom, near Croydon, in June of the same year. The social status of pugilism was assured by his example. So many men of power and influence took up the sport with the Prince that the prize-ring was well able to flourish when he personally turned away.

Given the Prince's fluctuating enthusiasms, he might well have deserted boxing at any time. He did so after witnessing a death in the ring at Brighton on 6 August 1788. A stage had been set up in front of the racecourse grandstand. The nobility and gentry took their ease, ready to savour the three arranged bouts and wholly confident that, illegal or not, the Prince's presence was a total guarantee that their sport would not be interfered with. Bob Watson, sponsored by the Prince's companion, Colonel Hanger, beat Bill Jones comfortably, and Joe Ward disposed of Tom Reynolds. The last fight was between the nimble and experienced Tom Tyne and a cumbersome country fighter called Earl. The newcomer appeared to be getting the better of Tyne, to the satisfaction of the crowd, who were not taken with Tyne's shifting and dodging or his adoption of Ward's stratagem of always having his knee near to the boards. A sudden blow from Tyne brought it to an end - Earl crashed against the rails of the stage as he fell, was knocked unconscious and died immediately. The Prince was so shocked that he vowed never to attend a prize-fight again and to settle an annuity on the wife and family of the dead man.[3] He did eventually favour pugilism again and never lost touch with it through his cronies, but for the next few years he devoted his esoteric energies to the promotion of Brighton rather than to the patronage of the ring.

The rest of the aristocratic following remained. Here was another opportunity for sporting participation, with which they were familiar from their horse-racing, cricket and cock-fighting. It offered another outlet for the passion for gaming, fed in recent years by increased income from their estates. Here were all the excitements of the cockpit in human form, with the added spice of illegality but virtually no danger of prosecution. They were used to having 'their man', a permanent employee, taking part in sporting activities, sometimes alongside them as in cricket, more often on their behalf. A groom would lead their racehorse from meeting to meeting, riding him in the races. More than one gamekeeper held his place because he was essential to his master's cricket team, and Sir Thomas Mann's Aylward was said not to be at his best in home games, where he enjoyed the right to run all the catering and drinking booths! Now, just at the time when pugilism was coming into vogue, a new relationship between master and performer was beginning to replace the old. The professional was being hired by the match, the race or the season, the long-term contract based on service and responsibility giving way to a short-term arrange-ment based wholly on fees - £5 a match, for instance, for Hambledon cricketers, with £3 for practice days.

Both styles of patronage found their way into pugilism. The Prince of Wales had his sedan chairman, Tom Tring. Lord Barrymore and Lord Camelford had Hooper and Richmond as their minders, and as late as the 1820s, in more anonymous times, 'a gentleman well known in the London Ring' was taking on young Edward Baldwin, a promising fighter, as groom. Some patrons regularly backed a particular boxer without taking him into their employment (Mr Brady1 with Humphries, for instance, and Mr Elliot with Tom Hickman) while others moved from boxer to boxer on a one-off match basis. One of the most active of the floating promoters was Mr Fletcher Reid, heir to considerable estates in Tayside, who appears to have had a genuine interest in promoting good matches. He staked both the Belchers, Jem and Tom, John Gully and Bill Ryan, as well as Bill Richmond who, after he left Lord Camelford, was also backed by Sir Clement Brigg. The most fickle was Lord Barrymore, who backed Gregson against Gully; when the latter won he paraded him around Newmarket in his coach the next day.

Barrymore would doubtless have claimed that he was displaying those first eseential qualities of the contemporary sportsman, the capacity to lose large sums of money and the strength of character to do so with good grace. The stake money involved in the various sports makes for interesting comparisons, with pugilism rarely at the top of the league. Cricket matches between wealthy patrons were frequently for £1,000 a side in the later eighteenth century, the 'side' being the patron himself. Individual horse-races were seldom for prizes of 200 guineas or more and sweepstakes, at their maximum, would rarely bring more than £1,000 to the winner. Most of the prizes for individual races were smaller, but the occasional outstanding horse, moving from place to place, would collect over £1,000 a season for its owner. Cock-fighting matches between the gentlemen of two counties were frequently for between 300 and 500 guineas, though at more modest levels the Gentlemen of Islington were engaging the Gentlemen of Hackney at the New Pit, Hoxton, in 1794 for 50 guineas.[4] Pedestrian feats were usually tackled for wagers, and were often for highly idiosyncratic performances - an unnamed duke staked 1,000 guineas against an unknown baronet to find men to walk ten miles in three hours, taking four steps forward and one back![5] Rowing and sailing contests, either time challenges or competitions, were usually for up to several hundred pounds. The sums at stake in pugilistic encounters were therefore by no means outstanding for the times, and the great majority of contests,like the great majority of horse-races, were for no more than 25 or 50 guineas.

Stake money, though, was not the only interest of the wealthy in sporting events. Reliable figures are hard to come by, but the sums wagered on important events, seen to have far exceeded the actual stake money. Mr Bullock's £20,000 winnings from Johnson's defeat of Perrins can be matched by the £10,000 racing bets familiar to Tattersalls, Lord Barrymore's loss of 2,800 guineas in a single night at whist and the fate of Baron Foley of Kidderminster. The Baron's obituary notice recalled that he 'entered upon the Turf' with an income of £18,000 a year and capital of over a million pounds, only to quit his life without ready money and an 'encumbered estate, and with a constitution injured by the labour and cares of a business unsuitable to the benevolent character of his mind'![6] All of this implies that the £30,000 to £40,000 said to have depended on the Humphries v. Martin fight is quite conceivable, even if the £150,000 'calculated' to have been involved in the Neat v. Hickman bout a quarter of a century later borders on the fanciful. Only the long odds sometimes given and take - remarkable for two-horse races - make the figures plausible.

Why were many of the socially eminent and the wealthy prepared to invest large amounts on men hitting each other, often under physically difficult circumstances and on relatively isolated occasions, when they could gamble at cards in comfort and without restriction, or back their fancy on the racecourse for most of the season? Love of gambling alone is clearly not the answer, although pugilism or indeed any other sport would have been unthinkable without gambling. There were other motives behind their patronage of prize-fighting - at first, the excitement of a new sport; then the sense of physical combat and involvement, even at second-hand. There was the opportunity it gave for conspicuous display, the build-up of the pugilist's reputation and then the share in his reflected glory. For Lord Barrymore it was showing off John Gully in his barouche. Later there was the deeper commitment of some backers, most conspicuously Captain Allardyce Barclay, who undertook oversight of a fighter's training. Patronage, in its turn, not only brought money and status to the sport, it made large-scale contests possible in spite of the law. It did so by influence, and where this could not sway the added opposition aroused by the biggest fights and the treat of extraordinary crowds, there would often be a gentleman at hand to lend his estate for a fight venue. Mr Thornton's park, near Stilton, housed the first Humphries v. Mendoza match, Captain Mellish's estate saw Pearce v. Belcher in 1805, and Gregson and Gully fought in Sir John Sebright's park near Woburn three years later. Most sustained of all was the unofficial protection afforded by the Duke of Clarence's estate at Bushey Park for some twenty years in the early nineteenth century.

It was a natural enough gesture of hospitality. The gentry were accustomed to providing cricket grounds and accepting that there would be invasions of spectators, and even though pugilism happened to be illegal, they were strong enough on their own land to keep the magistrates at a distance. It was predictable that they would carry their habits of patronage, the same approaches and attitudes from other sports into the prize-ring. Many of them were also caught up in other sports themselves. The Duke of Hamilton, Sir Charles Lennox (who became the third Duke of Richmond) and the seventh Earl of Barrymore were all keen cricketers; Barrymore was reported to be an excellent bowler, and the Duke of York was an excellent batsman. The Prince of Wales himself was so much at home with the game that, even after a fourteen-year lay-off, he 'displayed as much spirit, activity and skill as the most scientific player on the ground', at least according to the contemporary press. The Duke of Hamilton's sporting tastes were so catholic as to take him also into cock-fighting - he was a regular attender at the Cockpit Royal, along with Tom Johnson's backer, Mr Bullock, and another patron of the ring, Colonel Lowther. Hamilton and Richmond were just two of the ten dukes in the *Racing Calendar*'s list of subscribers for 1797, when followers of the prize-ring racing their own horses included the Honourable Charles Wyndham, the ubiquitous Mr Bullock, Sir Watkin William Wynn and, of course, Colonel O'Kelly, whose greatest claim to respectable fame was as the owner of Eclipse. The common interest shared by followers of the turf and of the ring shows in the ease with which subscription purses could be collected at meetings to finance a pick-up fight once the day's racing was over.

Most attention has been given to pugilism's aristocratic patrons and particularly to the more outrageous and raffish of them, such as Lord Barrymore and Lord

Camelford. The three notorious Barrymore brothers enjoyed the soubriquets of 'Hellgate', 'Cripplegate' and 'Newgate' (to which the Prince added the ungallant suggestion that their sister ought to be 'Billingsgate'). The first of the three, the seventh Earl, the backer of Bill Hooper, shocked even Brighton by his arrogant, bullying behaviour, and met an apposite end when he was accidentally shot by his own loaded gun as he drove in his curricle back to Brighton after a day's duty with his Berkshire militia. His judgement of boxers was as deficient as his judgement of playing cards and his handling of firearms, and he ridiculously overmatched Hooper with the champion, 'Big' Ben Bryan. Hooper bravely kept the better man at bay until darkness stopped the fight, telling his master that if he couldn't win for him, at least he wouldn't lose his money. The Barrymore family did not return the same fidelity and Hooper died a broken and diseased alcoholic in the poorhouse. Thomas Pitt, second Baron Camelford, whose livery Bill Richmond wore for a time, deserted Joe Bourke even more abruptly after his defeat by Jem Belcher and the seizure of both fighters by the Berkshire authorities. Camelford had backed his man for 100 guineas and put him out to a trainer, but Bourke proved untrainable in everything except courage. While Belcher was bailed at once by his backers, Bourke was left to lie in Reading Gaol. Camelford had a stormy naval career, followed by riotous years in London, 'where he achieved an extraordinary notoriety by disorderly conduct', ending with his death in the duel that resulted from one of his several stormy quarrels.

The ring attracted more than its share of such odd characters as Mr J.J. Brayfield, whose eccentricity was even admitted by his *Sporting Magazine* obituary, in March 1821:

almost from infancy attendant upon all the fairs, boxing matches, races, and diversions of every kind round London from the ring made by the first rate amateurs of the fancy down to the weekly badger-baiting in Black Boy-alley. Also constant at Newgate executions[7]

Among the landed gentlemen of the fancy, though, there were many worthy and otherwise respectable members of society, not least of them Lord Thurlow, the Lord Chancellor. Sir John Sebright, who lent his park for the Gregson v. Gully fight, was a liberal-minded Member of Parliament (even where the game laws were concerned), a free trader, a philanthropist who built and endowed a local school and a writer on hawking and animal breeding and behaviour. General Tarleton had distinguished himself less as MP for Liverpool for twenty-two years - it was re-marked that lack of acquaintance with commerce and manufacture coupled with love of pleasure made him a most inappropriate member for that city! The same could not be said of the Honourable William Wyndham, Macaulay's 'first gentle-man of the age', as passionate a fighter in the House of Commons for the suppression of the slave trade as he was to prevent legislation against what he saw as traditional English sports like bear- and bull-baiting.

The point has already been made that the landed classes had no monopoly of prize-ring patronage. There were strong links between the stage and the ring, and the literary and theatrical worlds were well represented. The theatre was still viewed with suspicion by the more austere, and the two were readily thought of in the same breath.

It was not to his credit that Barrymore,

> seldom made a public appearance without a *theatrical* or *pugilistic* companion; whether upon the turf, in the *chace*, at the *election*, the *debating* society, the *billiard* room, or the *bacchanalian* institution.[8]

Bill Oxberry, one of the sport's first chroniclers, was an actor and theatre manager, and among its supporters around the turn of the century were the player and dramatist, John Fawcett, and the writer, John Taylor. The web of relationships around the stage and the ring was spun in many directions, with the Duke of Clarence producing ten children by his mistress, the actress Mrs Jordan, and General Tarleton marrying that other lady of the stage, Mary Robinson, who had been the Prince of Wales's first love!

The resplendent and the raffish, the wealthy and the charlatan made up the broad vanguard of boxing's social leadership and gave it a precarious credibility which was to last for some thirty years. Some important reasons for its sudden rise in status and popularity in the late 1780s lie in the sport itself with its new performers and new techniques, but without deeper shifts in the national mood it might still have remained the obscure amusement of a small band of isolated enthusiasts. It was because the people were ready to play, because all sports were flourishing and new sports were being welcomed, that pugilism found its chance.

The country was at peace and prepared to enjoy itself. The disastrous affair with the American colonists was over, and defeat had left little bitterness, and had been softened by naval success in the West Indies and the lifting of the siege of Gibraltar. The New Plan of the Constitution of the United States was published in full in the *Daily Register* of 1 November 1787, with amiable comments and without recrimination. Humphries and Mendoza were about to sign articles for their first contest, and the Johnson v. Ryan fight was only six weeks away. The first rumblings of discontent were sounding across the Channel in France. There was anxiety lest the same mood should grow in Great Britain. Popular amusements might be under long-term threat but, for the time being, the pressures were relaxed. There was a feeling that the economy was on the move. The new turnpike roads and stage-coach services were making travel much faster. Cities, especially London, were growing rapidly, and the metropolis already had many of the features and most of the problems that the manufacturing towns of the North and the Midlands were to develop during the next fifty years. It had that rising thirst for new amusement which was to be a characteristic of later urbanisation.

This craving for excitement and spectacle is part of the explanation for the resurgence of interest in sport. It is true that the old communal sports continued to be under attack and that attrition was still weakening their hold. It is true, likewise, that hunting, a participatory sport, was becoming more widespread and being more systematically organised over much of the country. By and large, however, it was the spectator sports, both old and new, that were making great strides in popularity. This has been largely ignored, following the lead of the splendid but pessimistically conservative Joseph Strutt and the labour historians who have rightly traced the decline of traditional recreations. In his pioneering work, *The Sports and Pastimes of the People of England*, Strutt has no word for pugilism and few for other newly arrived sports.

Rowing and sailing, for instance, captured interest as competitive sports almost as suddenly as pugilism. The Cumberland Club had laid down the rules for Thames sailing races and the proprietors of the Vauxhall Gardens were donating generous annual prizes for both yachtsmen and scullers. All the races were attracting large crowds, whose best views, as may be imagined, were afforded by the gardens themselves. Nor was it just a Thames sport, catering for the sophisticated metropolitans; silver cups began to be sailed for up and down the coasts.[9]

It was, too, the age of the new classic horse-races - the St Leger, first run in 1776; the Oaks, in 1779; and the Derby, in 1780. Pedestrian contests were growing in number, in the wagers they involved and in their eccentricity. Betting was rising to the fever pitch it reached in the early years of the nineteenth century, when the gambling clubs of St James could regularly see a player lose £30,000 to £40,000 in a single night. More gambling nourished the appetite for more sport at a time when the two were considered inseparable, so much so that the *Sporting Magazine*, on its first appearance, promised to set out the circumstance of every match, event and wager as it was made. The publication of a monthly sporting journal was itself a remarkable development, its editor claiming to be 'astonished' that among all the magazines there was not a single one 'expressly calculated for the sports man'.

The birth of a specialist sporting press was both a symptom of the burgeoning interest in athletic and other contests and an encouragement to further growth in old and new sports alike. Captain Topham's *The World* had enjoyed a brief life in the late 1780s, before the captain had retired to care for his Yorkshire acres; the *Sporting Magazine* itself began its long career in 1793 and *Bell's Weekly Messenger* began its even longer one in 1796. In its very first number, the *Sporting Magazine* not only reported three prize-fights in some detail, but also embarked on the first instalment of a history of the ring. The general press had already led the way by its growing interest in pugilistic affairs. Whatever it might loftily say about 'bruising' in its editorials, the *Daily Register*, in the month before it became *The Times*, was acknowledging that pugilism was now the fashion and deserved notice. The notice was certainly given with little stint. There is mention of the sport in virtually every one of eight issues, between 20 December 1787 and the end of the year, with a deliberate build-up of excitement over the forthcoming Humphries v. Mendoza fight. Humphries had gone into the country to train. Mendoza had given up teaching at his boxing academy to concentrate on the fight. The outcome would decide which of the two men's schools would be the one to flourish. The betting was reported as 6 to 4 on Humphries, but Mendoza had 'increased in bulk and strength', and had 'improved in fighting' and was said to have 'adopted' a new blow from Broughton.

The sport itself responded by polishing its style and rituals. Tom Johnson had introduced the practice of wearing personal colours, ribbons which were tied to the fighter's corner-post when he entered the ring. The winner brandished the loser's colours as a trophy of victory, wearing them around his hat or his neck as he made his conqueror's way back to his London headquarters. Soon the yellow favours of the Bristol fighters were to be a common sight, victorious more often than not. The ring heightened its sense of theatre and ritual. The fighters became proud of their appearance, though it took some time to find a workable compromise between dandyism and practicality. Humphries' fine flannel drawers, white silk stockings with gold-coloured clocks, pumps and black shoe ribands made him a dashing sight at the start of his fight with Mendoza in January 1788, all the more so because his plainly-kitted-out opponent was the one with the colourful reputation. However, the slippery boards of the stage in the rain forced Humphries to take off his shoes, only to find that the silk stockings presented even greater problems. He had to put on coarse worsted before he found his feet and moved into the ascendancy.[10]

As the fight itself encroached further into theatre, the fighter himself became the dramatic hero. Any hints of nobility of character in the pugilist began to be lauded to the skies. Isaac Perrins, the Birmingham Goliath who fell to Humphries's David, was, it was pointed out, the highly regarded foreman of the factory where he worked. He was trusted by his employers and respected and liked by the workers, and had a taste for music that had made him the leader of a church choir. His death came about in consequence of giving help to put out a house fire. Humphries' good manners and polite behaviour became a byword, however much his record as a second sows doubts about his notions of fair play, as later generations have conceived it. Sportsmen began to counter evangelical tracts, with their warnings of the effects of gambling and drink, by citing such instances as that of Tom Johnson. He, while working as a corn porter, was said to have taken the place of a sick colleague by carrying twice the normal load, covering for his absence so that his wages would continue to be paid and his wife and children sustained. Here, even in one of the ring's older rough diamonds, was an instance of physical strength put to the undoubted service of virtue. If the sport's new social leaders felt any need to defend boxing beyond the resort to manliness, national character and fair play, here was the evidence. In a fashionable sport, the boxer had become hero. It was the final justification for pugilism, one in which all the bruises, the blood and the fatalities could, in a crude and cruel age, be forgotten.

4

Bristol's Crown and the Geography of Pugilism

London dominated the country's social and political life more completely in the late eighteenth century than possibly at any other time. The capital's sheer size ensured its pre-eminence - it housed almost one-eighth of the total population in the middle of the century and nearly a million people by the end of it. It was little wonder that it stood head and shoulders above the rest of the country in the newly developing sports, though sometimes at a certain remove. Newmarket, for instance, might be a good half day's coach ride from the capital, but it was the undisputed home of horse-racing for the London gentry and the frequency and quality of its racing set it quite apart from other meetings. Cricket was very much a sport of the south-eastern half of the country and standards of play tended to decline - Hambledon excepted - the further west and north the game removed from London. Competitive boating was organised earlier and more thoroughly on the Thames than anywhere else, while even truly provincial sports such as Cumberland or Devon and Cornwall wrestling only caught the national eye when their exponents came up to London to perform. If pugilism was to be a national sport, it had to be London based.

London itself consistently produced more prize-fighters than any other area (see Map 1), again a function of its size and the availability of opportunity, although by the 1790s there were also flourishing provincial centres, notably in the West Country, in and around Bristol and in the rapidly developing West Midlands, based on Coventry and Birmingham. Norwich, always a jealous rival of Bristol as a regional capital, also had its pugilistic ambitions, though these were only fitfully realised until the early nineteenth century. Out of 112 native-born pugilists fighting between 1780 and 1824 whose place of origin can be firmly identified, the majority came from the three urban areas - thirty-six from London, twenty-six from Bristol and Bath, and ten from the Birmingham district.

Initially, provincial competitors in all sports usually had a hard time of it against London opponents. It would be decades before cricketers from the Midlands and the North could meet those from the South-East on equal terms, and Newmarket horses had a high success rate when, as they often did, they toured the county meetings. Certainly Jack Slack had come up from Norwich to dethrone Broughton, but the early excursions of Bristol boxers into the reviving London ring were inauspicious. As well as the unfortunate Sam Martin, who came up against Humphries and Mendoza, there was Will Ward, who had the ignominious fight against Johnson, and Bob Watson, who did win his first three fights before being beaten by Hooper in 1790. All three rehabilitated themselves in time. Martin reasserted the West's provincial superiority by defeating Blight, the Coventry weaver; Will Ward became a central figure in the prize-ring's management; and Watson resumed his regional career before returning to London. His continued involvement with the ring was virtually guaranteed by his family connections - his wife was a sister of the Belchers, and his daughter married Jem Burn! There was also the relatively unregarded Ben Bryan (inevitably known as 'Big Ben', even though he was no bigger than the usual heavyweight), Bristol born and bred although he had spent most of his adult life in London. While Humphries and Mendoza were still battling out the right to challenge for the title, Bryan stepped in and beat the waning Johnson, but his health soon failed and he died without defending his championship.

Bristol men took the crown in earnest in 1795, on the retirement of John Jackson, and held it for the next twenty-five years. Jem Belcher, Henry Pearce, John Gully and Tom Cribb all emerged from the West to take the championship in turn. Even in 1820, at the end of Bristol's reign, the new hero, Tom Spring, turned out to be another west countryman, this time from Hereford. Bristol's pre-eminence in pugilism over this period is reminiscent of Hambledon's success in cricket, and it began just as the Hambledon Club's fifteen or so years of glory were coming to an end. Hambledon's success on the cricket field had been the result of the vigorous patronage of a few noblemen allied with local skill and enthusiasm. Bristol's success in pugilism is harder to explain. Better physique may have been one of the foundations on which it was built. London employers were always on the look-out for youngsters from the country (the North and Scotland were the most favoured areas), convinced that they would be fitter than those reared in the crowded, smoky capital. While Bristol's working-class areas were hardly salubrious, the fresh winds blew up the Channel from the Atlantic and the airy downs were close at hand. It was a place where the hills made sturdy limbs a necessity, and it was a prosperous city where men had some leisure and an eye for sport and entertainment. There was a well-established pugilistic tradition, which local fairs helped to foster, and a growing network, centred on the butchery trade, of known fighting men. The Bristol pugilists with their yellow favours became a close-knit community, whether at home or in London, and many of the ties were those of kinship. The Belcher brothers were grandsons of Jack Slack and as well as the sister who married Bob Watson, they had another who was wife to another fighter of minor fame, Pardoe Wilson. Joe Ward followed his brother, Will, to London, and it was to Will that Jem Belcher went for an introduction to the London boxing scene. Joe Ward was his regular second from his first major fight onwards and, in turn, John Ward, Will's son, was one of young Tom Belcher's early opponents.

Many boxing commentators have regarded the older Belcher, Jem, as the greatest exponent of pugilism ever. As a newly arrived teenager, he amazed Will Ward when they first sparred together in his tavern, but 1799 was not a time when the pugilistic world was as hungry for champions as it had been when Humphries and Mendoza first blazed their ways on to the stage. There was a certain war weariness in the air after two naval mutinies and some depressing military enterprises against the French. Belcher had to prove his worth in two bouts against tried but ageing boxers of the past generation, fighting for low stakes, before he caught the sporting fancy's eye. His hard-won victory in the second of these, against Jack Bartholomew, a long-time favourite,

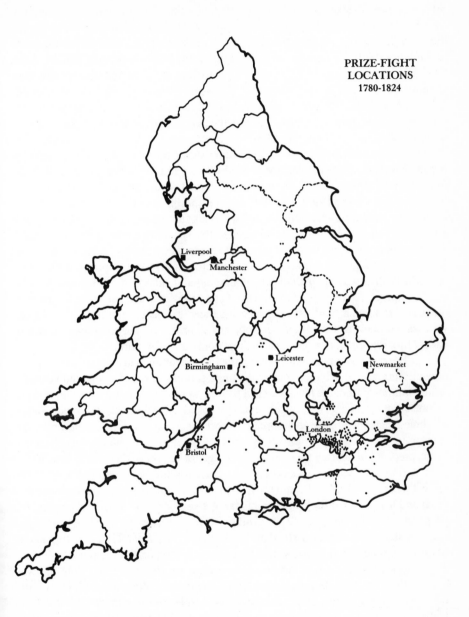

PRIZE-FIGHT
LOCATIONS
1780-1824

brought out the backers, and the two were rematched for 300 guineas to meet on a stage erected on Finchley Common in May 1800. Victory here, and the defeat of the Irish champion, Andrew Gamble, a few months later, meant that the only possible rival left for Belcher was Joe Bourke and the prospect of their meeting aroused more excitement than the ring had known since the Humphries and Mendoza days.

Something of the same glamour surrounded their encounter. There was again the contrast in style and personality, again the build-up of moneyed support for both sides and again a long anticipation before the outcome was finally settled. The appeal of the contest is easily understood. In the one corner was the bright young man, the recent arrival in the London ring, fresh, good-looking and with a fine physique. Belcher had made a highly favourable impression on account of his poise and grace in the ring and his easy manner outside it. Affable and smiling, he was none the less ready to put up his fists without undue ceremony and without a first regard for the size of the prize money. His skill was already acknowledged, with its novel speed and mobility, its rapid, hard punching, its elusiveness and strength. Yet there were many doubters about how he would stand up to the tried and hardened Joe Bourke, his opposite in so many respects. Bourke was squat, thickset, pugnacious and unpolished, loud mouthed and quick tempered. No one would make any claims for science in his fighting, but he held the palm for stamina, hardness, resilience and sheer unflinching courage. Their clashes were soon to show that Bourke never stood any chance of beating the young Bristolian, except by a random lucky blow, yet he kept coming up for more.

The one major benefit that Humphries and Mendoza had enjoyed and that was now missing was such backing from the highest ranks of society as would virtually ensure immunity from the law. Powerful patrons were still there, but the times and the manners were changing. Large-scale fights provoked rising opposition, so much so that the three Belcher v. Bourke contests came to belong as much to the legal history of the sport as to its athletic development. Belcher, meanwhile, wore his crown at a jaunty angle, prepared to fight off the cuff, as he did against Bourke in their second encounter after a chance meeting at Camberwell Fair. Only the persuasion of colleagues made them put off the battle until the next day, when they fought, almost unnoticed, in Hyde Park. Even at the height of his fame a year later (1803), Belcher was still prepared to take on John 'The Young Ruffian' Firby for a purse raised by enthusiasts at Newmarket, instead of the usual set high stakes. The purse turned out to be 100 guineas, but it was a speculative venture, typical of the man.

Belcher's end was a sad one. In the summer after the Firby fight, he was accidently struck in the eye with a ball while playing racquets at the St Martin's Lane court, an injury that cost him the sight of that eye. He became landlord of the Jolly Brewers in Wardour Street, Soho, and the boxing world assumed that he was retired. Instead, he came back for three sad fights, one against Henry Pearce and two against the up-and-coming Tom Cribb, all of which he lost. In spite of his claims to the contrary, his partial blindness clearly made it difficult for him to judge distance and he was beaten with relative ease. His disposition too was changed. His geniality gave way to irritability and depression. The ale and the spirits were too close at hand to be resisted and his decline was rapid. Jem Belcher, the paragon of pugilism, died at the age of 30.

Immediately after his eye injury, while his judgement was still sound, his own intention had been to retire and he had looked for a fighter he could sponsor for the championship, which was being claimed by his old unloved antagonist, Joe Bourke. Bristol was the natural direction for the search, and he came up with Henry Pearce, five years his senior and highly regarded in the West Country. The strength of the region's boxing was demonstrated when Pearce (known as Hen Pearce, hence 'The Game Chicken'!) convincingly beat the redoubtable Bourke in his very first London fight. He also won a return match with Bourke, and from then on his only serious challenger was yet another Bristolian, Tom Gully, who was destined to stride defiantly over the sporting and social life of the country for much of the nineteenth century. At this stage, the butchery business he had launched in London had failed. He put the mufflers on to spar with Pearce and so took the fancy of the champion and the bystanders that the two were immediately matched to meet in the ring. Pearce won a brave fight, while Gully's skill and courage stood him in good stead when the championship became vacant not long afterwards. 'The Game Chicken's' last fight was a reluctant response to the challenge of his half-blind promoter, when the only alternative was to give up the title. He won so easily that few questioned his claim that there were times during the fight when he could have killed Jem had he been so minded.

Pearce's own end had its pathos. He had his two brief years wearing the hero's mantle. He was a hard-hitting boxer with a stunning left hand, popular for his generosity towards opponents and his modesty about his own achievements. After beating Gully, he retired to Bristol, taking in a successful sparring tour on the way. In retirement, he performed two acts of heroism which soon entered the annals of pugilism as proofs of the sport's character-building qualities - he made a dramatic and public rescue of a servant girl from the attic of a blazing house and a few months later saved another damsel in distress when she was being pestered by three men on Clifton Downs. Sadly, the idyll could not last. His domestic life became unhappy, he shook the dust of Bristol from his feet, returned to London and became consumptive. He died on 30 April 1809 at one of his sport's main meeting places, the Coach and Horses, St Martin's Lane.

John Gully was on hand to maintain Bristol's hold on the title. Although Pearce never formally retired, Gully was the acknowledged champion until he announced his own retirement shortly afterwards. Bob Gregson, who had fought unavailingly under the banner of Lancashire in two cruel battles with Gully, now found that yet another Bristolian stood between him and the championship - Tom Cribb, who, for the past three years, had been working his way through the ranks of the London ring. When the two met, at Molesey Hurst on the Thames on 25 October 1808, Gregson suffered almost as bad a mauling as he had previously received from Gully. Tom Cribb was champion. He was never to be beaten, retiring at last at a splendid exhibition night at the Fives Court in May 1822.

Bristol's domination of the prize-ring had, paradoxically, covered the period when the sport was most firmly London centred. The ring depended on the capital for financial backing and for such social status and national organisation as it could muster. London, too, could provide a massive potential audience, a useful sign of public interest though economically only a relatively minor benefit, given the frequent difficulties in the way of collecting gate money. With its wealth and growth during the Napoleonic wars and its thirst for sensation and drama to fill the extended leisure that could be squeezed out from prosperity, London was the irresistible magnet for the aspiring pugilist. Its dominance was so complete that the regional boxing scene, on which it thrived, was only sketchily and fitfully recorded. Even in the case of the Bristol champions, little detail is known of their fistic achievements in the West Country before their appearance in the London ring. Standards there had obviously risen further since the days of Will Ward and Sam Martin, so that Henry Pearce could come, at one move, straight from Bristol into the top national ranks.

Champions from other provincial circuits tended to fare less happily. Noah James, for instance, the Cheshire ex-guardsman, fought seventeen bouts before attempting to make his mark in London in a match with Andrew Gamble, when he discovered that immense courage alone was not enough. In the twelfth round Gamble 'cut his nose dreadfully', in the twentieth he broke his collar-bone and in the twenty-first his jaw, yet James fought on gamely for four more rounds.[1] Birmingham boxers fared no better and, apart from Ben Stanyard, who became an occasional second and exhibitioner, had temporarily disappeared from the London scene by 1800. Ten years earlier the Birmingham sportsmen had been well organised enough - and confident enough - to put forward a joint challenge of no fewer than five of their champions, Isaac Perrins, Jacombs, Pickard, Tom Faulkner and Thornhill, against London boxers, but all the three challengers that were taken up resulted in wins by the London boxers, with defeats for Perrins, Jacombs and Pickard. Regional interest, however, was not extinguished, even when the much beaten Sam Martin underlined Bristol's provincial superiority by defeating Bligh, the Coventry weaver, in a contest which, incidentally, illustrates the vagaries of reporting out-of-town events. The fight was variously located at Ensham, Oxfordshire, and Evesham, Oxfordshire, when it almost certainly took place at Evesham, Worcestershire, which was conveniently midway between the home bases of the two fighters. The occasional purely domestic battle in the West Midlands could still attract high stakes, heavy wagers and large crowds. The 100 guinea fight between Thorney and Alcock, two Birmingham shoemakers, brought such a following to the nearby Lickey Hills in February 1793 that constant interruptions prolonged the contest from 1 p.m. to 5 p.m., with Alcock claiming victory as darkness fell. Nearly a decade later, the contest between Tom Cart and James Sidwell, near Nuneaton, was backed by wagers of above 100 guineas, but none of these local heroes went on to make any national impact.

Norwich, as a flourishing and fashionable provincial city, was soon to be making deliberate efforts to establish itself as a pugilistic centre. Meanwhile, commentators remarked that 'more valour than skill was displayed' when Benjamin Pile ('The Young Big Ben' as he was hopefully dubbed) beat James Harmer near there in 1797. Devon was always a wrestling rather than a boxing area and a fight at Moulton in 1794 between Greenway and Snokell was marked by such crudities as grabbing the opponent by the hair and striking him 'several very severe but unfair blows'. In this case the offender got his deserts when the victim extricated himself and with two powerful blows laid his rival 'senseless at his feet'.[2] Such differences in standards between sport at the centre and sport in the provinces, which were to be a common feature of the developing

3 Thomas Cribb, unbeaten champion of England (From the painting by De Wild, 1811)

spectator sports for many years, made the pugilistic superiority of Bristol all the more remarkable. The disparity between the Bristol ring and the rest of regional boxing was nowhere better emphasised than in a challenge issued in January 1805 by Burkitt, the Cheshire blacksmith, after he had beaten the Cornishman, Cavallin, in a much-heralded match in 'the wild mountains of Wales' (it was, in fact, in Merioneth!). Burkitt offered to fight, for 50 guineas, in many of the six western counties, Cornwall, Devon, Dorset, Gloucester, Monmouth and Somerset, 'the inhabitants of Bristol and Bath excepted'. The fact that Burkitt was, incidentally, seconded by another Cheshire man, Williams, whom he 'owns his superior' indicates that there were some established regional hierarchies.[3]

When provincial fighters did come up to London, they could still expect, as relative unknowns unlikely to attract vast crowds, to make their ring debuts fairly close to the city centre. The favourite venues were at most a couple of hours' brisk walking away - Wormwood Scrubs (until magisterial interference began there in 1802), Wimbledon Common, Hounslow Heath, Islington and sites along the Edgware Road (see Map 2). Minor (and impromptu) bouts could still take place in even more central settings such as Hyde Park, where the most important encounter was the hurried affair between Belcher and Bourke. As late as 1804 it was possible to mount a fight of some importance in Tothill Fields, one of the nearest rough spots to the city and a favourite place for bull-baiting. Tom Belcher, Jem's younger brother, fought John Ward there for a purse of 50 guineas on a June afternoon that year. Old Oak Common, Willesden Green and, just south of the river, Kennington Common, were other nearby sites, but it became increasingly difficult to sustain such venues as these as London expanded, the sport attracted bigger crowds and suspicion of all recreational gatherings grew stronger. Any regular prize-fighting near to large centres of population was likely to be stopped by the justices and their constables. These inner-London contests were, in any event, seldom the cream of pugilistic fare. They were the bread and butter of the sport, fights for low stakes mounted throughout the year, not just in pugilism's high winter and spring season, and rarely attracting more than a handful of upper-class enthusiasts and backers. The occasional presence of gentry supporters was rare enough to be remarked upon, as when the Duke of Hamilton, Colonel Hamilton and 'many other amateurs' were spectators on Hounslow Heath for the Cooper v. Wood fight in June 1795. Even where comparatively high sums were at stake, such as the 100 guineas between Cordy and Haines the next year, very few of the upper-class enthusiasts were attracted to these fights.

The location of prize-fights became much influenced by the attitudes of the local and legal authorities (see Map 3). It was accepted that major fights, those with any bearing on the championship, had to be well away from London, though preferably within a hard day's riding, which would allow the sportsman to be back home for dinner. These big fights were the hardest to stage. Some county justices, notably those in Buckinghamshire, Suffolk and Cambridgeshire, were consistently antagonistic. Others blew hot and cold from year to year, but Berkshire, Sussex, Kent and Hampshire were generally tolerant, while Surrey and Hertfordshire were unpredictable. Sites to the south and west of London were the most popular with the gentry - they disliked Essex because it meant a long ride over the cobbles of the city streets - but they were

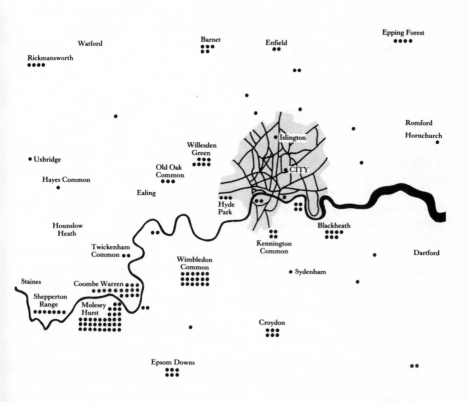

PRIZE-FIGHTING
LONDON LOCATIONS
1780-1824

prepared to support fights based on important race meetings such as Newmarket or Doncaster (until the corporation authorities stepped in). Crawley Downs, convenient for both London and Brighton, and sites just across the Surrey boundary in Berkshire and Hampshire were most favoured for the big matches.

It was the search for regular locations for substantial non-championship fighting that proved particularly difficult. The pugilists and their supporters found themselves pushed further and further away from the city (see Map 3). When the crowd made its customary way to Wormwood Scrubs for the match between Pittoon and Maddox in December 1802, they found the ground occupied by Bow Street officers and a large band of constables. Lock's Fields, off the Kent Road, were barred the next year, a Paddington fight was moved on and a magistrate's warrant on the eve of the fight prevented O'Donnell from meeting Henigan at Dulwich. London racegrounds also became too public for mounting set-piece contests and although bouts continued there, particularly on Epsom Downs, these were usually pick-up matches at the end of a day's racing. Wimbledon Common continued to be a regular resort, but freedom from police interference could no longer be guaranteed there after Bourke's fight with Henry Pearce in 1804, when the crowd had moved from one part of the common to another in their attempts to elude the constables. This was one of the rare occasions when the prohibitions of the law officers went unheeded. Tom Owen, as one of the most vociferous of the seconds, was made the scapegoat for the defiance and sent to prison for three months.[4] Old Oak Common managed to survive as one of the nearer venues, but that flat and inhospitable waste seldom catered for more than the rougher end of the market.

Eventually it was royalty which afforded pugilism the convenient venues it sought. There was never any formal agreement, still less any public announcement, but it came to be accepted that fights in the vicinity of the Duke of Clarence's estate at Bushey Park would go unhindered. The Duke, later to become William IV, had enjoyed the sport from his youth. He was a bluff, uncomplicated character, a career naval officer, and his silent protection meant that for some twenty years from 1805 pugilism had more-or-less regular venues at Molesey Hurst - for many years a recreational resort, where David Garrick had played golf and cricketers pitched their wickets - and Coombe Wood and Coombe Warren, on the northern bank of the river. These sites became effectively the field headquarters of the sport, in some seasons mounting fights almost every Tuesday. The promoters were careful not to push their luck too far by mounting the really big fights there, and the proceedings went on undisturbed.

As to the actual ring practice during the period of Bristol's dominance, there was a refining of existing techniques rather than any outstanding innovation. Greater speed in both movement and striking made boxing at its highest levels a less cumbersome sport than it had been in the past. Jem Belcher's excellence set standards which others sought to emulate but all agreed that his ring style was remarkably individual, owing more to intuitive mobility and reaction than to any definable advance in technique. Wrestling throws remained important and for all his punching ability Belcher was known too for his wrestling skills. When O'Donnell was described as throwing Smith with 'a cross buttock something in the Belcher style', this was praise indeed. It became

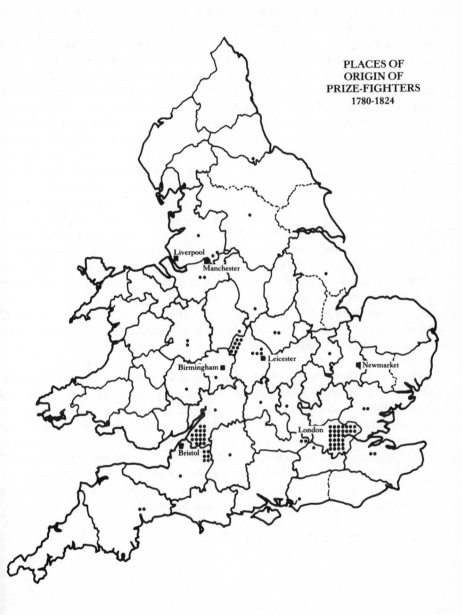

**PLACES OF
ORIGIN OF
PRIZE-FIGHTERS
1780-1824**

common to land heavily on top of a thrown opponent, while hugging, mauling and clinching increased, to the crowds' distaste. Defensive skills improved, with much more frequent reference to the parrying of blows. Many of them still landed though, and the risks to the pugilist remained as great as they had always been. A broken leg in Islington; two pugilists in Bath, after nearly two and a half hours in the ring, described as both being near to death and one not expected to recover; the sort of battering received by Noah James at the hands of Gamble;[5] and dreadfully contused faces and bruised hands were the common outcome, as was damage to internal organs from constant pummelling. And as if this punishment to the body were not enough, there could be the cruel desertion of the loser by his sponsors. Bourke was left to languish in jail after his fight with Jem Belcher at Maidenhead, while the winner was bailed out, and there was the callous neglect of O'Donnell after his hard-fought contest with Caleb Baldwin in September 1803, which was considered to be even worse. He was at length brought down with such a violent blow to the kidneys that he could scarcely stand at the scratch for the last round, when more heavy body blows from Baldwin and a violent cross-buttock finally flattened him. The poor man was then left alone in a coach without any assistance for nearly two hours while his so-called friends continued to enjoy themselves with some crude and second-rate competition which followed.

More thought did begin to be given to actual training. A reduction in alcohol intake (but not to the use of the brandy bottle between rounds) and some sparring practice had generally sufficed in the past. Now attempts began to be made for a more methodical approach and some of Bourke's sponsors tried to take him in hand for his fights against Belcher. Bourke's usual way of life was certainly not conducive to fitness, so he was taken into the country and put on raw eggs to improve his wind and raw beef to make him more savage, though it was never courage he lacked but the skill to use it. The news of Bourke's regime was not sufficient even to swing the odds against Belcher, let alone to secure victory against him. The opinion was that Belcher, even if not under a regular training system, lived a temperate life, was in good condition and 'full of stiff meat'.[6] The age of the scientific trainer had not yet arrived in Belcher's fighting days, but it was just around the corner, and Tom Cribb, the last wearer of Bristol's crown, was to reap its most conspicuous first benefits.

5

The Sport and the Law

This is a practice certainly which must be repressed - it is infinitely mischievous in its immediate effect to the limbs and lives of the combatants themselves. It draws industrious people away from the subject of their industry; and when great multitudes are so collected, they are likely enough to be engaged in broils. It affords an opportunity for people of the most mischievous disposition to assemble, under the colour of seeing this exhibition, and to do a great deal of mischief; in short, it is a practice that is extremely injurious in every respect and must be repressed.[1]

So pronounced Lord Ellenborough at the conclusion of the trial in May 1803 of James Belcher, Joseph Bourke (erroneously, and perhaps ironically, referred to as Edmund Bourke!), Joe Ward (in another error, called James Ward) and Henry Lee. They were charged with conspiracy to fight a duel, riotous assembly, fighting a duel and breach of the peace. If any eyebrows were raised by the noble judge's comments, it was because he gave as his first objection the damage suffered by the boxers themselves, usually a low priority in the reasons for complaint. Many voices were regularly making similar accusations against all popular sports. They took people away from work, attracted unruly crowds and generally promoted criminal behaviour. Racing could defend itself on the grounds that its meetings were seldom more than annual affairs and could claim, often spuriously, the justification of tradition. Cricket had for its defence gentry participants, its stature as 'the fine old English game' and the fact that its crowds seem to be smaller, and therefore less threatening, than in the past. Only pugilism was actually unlawful, and it therefore had to bear the legal brunt of the general attack on spectator sports.

There are some remarkable aspects of the survival of pugilism in the face of its total prohibition. There was the establishment of a whole set of conventions for the cat-and-mouse game with local law authorities; the remarkable complaisance of often vast and allegedly unruly prize-fighting crowds, opposed often by only one or two law officers; the existence not only of rules within the sport but the courts' acknowledgement of those rules; the general immunity from prosecution of both the sport's greatest champions and its upper-class sponsors; and the surprising decorum of some of the sport's own practices - it never, for example, mounted a fight on a Sunday!

The major handicap presented by the sport's illegality was, of course, the absence of fixed and readily controllable venues, especially the lack of indoor facilities for matches, which would have allowed the sport's energies to be given to better regulation and to improvements in control and practice. As it was, matches could not be formally advertised; time and place had to be notified by word of mouth. They attracted those whose respect for the law was less than total, either because they felt themselves to be above it, or because they sought to ignore it or lived outside it anyway. Not that breaking the law by attending a pugilistic match was regarded with any seriousness. In spite of warnings from the courts that everyone present was guilty of at least aiding and abetting and possibly of conspiracy, no mere spectator at a prize-fight was ever prosecuted. In fact, the great majority of fights passed off without interference by the authorities, although that did become more frequent after 1800. The organisers usually knew which places were likely to be safe and which were not, and it was often when local policy changed that they faced problems. Within months of the Prince of Wales's renunciation of pugilism, for instance, the Cambridgeshire justices were making it clear to the Newmarket sportsmen that they would not have the Johnson v. Perrins fight within the county. Such problems always tended to beset the biggest fights, those likely to bring in many thousands of followers, commotion and damage, and to be a very deliberate and visible affront to the rule of law.

Serious skirmishing between pugilism and the law began with the rise of Jem Belcher and the revived interest in the sport that accompanied it. Already his rematch with Jack Bartholomew had attracted the attention of the authorities because Bartholomew was currently bound over to keep the peace, i.e. keep out of the ring, and the humiliation of defeat was exacerbated by the frustration of brief imprisonment, until he was bailed by his backers, for breaking his undertaking. It was Belcher's contests with Joe Bourke, however, which constituted the central saga of the sport's conflict with the law. It began when the two men met at The Sun, Spitalfields, on 10 September 1801 and agreed to set out from there to do battle exactly one week later. In spite of the short notice, the magistrates heard of the proposal and issued a warrant to prevent the fight which was accordingly put off to 12 October. Again one of the Bow Street magistrates intervened with a warrant forbidding the fight, and this time Belcher was arrested on the evening before the fight and kept in custody until the next lunchtime, when any hope of bringing off the fight was gone. When it did take place, near Maidenhead in Berkshire, the location was not decided until the eve of the contest, too late for it to be prevented but not too late for the Lord-Lieutenant of the county to issue warrants against the two fighters and their seconds for 'unlawfully assembling and publicly fighting'. They were arrested in London and bailed for £200 each to appear at Berkshire quarter Sessions. Belcher's bail money was at once forthcoming, paid not by his noble supporters (at least not openly) but by a publican and an oyster merchant. Bourke, deserted by his backers, could not raise the money and landed in Reading Gaol. He had three months in prison before the case came up, while Belcher, although free, was still closely watched by the London magistrates. Sparring displays were usually tolerated as legitimate entertainment, yet when Belcher, Andrew Gamble and other pugilists exhibited at the Peahen Tavern, Gray's Inn Lane, in April, the premises were raided and the whole company, pugilists, spectators and all, found themselves in prison for the night.

At the quarter sessions, Belcher and Bourke were let off lightly. The chairman of the court acknowledged that they had surrendered themselves willingly to the law, trusted that they would no more disturb the peace by fighting, and on that understanding dismissed them from the court. He paid particular tribute to the good reputation of

4. 'Returning from the intended Fight, Oct 12, 1801' from the *Sporting Magazine* of that month. The fight was that arranged for Belcher and Burke and the chaos of the journey is well illustrated. Such scenes of disorder contributed much to pugilism's ill repute.

Belcher, who consistently came off better than his opponents in these brushes with authority, such were the rewards of being a popular champion with influential friends. Their influence, though, had its limitations. A match was made at Newmarket for the two men to fight again for £200 a side. The assumption that this would be a safe area, well away from both London magistrates and the county of their last offence, proved mistaken as all the neighbouring justices made it clear that the fight would be prevented. Accordingly it was agreed to hold it in June in Yorkshire, near Ripon, on the boundary between the North and West Ridings. The stage was erected, the crowd gathered and then up rode the Dean of York with magistrates from the two counties. He had the Riot Act read by the magistrates' clerk, and the disgruntled throng dispersed. It was later suggested that Bourke's refusal to fight because of dissatisfaction with his seconds was the real cause of the fight's abandonment and that otherwise the appearance of the magistrates, without any military or police support, would have been disregarded. This, though, is at odds with the general experience; contests were often called off at the intervention of a single brave magistrate. The allegation seems to have been a further attempt to blacken the character of Bourke, a task in which he himself regularly assisted.

That the fight eventually took place in Hyde Park, if only before a small impromptu crowd,[2] hardly made the London guardians of law and order better disposed towards the two men or towards their sport. Belcher was prevented from appearing at an exhibition at the Sadler's Wells Theatre and the magistrates went so far as to close down the theatre for the whole of the rest of the season. It was not the end of sparring exhibitions in theatres, for boxers sometimes went to show themselves off in theatres in the provinces, but pugilism tended to have its later displays in such venues as the Fives Court, which were free from the strict magisterial control imposed on theatres. Meanwhile, the Berkshire legal proceedings were revived on the grounds that Belcher and Bourke had broken their undertaking not to fight, an undertaking that had always been given somewhat lightly by pugilists in the past, with little fear of the consequences of breaking it. Belcher's friends had the case moved to the King's Bench in London, where they looked to a more sympathetic hearing. They were not disappointed, in spite of the fact that the public motive for moving the case was to demonstrate that a higher court was prepared to give full backing to county magistrates. In spite of Lord Ellenborough's stern words, the day ended with the two principals being called upon to place bail of £400 each, to attend to receive the judgement of the court when called upon and in the meantime to keep the peace. Two months later Belcher received his eye injury, which effectively ended his role in the legal proceedings.

For Bourke, the skirmishes with the authorities continued. Eventually, when the case was thought to have lapsed (when 'time at length eradicated all fear of that process', according to a contemporary account) he ventured to fight Henry Pearce on Wimbledon Common. This was the occasion when the police officers arrived after the fight had started and were unable to put a stop to it - perhaps surprisingly, Tom Owen rather than the traditional villain, Bourke, had to pay the penalty.[3] Bourke had at least shown some deference to the law by having his earlier fight with Pearce in the upstairs room of a tavern, the select gentry being invited by word of mouth, so as not to break his undertakings too early and too publicly. His brave but largely unsuccessful career in the ring was, in any case, nearing its end. His in-built propensity for attracting the attentions of the keepers of law and order followed him into retirement, where poverty led him to theft and further imprisonment. John Jackson, among his other charitable acts, organised a petition for the release of Bourke, who made amends afterwards by serving as a non-commissioned officer in Wellington's army during the Peninsular War.

The local harassment of prize-fighting, and particularly its gradual exclusion from many inner London sites, demonstrates the effectiveness of the Lord Chief Justice's promptings to magistrates. The county justices could be just as active as their urban colleagues, although distances and divided jurisdiction made their task all the harder. The pugilistic world had learned long ago the advantage of sites near points on the map where three counties met and where three sets of magistrates had to be on the alert to prevent contests - it was to meet this difficulty that the prosecutor at the Belcher v. Bourke trial called for magistrates to be given the right to cross county boundaries if an offence originally planned for their county was, on prevention, transferred over the border. The practice was commonplace. For instance, the match between Jem Belcher and John Firby was made at Newmarket. Hopes of mounting it in Cambridgeshire were slim, but Suffolk was more promising. When the Suffolk authorities intervened, the retinue slipped southwards to the nearest point in Essex and the fight took place near Linton. The Essex magistrates were not particularly tolerant, they were merely taken by surprise - in August 1804 they prevented the fight between Caleb Baldwin and Sam 'Dutch Sam' Elias from taking place within the county boundaries and the pugilists retreated back into Middlesex, where they were more successful.

The fight promoters sought to avoid the law by keeping their proposed locations secret. The greater the threat of interruption, the later the word would be passed around, often not until the eve of the fight itself. The articles governing individual fights - themselves, paradoxically, in the form of legal contracts and up to a point recognised by the courts as such - usually stipulated a site, say thirty or forty miles from London, or sometimes a site midway between two places. The main concern was that the moneyed followers should know where to go. For those with less speedy transport, or none at all, it often meant a speculative excursion on the day before the fight - to the consternation of the local populace and the profit of local innkeepers (who were usually drunk dry) - and a night spent in a barn or a stable or even under the stars. On the day of the fight, the organisers would seek out the favoured place, often posting outriders to give early warning of threatened interference. Well-known figures from the ring, like the white-haired black, Bill Richmond, would sometimes stand conspicuously on point duty, directing the crowds, though this was a mixed blessing to everyone except the carriage trade. One of the reasons for holding many fights on Tuesdays rather then Mondays, a practice which firmed up in these early years of the nineteenth century, was to reduce the offence given by mass migrations on the eve of fights by moving those migrations away from the Sabbath. Another consequence of the policing pressures was that the need for speed meant the abandonment of the old practice of taking carpenters and planks along to erect a raised stage; the fighting usually took place directly on the turf. It was a change not unwelcome to the boxers themselves; they found the sods a much easier bed to fall on than the deal boards of a stage. Spectators were less happy as fewer of them could usually get a good view of the fight, suitable natural hollows being in comparative short supply, and the difficulties of crowd control increased accordingly. One further result of harassment was a later start to many fights because of the shifts from one venue to another. The articles usually required the men to present themselves in the ring between noon and 1 p.m., but increasingly a safe location was not settled upon until late in the afternoon, which gave rise to new hazards such as boxers being dazzled by low winter sunshine, or, more conclusively, the light failing before the contest ended. In this circumstance, fighting on until darkness fell became a new tactic enabling a defeated man to survive and draw. After the fight, crowds making their way home in complete darkness faced even more perils to themselves and threatened more to others than they did during the full light of day.

Given all the external obstacles it had to surmount in the early nineteenth century, the degree of regulation in pugilism, at least at its upper levels, is remarkable. Contention over the outcome of a major fight was rare. The sport's conventions were well established and there were always enough experienced men of authority, gentry and pugilists, on hand to make sure that the accepted modes of behaviour prevailed. Mounting a fight at all was triumph enough, and there was the feeling that time and energy could not be dissipated on internal squabbles. The old disputes over falling without being struck continued, and the habit was seen as discrediting a boxer, though it was still not illegal unless the articles for the fight specifically forbade it. Ned 'Hopping Ned' Morgan claimed victory in his hour-long struggle against Donovan in 1803 because his opponent had repeatedly fallen of his own volition as he delivered his punches; he had also irritated the crowd by his shifting and retreating tactics. Where the stakes went in this case - and that was the final mark of victory or defeat - is not certain from the accounts that have survived.[4]

Racing men for the most part, the pugilistic backers looked for the same strict interpretation of the rules of betting as applied on the course. There was no room for individual decision making if the system was to work and debts of honour had to be the first call on any sportsman's purse. Those who wagered on the abortive Yorkshire fight between Belcher and Bourke, only to find it coming off months later, virtually in private and in London denied the excitement of the fight itself, had the added mortification of losing their money if they originally backed the loser, since it was decided that all bets made still held good. Backing one's man also still meant giving support without qualification. Playing the field was so unacceptable that when the fluctuating expectations of the Pearce v. Gully fight allowed a Mr Chersey to lay large sums at good odds on each man in turn, it was decided that all bets on the fight were off. There was no room for a gambler who went into a two-horse race knowing that he was certain to make a profit!

Strangely, too, the courts not only recognised the gambling contracts in general and arbitrated on them but they also gave judgement on boxing wagers, in spite of the sport's illegality. The state of the law on pugilistic bets was agreed by prosecution, defence and judge alike in a revealing case heard at Chelmsford Assizes in 1811. Money placed in an illegal wager, e.g. on a prize-fight, could be rescinded at any time before the event took place and the contract was put into effect. A backer could not, though, 'take the chance of the event, and after that demand the money; because that would be - "Heads, I win; tails, you lose".' The particular point in this case was whether a minor fight between two volunteers, Smith and King, had actually taken place when it was interrupted by the constables. What had happened was that Smith had been beaten out of the ring and had not returned in due time, so King was declared the winner. Then Mrs Smith urged her husband to resume the battle. King raised no objection; they set to again and the peace officers intervened. Defending counsel argued that it was the laws of boxing which determined whether or not the fight had been concluded and that 'the Court then and there assembled' at the ring had declared King the winner before the fight restarted. Tongue in cheek, the judge claimed that this was too abstruse a point of law for him to determine alone. He put it to the jury, who found that Smith had, in fact, been beaten by leaving the ring.[5]

Even in its most repressive moods, the law consistently gave such recognition as this to pugilism as a sport. It was never dealt with merely as fighting, and if manslaughter charges were successfully brought against a pugilist - and this was seldom easy, whether on points of law and evidence or in terms of convincing a jury - the sentences were invariably lighter than those for inflicting much less serious damage in a plain brawl. This was vividly illustrated in two assize cases which came up within days of each other in 1827. A fight after a quarrel at Stafford races, fought according to the rules, was described by the judge as 'as mild a case as possible' and resulted in a month's imprisonment. In a Lancashire bout, though, where a man was struck and kicked while on the ground, his opponent was transported for seven years![6] There was, certainly, increased pressure on the sport from about 1800 onwards, pressure directed both at major national contests and at local fighting venues. The suppression of pugilism was seen as both a desirable and a feasible objective, part of the process of bringing leisure activities to heel and promoting a life style thought more appropriate to an enlightened, industrious and civilised age. The possibility of adapting popular sports to accommodate them to a new climate of opinion was as yet only envisaged by very few. Pugilism gave particular offence, though it is as well to remember that it was to many, only slightly more obnoxious than race meetings or pedestrian contests.

There was a rapid growth both in the number of prize-fights and in the excitement they provoked, and there was the appearance of a new generation of popular pugilists centred round the incomparable Jem Belcher. Tom 'The Tinman' Hooper, Jack O'Donnell, Tom Owen, Andrew Gamble, 'Dutch Sam' (probably the best of the bareknuckle lightweights), Jack Bartholomew and even Joe Bourke all had their enthusiastic followings. Such a revival was soon to be out of tune with the times. Nearly ten years of war had quickened the pace of social change. Industrial progress had been accelerated and people were more prosperous and eager for new leisure opportunities, yet at the very time when changing social and economic conditions were demanding creative attention from government, government was preoccupied with war and could see little answer to the 'leisure problem' but repression. Here, though, pugilism presented the authorities with a problem peculiar to it as a sport. It was considered, reluctantly so by many of its opponents even, to promote in both performers and spectators personal qualities invaluable for fighting men. Pugilism had often been winked at in wartime. It was its revival just as peace began to be talked about again that put pugilism quite out of favour and gave free reign to the incipient antagonism of all the governmental, magisterial and respectable classes. This was obvious to contemporaries, who saw that 'the late ratification of peace had tended to annihilate fighting', a reference to the Treaty of Amiens, the preliminaries of which were signed just a few weeks before Belcher and Bourke met at Maidenhead and set the machinery of the law in motion.

The pressures of authority could not, in fact, kill pugilism. They were too uneven and too spasmodic, inadequately backed by effective policing and faced by too substantial a body of support for the ring. What they did was to drive it, from time to time, further underground, making it more and more a forbidden activity and imbuing it with the sad attractions that frequently attach to sin, especially if the sin does not seem too venal or too damaging to the majority of participants. It gave rise to a cat-and-mouse game between pugilists, magistrates and police. The avoidance and defiance of the authorities added spice to the whole event. Often, the pursuit by supporters of the boxers and their retinues became reminiscent of a mass fox-hunt and could even find itself described in terms of the chase. Most damaging, though, to the potential development of pugilism into a legitimate modern sport was its deepening association with criminality and the increasing expenditure of its energies on actually mounting fights, leaving less and less possibility for any adaptation, liberalisation or advancement in the organisation, laws and manners of the sport itself.

6

The Black Challenge and Bill Richmond

Three remarkable characters played central roles in pugilistic affairs during its most flourishing decades in the early years of the nineteenth century. They were not necessarily its best fighters - Jem Belcher and Tom Cribb could doubtless have beaten any of the three - but Bill Richmond, John Jackson and John Gully all made very significant, and very different, contributions to boxing's history. Bill Richmond became the first notable black professional sportsman, Jackson's authority came as close as was possible to securing respectability for the ring, and John Gully demonstrated that professional sport could provide a path to wealth and worldly success.

Young Richmond's story began in a parsonage on Staten Island. He learned to read, grew up bright and cheerful and helped his mother when Parson Carlton had guests at the house. It was one such guest - a Lord, and a General too - who plucked the 13-year-old away from his childhood home at the height of the War of Independence in 1777. General Lord Percy, who was to become the second Duke of Northumberland, was struck by the liveliness and good manners of the curly-headed youth and mindful of the fashion to have a coloured servant or two. For his part, young William had listened to the tales told by the sailors down at the wharf, stories of voyages across the sea to Africa to fetch slaves for the cotton fields and to England where black men were not slaves and many strutted about in rich uniforms provided by their masters. The tales did not tell him of the thousands of black beggars in London, and when the opportunity came to go with the English Lord's retinue across the Atlantic it was one that he grasped eagerly.

His Lordship was a considerate and perceptive man. He was popular with his troops and opposed to corporal punishment. He sent home at his own expense the widows of men killed in the war. Closer acquaintance with his black servant persuaded him that the young man's talents would be wasted as a household servant. The same generosity which later prompted him to reduce his rents by 25 per cent in the hard times after the Napoleonic Wars marked his treatment of Richmond. He put him to school in York and, after school, gave him a head start over most of his fellow blacks in the country by indenturing him to a local cabinet-maker. The young man became a good craftsman, always giving satisfaction to his employers and their customers. He grew to know his own worth and to recognise his place in the world. He was better educated than most native-born Englishmen and graduated into the privileged end of the labour market. He was particular over his appearance, liked to dress as near to fashion as his means would allow and was a good talker, regaling his hearers with stories of his childhood in New York. He had grown up tall, long-limbed and athletic, as nimble on his feet as he was with his tongue. He learned to keep a hold on his quick temper, and he also learned how to use his fists.

What rankled some townsmen was not so much his colour but the fact that he was well groomed, well dressed and smart in his bearing and clearly had a good opinion of himself. It was just such jealousies which led him to fight with a heavyweight blacksmith, of some 14 st. against his own 10 st. 12 lb., when the smith railed at him in the street for leaving his workplace looking spruce and tidy. Bill told him that if he wanted to stick by these remarks he would see him next morning in the Groves, the local venue for semi-formal fights and other popular recreations. They met, and Richmond soon showed the smith that the tidiness of his appearance was matched by the smartness of his fists. There were other insulters. One, Frank Myers, offended at seeing him in company with a white woman on a Saturday evening, called him a black devil and added other such epithets. With due deference to the Sabbath, they agreed to meet at the Groves on the Monday morning to settle their differences. The day's wait having given time for the news to get around, this was a fight for which Richmond had an appreciable audience. Myers, in the meantime had had second thoughts about the encounter, but the spectators were not to be disappointed nor was Richmond to go unsatisfied. He and his supporters went round to Myers's house to remind him that they had business to do. The high spirits of Saturday night had sunk to a low ebb in the cold light of a new day's dawn, but Myers could not help but go with them; he took a severe drubbing for his pains. A similar affront led Richmond into the sort of fight that often developed at race meetings, as an entertaining postscript to the day's events. His opponent was 'Docky' More, a soldier in the 19th Regiment, known before he enlisted as 'the hero of Sheffield' and the city's champion. He was a big man and an experienced fighter, and therefore Richmond's friends tried to persuade him to back down, but to no avail and, as it turned out, to no necessity. A ring was formed, the gentry looked on from their carriages and their saddles and the plebians crowded for a sight of the match. It took thirty minutes or so of hard fighting for Richmond again to emerge the winner.[1]

Richmond did not yet see himself as a fighting man. He did what he had to do when the alternative, in his own eyes, would have been ignominy. His life-long quickness to take offence, though, was fed by his skill with his fists. And, dandy though he sought to be, ambitious and anxious to make the most of himself, there was something about the flash life style that he saw around him on the race course that drew him irresistibly. A well-set-up black man, handy in a fight, was always a prime candidate for the household of a sporting nobleman. Richmond was taken on by Lord Camelford as his minder and attendant, and found himself halfway into the sporting world. He had had glimpses of it in the North, but in and around London it was all on a bigger scale. He was on hand at cricket matches and became something of a cricketer himself. He was at race meetings - some of them glorious affairs like Epsom on Derby Day and Ascot, others little country meetings - and then there were the prize-fights, afterwards, leading to his growing realisation that some men made enough money to live comfortably on the proceeds of their skill with a cricket bat, in the saddle or with their fists.

BILL RICHMOND.
From a portrait by Hillman, 1812.

5. Bill Richmond

In January 1804, at the start of what was to be an important year for him, Richmond accompanied Lord Camelford in the scramble across Wimbledon Common, from one parish to another, for the fight between Henry Pearce and his master's sometime champion, Joe Bourke. Bourke showed his usual pluck and determination but the 'Game Chicken' wore him down in twenty-four rounds in an hour and a quarter, which left the fans looking for more. A hurried match was made, and old George Maddox faced up to Seabrook, a dustman, well known as a second-rate pugilist. It was a three-round farce, Seabrook making off with his £4 appearance money, claiming that his arm was broken. This was too much for Richmond. Here was old Maddox, nearly 50 and still fighting for a purse. Richmond was so little acquainted with the habits of the game that he challenged Maddox as he stepped out of the ring, not recognising the conventional rhetoric in George's boast that he was ready to take on any other comer. A whip-round among the onlookers produced another purse of a few guineas and Bill fought for money for the first time in his life, and he fought very painfully. He discovered that the London prize-ring, even when the opponent was a veteran like Maddox, was in a different league from his skirmishes at York. He found himself battered from the start, even his quick footwork offering him no escape from George's fists. In the third round he caught a heavy blow under his left eye - it closed, and he could hardly see. There was no alternative but to give in. He had had a lesson and he had also forged a firm memory of old George. Here was an insult which would need to be taken care of, but not today.

Indeed, many a man in Bill's position would have considered that there was no future in the prize-ring. One fight was the most that many of them managed. He was tempted himself - after all, life was pleasant enough doing the rounds with Lord Camelford and there was always his trade to fall back upon. The death of his patron, in fighting one duel too many, precipitated Richmond's decision. He had touched the edge of the ring's magic circle and would get into that circle, come what may. He knew that he had the speed and the strength, and he thought that he had the spirit. All he needed to do was to put all three together and learn the London style of fighting. He became an eager pupil at the Fives Court, where the best pugilists of the day exhibited their art. He saw that some blows were best parried and some best dodged, and that the safest way of fighting for someone not of the heaviest weight was to get into the attack and out again quickly, to avoid the tight clinches and the throws as far as he could. He trained and learned quickly.

His chance came the next summer, after the fight between the rising Tom Cribb, whom Richmond had admired at Fives Court benefits, and the Jew, Ikey Pig. The sporting world had gathered at Blackheath, Gentile and Jew alike, and when this first battle ended in Cribb's victory in less than half an hour, spectators on all sides were ready for more entertainment. A Jew known as 'Fighting Youssop' presented himself boldly as his people's next champion. Bill Richmond needed little encouragement to take him on, and a purse of 10 guineas was quickly got together for the men to fight for. Bill was nervous at first, knowing that another defeat would mean the end of his aspirations. 'Fighting Youssop' was not greatly skilled but he was a big man and did not give many chances. When Richmond launched his first attack he found himself brought up suddenly by a counterblow, driven back round the ring and almost knocked out of it. But that was the turning point. His next attack was successful: he was getting in blows to the face. 'Fighting Youssop' could not defend himself and at the end of the sixth round he threw in the sponge.

Bill Richmond's future was decided. Word of the contest passed around all the other pugilists and the gentlemen promoters. From being a figure on the edge of fights, Richmond was taken into the fold. A leading patron, Mr Fletcher Read, the most regular of fight supporters and always keen to bring on new talent in the prize-ring, backed him for 50 guineas against the well-known Jack Holmes, a coachman. This was his first match made in advance and when he stepped into the ring he had another time-honoured battler, Paddington Jones, as his second. It was the start of a friendship which was to last for over a quarter of a century. Jack Holmes, though, only lasted for thirty-nine minutes, and there was distinguished company to watch Bill triumph. Not only was there Mr Fletcher Read and the Honourable Berkley Craven but there was also Thomas Sheridan, Mr Upton and a panoply of fighters including John Gully, the two Belchers, Bill Ryan, Tom Cribb and Dan Mendoza. There could hardly have been a more knowing jury to weigh up Bill's performance.[2] His place in the pugilistic circle was confirmed rapidly as he made himself constantly useful and was civil and amiable to all who treated him fairly. In an age of great boxers, though, he soon came to realise that he would never dominate the prize-ring. This was borne in on him when he was completely over-matched in a fight with the rising Bristolian, Tom Cribb, in a contest following the tremendous battle between Henry Pearce and John Gully at Hailsham in Sussex in 1805 - just a fortnight away from the Battle of Trafalgar. The crowd was bubbling over with excitement of Pearce's hard-won victory and it was some consolation to Richmond that not much attention was paid to this second contest. What rankled even more than the defeat was the fact that he had been made to look foolish by the young, strong and dashing Tom Cribb.[3] Meetings between the two of them for the rest of their lives were always likely to flare into dispute of one sort or another. Bill may have arrived as a pugilist, but he had arrived too late.

And so he came to another point in his career for important decision making. He could go on taking fights at low stakes from established boxers, not of the first flight, or risk taking on newcomers who might turn out to be easy prey but who might equally prove to be yet more Tom Cribbs on their rapid way to the top. He could, on the other hand, continue to make himself useful about the prize-ring, at fights themselves and at the Fives Court, where benefits were becoming almost weekly affairs. He knew that his understanding of the fight game was growing better all the time, even if age was having some effect on his performance. He got on well with people and found that he had a talent for teaching. Everything seemed to point to caution as far as actual fights were concerned, and this caution was made easier by the fact that, like all coloured fighters, he lacked steady patronage. This too was something which added reputation might remedy if ever he had need to enter the ring again. He had too much to lose to risk that reputation in wasteful fights which might permanently damage his standing, and so he continued to make himself useful - indeed nearly indispensable - in and around the affairs of the ring. After all, 'Gentleman' John Jackson had become the indisputable governor of the prize-ring on the strength of a couple of fights. Bill knew now that he would never be the champion that Jackson had been, but at his own level he could also find himself a place. This he set about doing assiduously. He helped to throw the drunken Bill Ryan out of the Fives Court at Gully and Sprey's benefit in 1806, and he was the unmistakable human signpost placed at the Magpie Inn to guide the crowd seeking the Gully v. Gregson fight, directing them towards Sir John Sebright's park in Hertfordshire where the troubled contest was at last able to take place. In the park itself, his reputation was such that he stepped into the prize-ring before the contest in company with such estimable giants as Gregson, Gully, Mendoza, Henry Pearce, Cribb and 'Dutch Sam'. His reputation as a second grew and grew, until within two or three years he was in the corner for the most important contests of the day, even seconding Tom Cribb in his fight with Jem Belcher in spite of the antagonism between the two of them. This came to the surface again soon afterwards when he was in Gregson's corner against Cribb. Cribb was so offended by Richmond's behaviour - he threw taunts during the fight - that he immediately challenged the black to sort out their differences on the spot but (fortunately for Richmond, even after Cribb had had an arduous fight!) he was persuaded by his friends not to go through with it.

Bill knew he might never really be able to settle his score with Tom Cribb. In his cooler moments, he had sense enough to know that Cribb was out of his reach, but there was still his grudge against Maddox to be settled. By 1809 Richmond felt that he could take him on with no great risk of defeat and, if he did happen to lose, without serious damage to a well-established reputation. He had had a try out - it was no more than that, with the stake at only 10 guineas - against Isaac Wood, an unknown waterman, at Coombe Wood and had come through it virtually unscathed. With this confirmation that he was in fighting trim, Bill now had no problem in finding a backer - the sporting Baronet, Sir Clement Brigg - to put up £100 against his old enemy. Richmond might be past his best as a fighter but the game old Maddox was now in his fifty-fourth year. Such considerations did not deter the enthusiasts, and there was a crowd of over 3000 at Pope's Head Watchhouse, on the coast between Margate and Reculver, to see the fight, with many of the sport's noble and gentry supporters among them. Richmond, the report said afterwards 'displayed great superiority, both in science and strength and after good fighting threw his aged adversary with a force which astonished every spectator'. Maddox lasted for fifty-two minutes with great gameness, which was rewarded by a good collection on his behalf at the end of the fight. It was publicly declared by no less a figure than the Honourable Charles Wyndham, a notable reformer in Parliament and an equally notable sportsman out of it, to be a 'smart contest' and an example to the nation of the characteristics in men which should be promoted. Why discourage 'all the practices and habits which tend to keep alive the same sentiments and feelings' that British soldiers were displaying on the battle fields of the Peninsular?[4]

Richmond's fame was now secure. As landlord of the Horse and Dolphin, next door to the Fives Court, he was now at the very centre of the pugilistic world. The demountable 5-ft-high stage had been Richmond's idea and the exhibitions at the Fives Court were now the most regular events in this irregular sport. There could be no better

6. Tom Molyneux

venue than his house next door for his pugilistic school, held in the upstairs rooms. Here gentry came for lessons and hopeful young boxers sought an entry to the prizering. Suddenly, one such newcomer gave Richmond a glimpse of the championship itself. It could not come to him, but Tom Molyneux held out the chance for him to share in the crown. Tom Molyneux had two attributes which Bill himself had not possessed when he entered the prize-ring - youth and size. He was 26 years old, well on the way to being a six-footer and 15 st. in weight. He had learned fighting of a kind in Virginia and made his way somehow to England. He showed himself at the sporting houses in London, prepared to take on all comers, and naturally finished up with his countryman at the Horse and Dolphin. He displayed his talents at that rough corner of London, Tothill Fields, against an anonymous Bristolian seconded, perhaps inevitably, by Tom Cribb, and dispatched him after half an hour, his face reduced to a pulp. Cribb and Richmond, as the two seconds, had a quarrel over a foul blow and had their own inevitable turn-up which Richmond was bright enough to turn his back on after one round.

Molyneux was rough, raw and tough. His style, as yet, had little to commend it, consisting as it did of wild swings and a hugging, jabbing infighting, rushing his opponent off his feet. Richmond, though, was sure that what Molyneux lacked he could give him. He sang his praises to his upper-class patrons, and when he took him down to Reculver, where he had beaten Maddox, there was a large gentry following and no difficulty in putting up a £100 stake to match him against Blake, otherwise known as 'Tom Tough', a boxer of some considerable reputation although, at 40, past his best. Bill introduced his man to the crowd with due modesty, in spite of what he had been saying in private, and the betting started at evens. The fight only took eight rounds. In the sixth Molyneux gave Blake such a blow as to knock him completely off his feet, and at the end of the eighth he had beaten him into such insensibility that he could not make the scratch for the next round. According to Richmond's judgement, Molyneux was ready to go right to the top at once and there was plenty of money to back him to do just that. He let his young protégé brag about what he would do to 'Massa Cribb' and the black's challenge could scarcely go unanswered for long. The fight that took place at Cropthorne, near East Grinstead in Sussex, on 18 December 1810 was in many ways the highlight and peak of not just Molyneux's career but of Bill Richmond's as well. It was the fight for the championship which he himself had never got near, and it was against his old rival, Tom Cribb, who was out of his personal reach. What he had not been able to get in person he stood an excellent chance of gaining by proxy.

It was a bitterly cold day, with the wind blowing the rain in from the east. The two men were formidable opponents, both of much the same height and weight, with Molyneux's long arms suggesting that he might have an advantage in spite of his rawness. Molyneux glared at Tom as they shook hands and squared up. As far as Cribb was concerned this was an upstart novice. The champion had not prepared himself for the fight as he might have done and knew that he was carrying a good deal more weight than he needed. He knew, though, that, Molyneux's backers apart, the crowd was on his side, virtually to a man. It was a bruising fight which went first one way, then the other. When the scales were weighted on Molyneux's side the crowd lost no time in making its passions felt and the ring was broken at least once to save Cribb from possible defeat. Bill Richmond never had a more difficult task when he was in the ring himself. In the opposite corner there was the redoubtable John Gully and the cunning Joe Ward, while he had the trusted Paddington Jones, his old opponent, sharing the support for Molyneux. Every device was used against them. Apart from the breaking of the ring, there was the occasion when Cribb was having difficulty in making the scratch for the twenty-eighth round and Joe Ward complained to Richmond and Jones that their man was carrying weights concealed in his fists. This was a plausible allegation perhaps since Molyneux was known to have trained with weights in his hands. The delay in settling the matter was enough to give the champion the respite he needed. In the end, and in all the circumstance, the result was perhaps inevitable. Molyneux threw Cribb heavily but landed on his own head in doing so. He felt he could not go on, though Richmond urged him to the scratch once more. It was for the last time; he staggered and fell. He was accused of falling without a blow but no umpire's decision was called for as he declared that he could go on no longer.[5]

This was a bitter disappointment to the challenger and his seconds. Richmond knew the English well enough not to cry 'foul' too loudly at the way things had turned out at Cropthorne. He knew that newcomers to the ring, whether they were from Bristol, Staten Island or Virginia, often had a hard time of it against an established favourite. He saw to it that a courteous letter went to the press from Molyneux. He put down his failure to win to the bad weather and expressed the hope ('the confident hope') that his colour 'will not in any way operate to my prejudice'. The challenge was taken up, but Richmond remained cautious. At the Fives Court benefit, in the week after the fight, Molyneux had had a set-to with a large Lancastrian, Rimmer, brought forward by Gregson. The newcomer had challenged Molyneux and Richmond saw it as a safer match than a further contest with Cribb. He feared that the latter, now knowing the measure of his opponent, would prepare better for it than he had for the first match. When he found that he could match his man for £300 a side against Rimmer his mind was made up, and the rematch with Cribb was deferred.

These were hectic days for Richmond. Molyneux's fight with Rimmer came off on 21 May 1811. The venue was the classic home of Regency boxing, Molesey Hurst. Bill Gibbons, another veteran leader of the prize-ring, shared the seconding of the black with him, and Power and Paddington Jones were in Rimmer's corner. Molyneux started the favourite, before a good crowd from all quarters of society. Rimmer, coming like his trainer, Gregson, from Lancashire, brought the rough Lancashire style of boxing with him. Molyneux had improved as a boxer without losing the capacity to maul and bludgeon which he had always done. Even though the money was mainly on Molyneux, Rimmer still had enough support for the crowd to break the ring at the end of the fifteenth round with the white man apparently beaten. It took some time for the pugilists to clear the ring. Rimmer must have wished that they had not succeeded. He had to endure six more rounds of pain and suffering before he was reduced to helplessness and surrender.

There was over a year from then until the fight with Cribb, and Molyneux was enjoying the fame. He fell in readily with plans to tour the country giving sparring exhibitions and meeting all comers with the gloves off. Tom Belcher and Richmond went along with him, but Richmond had a divided mind over what was taking place. The sparring and the practice in the ring could be all to the good, just another means of keeping in training, but Molyneux was reluctant to accept the discipline which Tom sought to impose on him, both in and out of the ring. He responded to challenges too readily and was always likely to take matters more seriously than they were meant to be once he had the gloves on. His gluttony for fighting and for dishing out punishment was matched by an equal greed in virtually every other direction. His companions found him to be out of control. Fine clothes, endless food, heavy drinking and constant womanising were bound to damage his constitution sooner or later. Richmond, always a moderate and sober man - unusual in his day and quite exceptional for a pugilistic innkeeper - looked on with growing despair as the day of the return match with Cribb drew near. Molyneux was costing him more than he was making and the prospects of winning something back from the forthcoming fight seemed all the dimmer in the light of the news that Cribb had been training for over a month under the noted athlete Captain Barclay, who had reduced his weight and increased his stamina and would be sending him into the ring in a high state of fitness.

At Cropthorne it had been Molyneux who had been fresh and fit and Cribb overweight and out of condition. At Thistleton Gap near Leicester the positions were reversed and the result was decisive. Molyneux's jaw was broken and he was flat out after only nineteen minutes and ten seconds.[6] For once, Molyneux was fairly treated by the crowd, perhaps because they sensed that he could not win. The consequences for Richmond were punishing. There was tumult in his tavern in St Martin's Lane on the Saturday night: a crowd of disappointed supporters of the black had to be dispersed and the house closed. All Molyneux had from the fight was the £50 collection raised by 'Gentleman' Jackson. Richmond knew that some of the blame lay with him. He might at least have prevented his man from making a breakfast on the morning of the fight of a boiled fowl, apple pie and a tankard of porter. But he was becoming weary of trying to manage the unmanageable. Molyneux insisted on going his own way, becoming depressed at his own unpopularity but doing nothing to make himself more appealing to the crowds. He appeared always as the powerful, angry and uncontrolled black, a regular drinker and a man whose first inclination in any new town he arrived at was to seek out the local stews and the fanciest of their providers of comfort. He was still a source of curiosity, though. Thousands would pay to see the man who had faced up twice to Tom Cribb, champion of England. He began another tour, but this time Richmond had had enough. Molyneux still owed him money and eventually he put legal restraints upon him to try and get it back. Even after his release, Bill's unforgiving nature pursued the man he had fostered so hopefully and he made a match for Carter to fight Molyneux for 100 guineas. It was a dubious affair, both in the motives behind it and in its outcome, and not Richmond's most shining hour. Carter suddenly gave in at the end of the twenty-seventh round when he was clearly on top, falling insensible on Richmond's knee in the break between rounds. Certainly he had received a hard blow on the temple a little time before, certainly vigorous efforts appeared to be made to revive him by Richmond. The appearance of coma looked genuine enough and it was half an hour before he recovered his senses, but at the same time there was an air of suspicion about it all.

That was the last that Richmond had to do with his fellow countryman. Molyneux set out with his recent opponent, Jack Carter, on an extended sparring tour, taking in Scotland this time. The two were well suited. Jack was as hard a drinker as Tom and if anything rather rougher in his manner. Molyneux, while the money lasted, enjoyed acting the dandy, the boozer and the Lothario. He bestowed his amorous favours indiscriminately and his once excellent physique began to collapse. He was still good enough to take on and beat William Fuller, a Scottish hero who was so little acquainted with the ways of the prize-ring that he refused to go down to avoid punishment after sixty-eight minutes of fighting with only two rounds completed. To spare his man, Joe Ward, the old stager in his corner, seized him by the legs and pulled him down to get a pause. Molyneux's second complained, and the fight was given to him. By coincidence, he was the William Fuller who was eventually to cross the Atlantic in the other direction, to set up his successful pugilistic gymnasium and live out his retirement as a gentleman in New York. For Molyneux there was to be no long coda. From Scotland it was Ireland and further decline, and he ended his days only some eight years after his glorious battles with Cribb, deserted by all but a couple of his fellow countrymen in the 77th Regiment, then quartered in Galway. He died in the barracks bandroom on 4 August 1818.[7]

When he turned his back on Molyneux, Richmond was saying farewell to his highest ambition. The days of high excitement were over, and he would never produce a black champion. He would never to be as close to the pugilistic crown again, but neither would he die a quick death as a wasted giant. There was much still to live for. The Horse and Dolphin flourished, attracting a good clientele for its wares, Richmond's ready conversation and the chance to rub shoulders with the day's fistic heroes. There was also the profitable training school upstairs where Richmond's skill and courtesy as a teacher brought him some of the most rewarding clients of the day; they shared Pierce Egan's view that no one was better suited to teach the art.[8]

He was not even ready for an honourable retirement himself. After the dreadful Molyneux v. Carter fight he offered to fight either of them for £100, though whether this was any more than the braggadocio to which he was inclined after the excitement of a fight is hard to tell. His own thirst for the ring was certainly not quenched, and within a year, at the age of 50, he was back again, fighting Davies. This was a significant battle because it was the first arranged by the newly formed Pugilistic Club. Richmond, with his close contacts in the leading sporting circles, saw that the club, set up to promote and to some extent regulate pugilism, after the model of the Jockey Club, could be a powerful instrument. It was a body with which he, as one of the leading men of the prize-ring, should be closely involved. Its first meeting in the field, at Coombe Wood on 3 May 1814, looked doomed to disappointment when the expected Painter v. Oliver match fell through, but Richmond stepped in to fight for a purse of £50 raised by the club. It was an impressive occasion. The stakes of the 25 ft ring were painted in the club colours, with the initials 'PC' imprinted on them. Three rounds of the club ropes formed the arena. The members of the club were dressed in their blue and buff uniforms and the pugilists acting as stewards wore blue ribbons in their hats. In spite of giving Davies about a half stone in weight and over a quarter of a century in years, Richmond accounted for him in the thirteenth round. When he was declared the winner he demonstrated his fitness by leaping over the ropes, which were nearly 5 ft high, and he emerged from the twenty-minute battle with little sign of harm. He stayed for the rest of the day to enjoy the remaining fare. Even then he was not finished and a year later he beat Tom Shelton before a crowd of 10,000 or more at Molesey Hurst. It was his last fight, but Richmond never regarded himself as really retired. Given the opportunity and the purse, he would probably have gone into the ring again until the day of his last illness.

His know-how, his ringcraft and his capacity to urge on his own man and put off opponents meant that he was always in demand as a second. He promoted a string of black fighters after Molyneux, among them Kendrick, Robinson, Johnson, Stephenson and Harry Sutton, but the white men he also supported made up a pugilistic roll of honour of their own. They included Cribb, Gregson, George Cooper, Turner, Scoggins, Cy Davis, Oliver, Bob Baldwin and Alex Reid. He remained nimble and quick footed to the end, and this, together with his sharp in-and-out style of fighting, with rapid blows and smart retreats, made him a popular figure in sparring exhibitions. He was a willing worker for his fellow boxers, not even drawing the line at appearing at his old antagonist Tom Cribb's benefit. At both the Fives Court and, subsequently, the Tennis Court he could always be relied upon to be present. Indeed, the first benefit held at the newly opened Tennis Court in Windmill Street in 1820 was mounted for him. Other benefits followed, though none of them brought the rewards that he deserved. He made a 'neat' speech of thanks to his supporters at the end of the exhibitions on his behalf in February 1822, but we are told that they were 'not well attended'.[9] Indeed, pugilism itself had begun to fall upon less prosperous and often evil days. Fights had become less reliable, gentry interest had declined and the sport was looking less and less respectable. Four years later, a week after he had seconded Alex Reid against Gaynor, another benefit again drew few patrons and the quality of the sparring did not justify better attendance.[10] The end was not easy. Just after his death there was a benefit for 'poor Richmond's widow' and it typified the state of affairs into which the ring had fallen. It was the occasion when Jem Ward made a public apology for the fiasco of his so-called Leicester fight with Simon Byrne, with its bribery, corruption and double dealing.[11] These were not the pugilistic manners which Bill Richmond had known. He might have been ready to take all the advantage that the loose laws of pugilism allowed, and then some more, but downright cheating was outside his book.

Although he was not the first black to fight in England, Bill Richmond had opened the door to the ring for his race and held it open for a quarter of a century. There was little direct racial prejudice. With the upbringing, intellect and manners of an Englishman, Richmond could carry his colour with quiet pride, throwing roughnecks, white or black, out of his tavern without discrimination. As a promoter of black boxers, though, he faced the major problem of finding backing for them. The other minority ethnic groups in the ring, the Jews and Irish, could always be relied upon to back their man. The blacks, by contrast, tended to be scattered and low on resources of their own, and they had no community to fall back on. Such financial support as blacks could muster was always opportunistic and unreliable, likely to evaporate at the first hint of defeat. Their ring careers were haphazard and chancy. It was a difficulty which Richmond himself had faced and which Molyneux only surmounted by his obvious excellence and with Richmond's guidance. For the other blacks, boxing was a possible career but not an easy one.

Take, for instance, the career of a good average boxer like Harry Sutton. Lack of opportunity confined his pugilistic life to three years, but its high point was the defeat of the accomplished Ned Painter. Certainly he lost the return bout a few months later, but the two bouts were hailed as excellent contests and Sutton won high praise for his strength, courage and skill. Even so, at a time when the ring was at its most flourishing, he found it impossible to find further matches. All he managed was a pick-up contest against his fellow black, Kendrick, for a hastily collected 15-guinea purse, when a proposed Oliver v. Shelton fight fell through. He turned up without fail at bouts, was at all Fives Court exhibitions, at race meetings and anywhere else where there was the chance of making a match, but nothing came his way. Where they could get fights, blacks were more likely than most to be deserted by backers; after a good performance against Acton, Kendrick was left supported only by his second and scarcely conscious, until at last he was allowed 'to tumble into a vehicle'.[12]

It was the sort of fate which Richmond himself had always managed to avoid. Indeed, in his white-haired old age he could look back not only on fights for the championship but also to those occasions when his profession had taken him into the company of kings. By royal behest he had been called upon by John Jackson to display the art of pugilism along with other such stars as Belcher, Cribb, Painter and Oliver before the royal visitors there at the conclusion of the Napoleonic Wars. He had performed before the King, the King of Prussia, Crown Prince of Prussia, Princes Frederick and William of Prussia, the Prince of Mechlenburg and other such grandees of Europe. Again, he had been one of 'Gentleman' Jackson's team of pages commissioned to keep order at the coronation of that old patron of the ring, George IV, in 1821, and his final gratification came when his son was appointed pugilistic instructor to Prince William of Cambridge. But it was time for him to go. His age had passed and he had made his mark upon it. He had made no mean contribution towards establishing the worth of men of colour. He had shown that they could be as civil as any Englishman and more so than most. Entertaining, lively, always sober and drinking only to moderation, as honest in his family life as in his public, liking the rough sports of the bait and the cockpit as well as any man of his day, he had lived a life of solid sporting worth. He had brought pleasure to many and harm to few. The Elysian fields would be all the brighter for his presence there.

7

Mr Jackson and Mr Gully

The pugilistic subculture of Regency London was led by wealthy, influential backers, from the ranks of the nobility and gentry. They gave the sport its status, were the dominant element in its financial prosperity and afforded its bouts some measure of protection. With their sleek horses, their rich carriages, their liveried servants and their expectations of precedence, they were the spectators who caught the eye at any notable contest. Hardly less obtrusive were the men who were obviously handling all the arrangements on the ground. They were setting up the ring, manoeuvring their wagons into prime vantage points so that they could charge for places on them, collecting entrance money from as many spectators as they could and trying to keep them under enough control for the fight to take place. These were boxing's professionals, whose hold strengthened as their own numbers grew and as contests in and around London became more frequent. They included the pugilists themselves, the ex-pugilists, the landlords of the taverns where the sportsmen met and the various hangers-on of greater or lesser respectability.

It was a closed group, not always easy to break into, and much was made of the camaraderie which bound its members together. They had a common interest in protecting their sport and making it as remunerative as possible, a task that was, of course, all the harder because of pugilism's illegality. Each was expected to take his turn in putting on the mufflers to spar at benefits for fellow boxers. They were expected at other men's fights, to help keep order. Strong personal allegiances marked some of the relationships within the group, especially between Bristolians, though for a fighter to have the same second throughout his career, as Jem Belcher had Joe Ward, was exceptional. The services of seconds were usually to be had on a purely professional basis, and men moved readily from one corner to another from fight to fight. It was already as much a business as a sport. While matches were often spiced with loud assertions that the fighters had some personal score to settle, long-term animosity between individual pugilists was rare enough to be conspicuous - such as Mendoza's hatred of Jackson and Richmond's dislike of Tom Cribb.

Pugilists came from a variety of occupations before they began their ring careers. With rare exceptions, these were urban occupations, with butchery predominating[1] - apart from the physical demands made of them by their trade, butchers had a reputation for belligerence and defiance. Much the most popular occupation for pugilists after their fighting days was that of publican - by 1820 there were at least a dozen London taverns run by well-known ex-boxers.[2] Among these, certain houses became acknowledged meeting places for the sport. The

Coach and Horses in St Martin's Lane had a succession of pugilistic landlords; Jem Belcher had the Jolly Brewers in Wardour Street; and his younger brother eventually took over the most famous tavern of them all, The Castle in Holborn, for years the undisputed unofficial headquarters of the ring.

No matter how many of them finished up as publicans, though, there was no one mould for pugilists. There were all-round sportsmen like Faulkner, the cricketer and boxer; there were numerous pedestrians all through the sport's history right up to Jem Mace; and there was Tom Cannon, who would try his hand at anything from track-racing to quoits. Jem Ward was an artist of some quality, Tom Tring was an artist's model, Tom King was a keen gardener and William 'Bendigo' Thompson eventually became an evangelist. A few, like Richard Humphries, prospered in business after leaving the ring, but of all the sport's varied stars only John Jackson and John Gully earned the age's firmest accolade of respectability, the title of 'Mister'.

As active fighters, their careers were strikingly similar. Each fought only a handful of carefully chosen contests, and each retired, without taking a challenge, after winning the championship. Their paths then diverged, Jackson becoming a renowned teacher of self-defence and then the pillar of the prize-ring's organisation and reputation for nearly twenty of its best years. He won the highest regard from pugilists and peers alike, was looked upon as a model of honesty and was accepted as the final authority on all matters pugilistic. Jackson never married, and he devoted his middle life to selfless promotion of the sport he loved. John Gully, on the other hand, was an uxorious character, marrying twice and producing eleven children by each of his wives! Gully gradually diluted his attachment to the prize-ring, though to the end of his life he remained proud of his performances there and knowledgeable about what was happening. Not content with the simple retreat to a public house, he also gambled carefully and profitably, taking to the turf as easily as to the ring. He became a racehorse owner himself, and continued to accumulate wealth. He progressed to country landlord, coal owner, and Member of Parliament for Pontefract - and all this after running a butchery business which failed when he first arrived in London.

It was John Jackson who started with the social advantage, coming as he did from an unusually prosperous background for a pugilist. His father owned a thriving building business, notable for carrying out the arching of the Fleet Ditch. Jackson himself found his way into pugilism not through the usual street-corner fighting and casual, half-organised local brawls, but by way of his performance at sparring schools, where he was a frequent attender and a ready pupil. The brief and accelerated ring careers of both Jackson and Gully show that a man of outstanding promise could find very early backing for contests against the highest opposition. Johnson's superbly athletic physique and his obvious ringcraft attracted the support of the leading patrons of pugilism, with the upshot that he entered the prize-ring against Fewtrel, a match arising from the Birmingham challenge to the London amateurs.[3] Fewtrel was the taller man and much the heavier (he was even said to be 'corpulent') and onlookers thought that the 19-year-old Jackson stood little chance of landing his punches on him. It did take an hour and seven minutes to prove them wrong, but Jackson's performance was so impressive that the Prince of Wales, who had forgotten his previous disavowal of the ring, made a generous donation to the young newcomer.

7. Mendoza v Richard Humphries, 1798 - a more enclosed and regulated fight than was often possible in the later days.

After such a promising beginning, Jackson's next foray into the ring proved to be a disaster, but not a damaging one to his reputation. He was matched with George 'The Brewer' Ingleston but had to retire when he broke a small bone in his leg. His offer to continue fighting sitting down was, even for Jackson, smacking somewhat of bravado!

However, the man's quality as a pugilist was heavily underlined in his third and last fight when he took on Mendoza, the undisputed champion. It was a great occasion, with many of the quality, such as the Duke of Hamilton, Lord Delaval and Sir John Phillipson, present. Jackson had not fought for over five years, Mendoza had come to seem invincible and the odds favoured the champion. It was a brief, torrid encounter, all over in ten minutes. In the third round, Jackson attacked unremittingly, Mendoza's eye was cut and he fell to end the round. In the next came the well-known incident where Jackson held his opponent down by the hair and landed some heavy blows while doing so. The umpires rejected his opponent's claims of foul play, certainly a dubious verdict even if what Jackson did was common practice. Jackson's victory was decisive and seems to have been already guaranteed before this particular incident took place. His performance was so striking and the speed and strength of his blows so punishing that there could be no doubt about his pre-eminence. Mendoza never forgave him for taking away the championship and claimed subsequently, when Jackson had clearly retired for some years, that his challenges were ignored. The truth was that Mendoza could no longer command the backing that he had in the past for a contest against someone as formidable as Jackson, and the stakes that he could muster could quite legitimately be turned down. The two remained unreconciled throughout their lives, Mendoza being the one implacable enemy that Jackson made during all the years in which he was associated with the prize-ring.

Immediately after his championship fight, Jackson virtually disappeared from the prize-ring. Indeed, apart from the great occasion of his fight against Mendoza, Jackson had had little involvement in professional pugilism for a number of years. In his first year in the ring he had been much in demand as a second. He was in 'Big Ben's' corner in December 1788 and second to Tom Johnson a few months later; and he acted as bottle-holder to Mendoza for his second Humphries fight and to Will Ward when he, in turn, took on Mendoza in September 1791. Thereafter he concentrated on sparring and training amateur sportsmen. His athletic interests had never been confined to boxing, and he was himself a first-class sprinter and jumper. He retained a life-long interest in new developments in fencing, horsemanship and pedestrianism. His status as a teacher of self-defence was even more secure once he had won the championship, and Jackson's Rooms, 13 Old Bond Street, have become enshrined in boxing history as the social centre of the sport.

They were, in fact, as much if not more D'Angelo's rooms, with John Jackson joining an already thriving establishment. The D'Angelo family had been running first a riding school and then a fencing academy for the last thirty years or more. Harry D'Angelo moved his fencing academy, with its highly fashionable clientele, to Bond Street in 1789 after his Haymarket premises had been badly damaged by fire. Already fencing professor to a sizeable section of the aristocracy, many of whom knew him from their Eton and Cambridge days, Harry D'Angelo was not beholden to any outsider, and it was his initiative that took Jackson into the Bond Street rooms. D'Angelo had a keen eye for coming enthusiasms, and as Jackson shared his views on the character-forming nature of the combat sports, the two joined forces. Jackson brought the professional skill in teaching the noble art that the academy demanded and joined enthusiastically in the aim of promoting gentlemanly behaviour in sport. The gentlemen pupils were encouraged to practise with the foils one day and take a turn with the mufflers the next. The well-known relationship between Lord Byron and Jackson undoubtedly stems from the D'Angelo connection. Lord Byron had been instructed by the fencing master at Cambridge (pursuing a regime of exercise to strengthen his leg, crippled by infantile paralysis) and when Byron returned to D'Angelo's in London he put on the gloves, as did many other of the clientele. Always afterwards he was loud in his praise of Jackson's pugilistic skill, his teaching and his gentlemanly and generous conduct.

While he was building up his reputation through his teaching, Jackson's associations with the ring were quite muted and he came back into the centre of its affairs only gradually. He does appear, as he said in his reply to Mendoza's belated challenge to him in 1801, to have 'entirely withdrawn from a public life'. It was at the Belcher v. Pearce fight four years later that Jackson first took his characteristic lead on behalf of pugilists when he organised a collection for the defeated Jem Belcher and this, we are told, was 'very liberally supplied'. By 1807, he had the confidence to intervene in the disputed ending of the fight between Tom Belcher and 'Dutch Sam'. Belcher had aimed a blow at Sam and fallen to his knees as he did so. Sam's decisive counter-punch was delivered at almost the same moment, as Belcher was falling. Much of the money was on Belcher, and the two umpires disagreed. It was Jackson who came forward and said that the man was not considered down until his hand had reached the floor, so the blow was fair and Sam had to be acknowledged the winner. Jackson's authority, however, strong as it might be with the fighting world and his own coterie was not the final word and the umpires (Captain Barclay and the Honourable Berkley Craven) agreed to refer the matter to a referee, a task eventually undertaken by Lord Archibald Hamilton after Lord Say and Sele had turned it down.

Apart from its disputed ending, this bout had demonstrated the urgent need for better organisation. The ring, originally pitched at 9 a.m., proved to have been so badly sited that it left little room for protesting spectators, and it took two hours to find a more commodious site. A few months later Jackson and Will Ward were in the ring at the Gully v. Gregson fight, not as seconds but 'less the occasion might demand their services'. In the same year, in fact, Jackson played his last partisan role when he was Gully's backer in the return fight with Gregson, putting up the first 50-guinea stake and signing the articles with Major Morgan. Already, though, he was assuming the role of pugilism's national manager.

It was Jackson who announced to the assembled host on Molesey Hurst in April 1808 that the fights arranged for that day (between Tom Belcher and Dogherty and between 'Dutch Sam' and Cropley) could not go ahead on account of the arrival of Bow Street officers with a special warrant. He was soon looked to as the authoritative figure in the pugilistic world, heading the organisation of all major prize-fights. His concern for the sport and its participants left no room open for doubt. He was the first to initiate collections for defeated boxers. From his neutral position, with no suspicion that he had anything to gain by it, his was a persuasive voice urging defeated fighters to give in to avoid useless punishment, which was in defiance of the traditional practice of being held up to scratch until knocked into final unconsciousness. By the time of the famous Cribb v. Molyneux fight in 1810, the first black challenge for the championship, Jackson was clearly, and almost formally, established as the prize-ring's master of ceremonies. His own prestige and status, and that of his sport, were emphasised when he was called upon to organise a pugilistic display for the allied monarchs visiting London in 1814 to celebrate (somewhat prematurely) Napoleon Bonaparte's downfall. The visiting royalty also went to D'Angelo's rooms for more sparring displays. The royal connection was underlined even further at the coronation of George IV in 1821, at which Jackson was commissioned to supply uniformed ushers from among the pugilistic fraternity to keep order in Westminster Abbey.

For the ten years or so after his first royal appearance Jackson's authority in the ring was unquestioned. When a number of enthusiastic amateurs formed the Pugilistic Club in 1814 it was almost inevitable that Jackson should become its secretary and manage its day-to-day affairs. He became the interpreter of its rules, indicating, for instance, during the negotiations for a match between Oliver and Painter in 1817 that it was 'contrary to the rules of the Pugilistic Club to give a purse of 25 guineas when the battle money amounts to £100'. He was in a position to guarantee purses to ensure that desirable matches came off. He would be given the task of deciding where a fight was to take place, and he would frequently be the stakeholder and often the nominator of the referee. He saw to the good order of the fights themselves and was quite prepared, if that order broke down, to call off the contest and order that all bets be returned.[4] No longer was he merely an adviser of umpires - now they referred to him for a decision, as in the Sampson v. Belasco fight in 1820. By this time he stood apart from such workaday business as making the ring, but he was an imposing figure on all fighting grounds when major contests were taking place - a newcomer to the boxing crowd described him in 1823 'moving like one of Homer's heroes'.[5] If for some reason he was not present at a fight, his absence was always noted and any resulting shortcomings were put down to that. At one such, as a commentator said, there was no system of 'acting in concert in order to beat out a ring and all collapsed in confusion'.

John Jackson was undoubtedly, as Pierce Egan described him in 1821, 'the LINK that keeps the whole CHAIN together'. The histories have it that he cut himself off from the prize-ring when a backer demanded his money back in 1823, and that thereafter, in his absence, the standards shrank lower and lower. This is all too cut and dried. The incident of Martin's stake money for the fight with Randall was in itself a symptom of the growing unreliability of pugilism, and Jackson never cut himself off from the ring as completely as previous accounts have suggested. Gentry support was certainly waning and with the weight of organisation and control of pugilism being thrown increasingly on to fewer and fewer responsible shoulders, it was inevitable that much of its edifice should begin to collapse. 1822 proved to be a disastrous year for the sport, though for John Jackson it began brightly enough. He was awarded a subscription plate and silver service purchased by donations from the Duke of Clarence and other nobility and gentry. In June, he was organising a benefit for the 'starving peasantry of Ireland' and raising a purse at Molesey Hurst for a supporting fight between Scroggins and Cooper. There were ominous signs, though, from both sides of the law. The opponents of pugilism, increasing in number and influence all the time, were having their view supported by a judge's decision that even sparring exhibitions were illegal 'in as much as they are precursors of prize-fights, or breaches of the peace'. A few months later there was a warning from the Berkshire assize judge that it was not only the principals in a prize-fight who were subject to manslaughter charges if deaths occurred, but also their seconds and bottle-holders, and that all who attended a fight in any capacity could be guilty of aiding and abetting the offence. Significantly, too, perhaps, the *Sporting Magazine* itself began to reflect the changing times - it was under new editorship and its moral expectations were raised by several degrees. Matters such as bull-baitings, which had previously been reported in neutral fashion, now tended to be described as disgraceful episodes.

It was against a background of renewed pressure from the courts and falling gentry backing that the disastrous rigged contest between Ward and Abbott took place in October 1822, when Jackson and the remnants of the Pugilistic Club had the task of deciding what should be done with the stakes after Ward had blatantly given the fight away. Within days, Jackson accepted the 1000-guinea stakes for a third match between Randall and Martin, scheduled, perhaps fittingly as it turned out, for Guy Fawkes' Night, 5 November. Then Martin's backer, Mr Elliott, demanded the return of his cheque on the grounds that his man was likely to be sued for the stake money from his previous fight with Randall. An angry John Jackson declared that he would not act as stakeholder again. This was against all the practices of gaming: a man's word was his bond and a match, once made, stood, 'play or pay'. It was no longer a sport that he could be responsible for and by August 1823 he had given up the part of master of ceremonies. The withdrawal, though, had been gradual and was never complete. He acted as stakeholder for the Spring v. Neat contest in May 1823, superintended the setting up of the ring and announced at the beginning of the fight that all must stay clear of the ropes, other than the umpires and the referee - a comment pointedly addressed to the gentlemen present who took heed and retired, giving everyone a good view. Jackson was named as stakeholder for the major fight between Spring and Langan for £1000 and oversaw the arrangements for the fight, helped, according to his own account, by Pierce Egan. He was also active in 1824, supervising two meetings at Virginia Water and the second Hudson v. Cannon fight at Warwick racecourse, but thereafter his involvement in the ring's affairs was only spasmodic. He was always ready to support a good cause, such as the benefit for the Lancashire weavers at the Fives Court in 1826, which raised a mere £7, a reflection both of waning interest and of the poor quality of the boxing provided. Whenever there was hope of revival he did his best to encourage it. The Pugilistic Club had finally dissolved itself in disgust at the sight of the deceitful Jem Ward parading himself as champion. When Tom Spring sought to provide a similar beneficial influence through his Fair Play Club, Jackson was quick to accept an invitation to join the committee. He continued to be in demand to demonstrate his sport to visiting grandees, including the Prince of Orange in 1836,[6] and he even supported James Burke in his corner in 1839. By then, though, he was in his sixties, and he finally died at his niece's house in Lower Grosvenor Street in 1845.

Jackson had exerted a remarkable influence over the prize-ring during its most flourishing years. His record there, and his services to pugilism outside the ring itself, had brought him respect, prestige and authority. He was easy in his station in life, confident of where his power and authority lay and had no great ambition to move into any other sphere. He was variously referred to as the 'Commander-in-Chief' and the 'Commissary of the Forces', but he was, in fact, rather the regimental sergeant-major, the undoubted head of the non-commissioned officers who managed the arrangements for contests on the ground. Wholly at ease with all, he still had a clear view of where his role ended and where that of the amateur supporters began. He would pronounce readily and judiciously on disputes when they were referred to him, but he preferred not to act personally as referee - that was the office of a gentleman. He did occasionally accept an offer to be referee, for instance in the Neat v. Hickman fight in December 1821, but his usual response was to decline on the grounds that he was needed to manage such practical matters as defending the ring. It was Jackson who was in charge of the arrangements for the Randall v. Martin fight in 1821 - but when there were doubts over whether it would be allowed to take place, it was a general in the cavalcade who rode off to negotiate with the local JP! Jackson wholly accepted the rightness of this. As for himself, his easy manner, authoritative on athletic matters but modest and unassuming in all others, won him the affection of sportsmen of all classes. He could urge defeated pugilists to give in without any fear of a charge of softness or cowardice. He had the strength of leadership to maintain order in all but the most trying circumstances, though it is as well to remember that the final means of doing so was by horse-whipping, the ornamental whips of the Pugilistic Club having been designed for just this employment. Pugilism's methods of crowd control were just one of its practices serving to keep it at arm's length from an increasingly polite society. The task of reconciliation was a formidable one, and it was made the harder with every passing year. The gulf between pugilism and acceptablility was bound to be wide as long as the sport had to operate outside the law and create its own disciplines. But the man who came nearest to bridging the gap, the only man in the whole history of the sport who might have done so given more consistent support, was John Jackson.

After the hard-fought championship battle between Spring and Langan on Worcester racecourse in January 1824, Jackson collected a few pounds for the gallant loser from spectators on the ground near the ring, while Pierce Egan got together £12 16s. from gentlemen on the stage. The total included £5 from Mr Gully. Nothing could better typify the divergence in the life-styles of the two former champions, whose fighting careers had been so similar and who, incidentally, remained on the best of terms for the whole of their lives. But Mr Jackson remained in charge on the ground while Mr Gully asserted his place on the stage. By birth and general acceptability, Jackson was apparently much the better equipped to climb the social ladder, but it was Gully who forced his way into the ranks of the gentility. Many would say that he bought his way there and he was by no means always welcome, but there, indisputably, in terms of wealth and power he most surely came to belong.

Gully came from the same tradesman background as Jackson, but his was much the less successful family, and his early adult life was far less auspicious. He was born at the Crown Inn, Wick, between Bath and Bristol, before his father moved into butchery, not apparently with great success. After his father's death, he moved to London, only to fail, in his turn, in a butchery business there. So, at the age of 21, John Gully found himself in the King's Bench Prison as a debtor. He used the ample leisure there in playing racquets, keeping fit and sharpening his wits. Henry Pearce, helping a fellow townsman in distress, was among his visitors, and he put the mufflers on with Gully. It seemed inevitable that every butcher who came up from Bristol or Bath was a potential champion of the ring. Pearce was much impressed by Gully's performance and so were the onlookers; word reached the amateur backers that here was a potential challenger. Mr Fletcher Read, always a keen supporter of new talent, took the lead in discharging Gully's debts, releasing him from prison and putting him in training at Virginia Water.

Gully was confident that he could stand up to Pearce. The rewards that a successful fight promised were such as to dispel all his doubts. The urging of patrons - and the absence of any other serious threats to 'The Game Chicken's' title - resulted in a match between the two, for 600 guineas on Pearce's side against 400 on Gully's. A great day's fighting was planned for 20 July 1805. There would be two other matches, one between Jem Belcher and 'Dutch Sam', and another between Bill Ryan (the son of Michael Johnson's past challenger) and Caleb Baldwin. Like so many high pugilistic hopes, though, the actuality fell far short of the expectation. The main fight was called off when it was discovered that the enterprising Mr Chersey had backed both boxers at different times, securing good odds on each.[7] While the gentry backers were debating how to proceed, news came that the Surrey magistrates were on their way. Only a remnant of the cavalcade moved on to Blackwater, where the sole fight that came off was a scratch contest for a hastily collected purse - but it was a remarkable one, Tom Cribb's debut and his only defeat, at the hands of his fellow Bristolian, George Nicholls.

The fight for the championship between Gully and Pearce eventually took place at Hailsham, a small village in Sussex between Brighton and Lewes, remote enough to be safe from intervention. That safety was ensured by the presence among the spectators of numerous gentry and nobility, including the Duke of Clarence, the future William IV. Pearce won, but only after a gruelling struggle for well over an hour, at the end of which he declared that Gully was the only man ever to have stood up to him. The general verdict was that 'The Game Chicken' was the only man capable of beating young Gully. Such was the impression that he made that, after Pearce's retirement on the grounds of ill health in December 1805, Gully was regarded as the champion, although it was not an honour that he immediately claimed. The championship was still, in any event, quite unofficial. There was no ruling body to arbitrate, and the title depended upon a combination of consensus and the readiness of patrons to back the contenders. It was to be another quarter of a century before attempts were made to regularise the process of challenging for the title, in order to prevent the current champion from avoiding unwelcome rivals!

Whether formally champion or not, John Gully kept himself at the centre of pugilistic affairs, and he had a busy year in 1806 supporting other fighters. In February he was with Tom Belcher against 'Dutch Sam', in March with Harry Lee in the unnecessary contest with the ageing Mendoza, and in June in Joe Ward's corner for his fight with Quirk. In June, too, he took his first benefit at the Fives Court, shared with Elias Spray (another unsuccessful challenger of Pearce), and by October in the next year he was ensconced in his own hostelry, the Plough, ironically in Carey Street, the thoroughfare synonymous with bankruptcies. He grew ever more worldly wise, learning one useful lesson, for instance, from crafty old Will Ward, when the two of them were seconds in the Belcher v. Cribb fight. After eighteen rounds Cribb was near to exhaustion and Gully offered odds of 5 to 1 that his man, Belcher, had won. Ward accepted, insisted that the stake money be produced and by so doing gave his man time to recover and eventually win both the fight and the bet, at handsome odds.

Up to this time, Gully had, of course, only fought in the ring once, and then had been defeated. It was an amazing tribute to the strength and potential that men saw in him that he was universally acknowledged as Pearce's successor as champion. He was eventually put to the test in two fights against Bob Gregson, a Lancastrian well over 6 ft tall who was credited with prodigious strength. The first fight, near Newmarket, saw thirty-six strenuous rounds during which both men took much punishment, with Gully winning only by sheer will-power and determination. In the return match in the following year, Gully got on top in the first round with strong rapid punching which broke through Gregson's guard. The Lancastrian never wrested the initiative back from Gully, though he survived bravely for an hour and a half.[8] Throughout, Gully's confidence in himself was supreme - just as he was entering the ring he offered to back himself for £50 against any taker. This second fight was one of the great pugilistic occasions. Barred from the intended Buckinghamshire site by order of that county's Lord-Lieutenant, the cavalcade made its way to Sir John Sebright's park in Hertfordshire, Gully riding splendidly in Barrymore's own coach, alongside His Lordship. Over 150 of the gentry and nobility were said to be there, mounted on horseback. The crowd was kept well back from the ring, which was itself extraordinarily large 40 ft square. It was a fine stage for Gully's farewell. After his first fight with Gregson, he had cut a great figure next day at the racecourse. Now, after his second victory, he announced from the ring that he would not fight again, and invited all and sundry to come and drink at his public house. A well-attended benefit, shared with Tom Cribb, entrance 3s. 6d. per head, added further to his prosperity.[9]

So ended the active fighting career of John Gully. Challenges came, but he refused them consistently and by 1810 Tom Cribb was regarded as his successor as champion. It was a title of which Gully had shown himself to be wholly worthy. The high promise that he had given in his fight with Pearce had been more than confirmed in his two sterling contests with Gregson. The hard grit, determination and sharpness that would mark his later life were all evident in his fighting career and were major contributors to its success. In spite of being tall and well built, he was remarkably quick on his feet nd a strong, rapid puncher. He was adept at parrying and avoiding punches, and his own weakness was as a wrestler. Several rounds in his bouts with Gregson ended with his being thrown heavily, but he usually managed to avoid grappling and if he was thrown he had the strength and resolution to recover.

Once he had retired, Gully cut himself off from physical participation in the ring's affairs much more completely than most. He made a single sparring appearance with Tom Cribb at Will Ward's benefit in December 1808. He also acted as second on several occasions, notably to Cribb for his fight with Gregson and his two famous encounters with Molyneux. It was the start of a close lifelong companionship between the two West Countrymen, highlighted when they danced a Scotch reel' together in the ring after the second Molyneux battle and enduring strongly through all the years when the gulf of wealth and power grew wider between them and might well have pulled others apart. Gully soon had an eye for more profitable prospects than the prize-ring offered. He looked to Newmarket. His knowledge of the turf grew steadily and with his profits from his public house and the proceeds of astute betting he acquired his first racehorse, Cardenio, in 1812, when he was still only 29. His career as racehorse owner was to last fifty years and, one or two disappointments and failures apart, it was marked by conspicuous success and prosperity. It was twenty years before he won a classic race (with St Giles, whose ownership he shared with his betting partner, Robert Ridsdale), but by 1827 he was able to carry a loss of £40,000 on the St Leger. A dozen years earlier, he had translated himself to the amateur side of the prize-ring when he was one of Scroggins's backers for his fight against Eales. Jack Scroggins appeared to be a rising star, and this was another of those contests to attract the nobility and gentry, company which Gully was increasingly making himself at home with. Continuing his role as patron, he was advising Neat on his training in 1818 and umpiring the Scroggins v. Martin fight in the same year. He was noted as being at the head of the 'Newmarket people' at the Neat v. Hickman fight in 1821, 10 at that time backing Neat. A couple of years later he switched his allegiance without compunction to Tom Spring and won what had become for him a minor prize of £100 on Spring's victory.

He remained proud of his pugilistic past, never boastful about it but always prepared to recall the old days with friends from the sporting world. His formidable physical appearance and his thrusting personality made him a man to be reckoned with. Apart from his horse-whipping of his former partner, Ridsdale, after a quarrel on the hunting field, he generally kept his temper under control. That episode cost him £500 damages for assault, but it was a time when a brisk defence of personal interests was essential. The 1830s and 1840s were decades in which honesty in horse-racing was at its lowest ebb. It was a climate in which Gully was well fitted to survive and prosper. He was not obviously dishonest, but he was prepared to take the world as he found it. In 1832, his most successful year on the turf, he took it to the tune of nearly £100,000 through being joint owner of the Derby winner and sole owner of Margrave, victor in the St Leger. He purchased Upper Hare Park, near Newmarket, from Lord Rivers, shortly afterwards selling it to Sir Mark Wood and moving to Ackworth Park, Pontefract. He had not had distinguished success at Newmarket up to this point - his two victories in the 2000 Guineas came in 1844 and 1854 - and he could never work his way into the good graces of the Jockey Club. However, Newmarket itself was faded. The major opportunities it still presented to the astute backer often lay in the old two-horse challenge matches, and Gully took full advantage of these. Apart from the overwhelmingly popular Derby week at Epsom, the focus of racing attention had switched to Doncaster, where the prizes were high, the facilities good and the betting highly organised. There is little doubt that this consideration weighed heavily in Gully's move to Ackworth. Shortly after moving there he became Pontefract's Member of Parliament, not, as historians have usually suggested, because he bought a pocket borough together with his estate but as an elected member of the first reformed Parliament with a wider franchise under the Reform Act. Those who feared the worst from the widening of the electorate saw these fears confirmed in such a result - Greville remarked of the new Parliament 'some very bad characters have been returned; among the worst - Gully, Pontefract'. He held the seat for five years, with no particular distinction apart from entering into a dispute over the regularity of the election that had brought him there. He put up again in 1841, but this time the electors rejected him.

Mr Gully - and there came a time when even he had to be granted the title - continued his highly successful racing career throughout his life. In 1854 he won the 2000 Guineas with Hermit and, in partnership with Mr Henry Padwick, the Derby with Andover. In the meantime he had turned to prosperous investment in heavy industry. His racing winnings went into coal-mining and land. He purchased shares in the Hetton colliery, then being sunk, and held them until their market value rose, turning the profits into a share in the company sinking the Thornley collieries and other such ventures. In 1862, the year before his death, he became the sole proprietor of the considerable Wingate Grange Estate and its collieries. He died in Durham in 1863, a highly successful business man and the epitome of the capitalist entrepreneur, but at the same time the despair of the evangelistic tellers of moral tales on the ruination and dangers of gambling, horseracing and pugilism.

Within four years of his death the Marquess of Queensberry was framing his new rules for boxing. It is an interesting speculation that John Gully, as a young man, would have been an even greater fighter had he been given the protection of gloves and spared the necessity of wrestling. As it was, no other pugilist approached him in terms of making a commercial and economic success out of the bareknuckle sport. In their very different ways, Jackson and Gully greatly enhanced the prestige, standing and promise of the prize-ring. They demonstrated that it could bring to its practitioners esteem, wealth and influence. Worthy as the publican's trade might be (and some, like Tom Cribb, could be blissfully happy in it), Jackson and Gully showed that it need not be the height of a pugilist's post-ring ambitions. They presented to the eyes of adventurous young fighters, for over half a century, vivid pictures of where success might lead.

8

The Hollow Crowning

Shortly after midnight on 19 July 1821, John Jackson mustered an extraordinary corps
of muscular royal pages in Westminster Abbey. They were the men he had been
commissioned to provide to keep order at the coronation of George IV, that old erratic
patron of pugilism as Prince of Wales and Prince Regent. Some of the band wore the
livery of the Crown with impressive ease - Tom Spring, not quite the undisputed
champion yet, but nearing his prime; the young Peter Crawley, 6 ft tall and upright as
a guardsman; Bill Richmond, at home as a uniformed retainer; and Jackson himself, on
nodding terms with many who scrambled through the crowd to their seats from the early
hours onwards. Others, like Tom Cribb and Josh Hudson, hardly had the waistlines of
young pages; while Jack Carter and Phil Sampson, reared in the hard schools of canal
navvying and a Birmingham button factory respectively, could scarcely believe they
were where they now found themselves.

The remarkable band of ushers performed its task well. It was not the pugilists' fault
that the Queen, George's estranged wife, Caroline, had to parade herself from door
to door, trying to gain admission without a ticket, before retreating home in humiliation. It was none of their business either to control matters at the coronation
banquet at Westminster Hall. There, after the royal diners had departed, the throng
of onlookers from the galleries descended like wolves on the remains of the feast,
drained the wine and gobbled up the uneaten food; then, in a mêlée familiar to
fighting men, they made off with gold and silver forks and spoons in their pockets
and unwashed pieces of royal plate wrapped up in their handkerchiefs. Grandeur
and farce had never been far removed from each other in the affairs of the new
monarch and the equal contradiction of bestowing the royal accolade on an illegal
sport caused little stir in the excitement of the day. A single gold coronation medal
between them was a modest reward for the fighting men's exertions, but they were
happy enough with it and it gave them the excuse for a celebration dinner, where
it was raffled off to Tom Belcher.

In the abbey, the King's brother, William, Duke of Clarence, had eyed them with
approval. He knew them all and would continue his patronage and the protection of
Coombe Wood for a few more years still, but as he grew conscious of his own nearness
to wearing the crown and more sensitive to changes in public opinion, he would
withdraw himself from a sport which was falling away rapidly from its best days.
Already, apart from Tom Spring, the bright stars in the Westminster band belonged to
the past - Jackson, Cribb and Belcher, all now with their fighting days behind them.
Jackson was on the verge of his own disillusioned renunciation of pugilism's leader-

ship; Belcher was happy to see his inn, The Castle in Holborn, used as the unofficial headquarters of the sport; and Tom Cribb, liked and respected, was content to preside over his Union Arms in Panton Street, Haymarket, never the same supremo out of the ring as he had been in it and not wanting to be. Richmond alone sought still to play the part he had played in the great days, but his was a supporting role and the drama lost its hold as the luminaries faded from the scene. And John Gully was just not there, having promoted himself out of the ranks of the performers but still not having arrived within reach of the guests.

They were harsh times, the brief prosperity of victory in the French wars having soon given way to higher prices, lower wages, unemployment and general discontent. The government was unpopular and the royal family was never held in such low esteem as it publicly flaunted its domestic quarrels. Sedition was feared and repressive legislation sought both to muzzle the press and prevent free assembly. When, on the eve of the Martin v. Hudson fight in December 1819, the crowd shuffled between Hounslow, Wimbledon and Colnbrook looking for a safe site, it was, according to the *Sporting Magazine*'s correspondent, 'not unnaturally taken for a brigade of Radicals on a march to join their brethren in other quarters', and sober folk hid their daughters. More seriously, the same issue reported a worried meeting at 'Belcher's Castle' of 'several of the most liberal patrons of the ring' to protest at the bills then before Parliament, which were to become the notorious Six Acts. They feared that their sport could be quite put down by the restrictions on meeting and the banning of drilling and training, a theme on which the pugilists were 'forceful rather than subtle'.[1] Although fears about the application of the new statutes against pugilism proved groundless - the law was already strong and embracing enough if justices sought to apply it - the meeting was right to be concerned over the ring's health. Economic depression was affecting it at all levels. Stake money was harder to raise and farmers became more antagonistic towards the destructive hordes of fight followers (or, alternatively, sought to exploit them by charging to allow fights on their land), while the temptations to fix fights by every sort of sharp practice were given the added spur of poverty.

There were already some ominous signs of deterioration. The fight between Ned Turner and Jack Martin had brought a huge crowd down to Warlingham, Surrey, in October 1819. It was said to be 20,000 strong, and this main fight was reasonably ordered. Turner was expected to win, but he had a suspect knee; Martin proved brave and elusive and lasted for thirty-seven rounds. The crowd grew restive at such a comparatively bloodless contest.[2] The usual purse was collected for a second fight and Phil Sampson, the newcomer from Birmingham, challenged the well-known London favourite, Josh 'The John Bull Fighter' Hudson, stout of both stature and spirit. While the historians of boxing report Hudson's victory in this fight only briefly and blandly, the contemporary press had no such reticence. It was a scene of the greatest confusion:

The immense multitudes closed in upon the inner ring in one mass, aided by plunderers of the most daring description, with whom and some of the fighting men a desperate affray occurred, which ended in many broken heads. Such disorder was never before seen at a fight, and it is hoped never will be again, or measures must be taken of a different kind.[3]

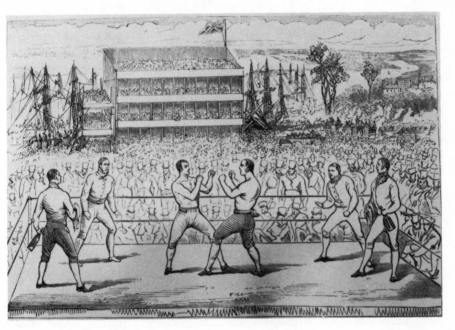

8. Spring's first fight with Langham on Worcester racecourse - spectators even crowded the rigging of ships on the river Severn.

It had to be a hollow threat in a sport which existed only outside the law, and such turbulence became increasingly commonplace at fights, so much so that good order was soon the exception rather than the rule. Nor was the reputation of the ring enhanced by the grudge match between the 57-year-old Daniel Mendoza and Tom Owen, only six years his junior. The contest brought out many of the ageing fight supporters, reviving memories of their youth, but it was repudiated by the Pugilistic Club and ended with the one-time champion being carried away in a coach, badly beaten and with nothing to show but his bruises and £20 collected for him by John Jackson. The club itself was fading away, with only seven members turning up for its annual dinner in 1820;[4] sixty or seventy would have been present a few years before. Even the West Country was failing to supply pugilism with its reliable import of new talent. The allegedly 'iron fisted' Strong (usually known as 'Cabbage' - the soubriquets became more extravagant as the fighting became less distinguished!) proved to be quite out of Jack Martin's class when they were matched in April 1820. He was dubbed 'the worst pugilist from the renowned Bristol nursery', though the state of the sport was such that he pursued his modest career in the London ring for several years with little on his side but courage.

It was not just boxing, or even just sport, which had lost its zest. There was a general air of malaise, disappointment and disillusion from which no aspect of life seemed to escape. The inns were going downhill, horses were not rubbed down properly, service was deteriorating and the large meat joints of yesteryear were no more, at least according to one complaining letter writer.[5] At Cambridge, sports had been curtailed and both the Union Society and the Fitzwilliam Museum had been closed, so that all the money and energies of the young gentlemen were going on dicing and cards. As for sport itself, it all seemed to be increasingly unreliable. Bets were being left unsettled after race meetings and the racing itself began to look more and more dubious. The St Leger, now the country's premier race, had also become the regular focus of controversy. In 1819, for instance, there was first the matter of the favourite, Sultan, pulling up in training, with the consequent rush of those in the know to betting rooms to cover their wagers before the news broke. Then there was the almost traditional chaos at the start of the race, with some horses failing to respond to the starter's signal while others completed the course. It was immediately re-run, with the owner of the original winner, Antonia, understandably refusing to let his horse take part, so that punters were left with the choice of refusing to recognise whichever running of the race best suited them! Of pedestrianism, it was alleged that 'so numerous are the frauds committed in these matches that they have created a general distrust', a comment prompted by an apothecary's attempt to drug a competitor (who accepted his 25-guinea bribe and the bottle of liquor that went with it, but threw the dose away, won and cost his tempter £500 in lost bets). Even cricket, going through a quiet period of recovery after the setbacks of the war years and with the rumpus over round-arm bowling still below the horizon, had its disputes over the terms of matches. These were typified by that between the aspiring Nottingham Club and the athletic all-rounder, Squire George Osbaldeston, marksman, racehorse owner, oarsman and master of foxhounds as well as cricketer, over the articles governing the contest with his All-England side. A crowd of 20,000 turned up to watch, but the club claimed that it would have been many more had the Squire himself played for the visitors, as they had expected.[6]

In the Squire's case, his own absence from the Nottingham match was not a sign of abjuring the sporting life. He continued to participate in everything from rowing to pigeon-shooting. More serious matters, though, or at least more sober sports, were drawing many of his class away from some of their old leisure pursuits and the less genteel the sport the more it was to suffer. Pugilism in particular found itself caught up in a vicious circle of decline from which it was hard to break out. The upper-class support which it had enjoyed for the past thirty years and more had ensured a degree of probity that came up to the undemanding sporting standards of the day. As this support diminished, the demands for fair dealing began to lose some of their force, and as pugilism became a less reliable home for a wager, more and more of the sporting money and influence turned elsewhere. The old brigade of ring enthusiasts was in any event gradually disappearing into the shadows and the young bloods of the new generation were disposed to find other more controllable outlets for their sporting ambitions. Their interest could still be fired by the occasional big fight, but as regular supporters of the prize-ring their numbers became fewer and fewer.

Not that there was any sudden desertion by the gentry. It was a more gradual process even than John Jackson's 'withdrawal', spread over more than a decade and never complete. As early as 1818, and in spite of a full bill of three minor fights, the 2000 crowd at Molesey Hurst on 29 October to see Eales and Hall consisted mostly 'of the lowest order'. Similar comments recur regularly through the 1820s. There was 'a motley multitude' at Josh Hudson v. Will Ward in 1822; there were 'many fighting coves' but few of the 'amateurs' at Alexander Reid v. Bishop Sharp in 1824; and there were 'no patricians' at Shelton v. Brown in 1825. There was 'scarcely one Patron of the Art present' at the first Brown v. Dobell fight in Shropshire in 1829, when the taint of dishonesty in the ring 'had an evident effect on the respectability of the meeting, for a more motley group was perhaps never assembled'. The changing patronage of pugilism was reflected in the actual promotion of contests by the 'humbler votaries of the sport', such as that between 'Young Dutch Sam' and Tom 'Gypsy' Cooper at Thurrock in 1826.

Just as a propitious pattern of circumstances had drawn the upper classes - or at least a significant section of them - into pugilism in the late 1780s, so another set of circumstances was pulling them away thirty years later. There was a new seriousness in the air. The long war years had kept attention away from the profound changes in methods of production that were taking place and from their sweeping consequences in terms of population changes and altered living and working conditions. There was real fear of social and political unrest. To this the only immediate answer was repression, though there was a growing humanitarian groundswell which had already engulfed the slave trade, was becoming sensitive to animal cruelty and would be concerned over child labour in the new industrial society. At the same time, there were demands for hard, regular work patterns - for an industrious life which rejected the old festivals, sports and feasts as relics of a primitive past. It was a climate in which the Bank of England's holidays were to be reduced from forty in 1825 to four by 1834, in reflection of what was happening throughout the land's working practices. There were insistent demands for order and control, which could not bode well for a sport which was both illegal and also always an occasion for actual or potential disorder. The gentry, while seeing no need as yet to abridge their own sporting activities, were inclined to make them less conspicuous by making them more exclusive as their own 'idleness' was becoming a matter for critical comment.

That monthly chronicle of the gentleman's leisure pursuits, the *Sporting Magazine*, had its occasional pleas in defence of popular sports. In May 1823, *Vox Humanitas* was supporting the traditional seasonal festivals as opportunities for the lower orders 'to lay aside their implements of labour, and for a short time enjoy those festivities which their inclinations may lead them to prefer'. He asked whether gentlemen, who could sport throughout the year, were right to oppose 'the rare sports of those who engage in labour'. More typically, though, the *Sporting Magazine* was itself reflecting changing attitudes, reporting the animal sports of the workers with increasing distaste while still accepting cock-fighting and hunting with equanimity. Bull-baiting in particular came under the editor's attack, more so if it was part of some traditional merry-making than if it occurred, as it often did, as a follow-up to a fist-fight. And the magazine did still help to publicise the feats of one of the most bizarre sporting heroes of the 1820s, the dog Billy, whose repeated speciality was to kill fifty rats (probably doped) in less than a minute and who finished up, stuffed, on the bar of Tom Cribb's Union Arms in Panton Street.

The new respectability came only fitfully into vogue, but one of its features was to be a new concentration of attention on the family. There are signs of this in the growing demands of women to share in the sporting pursuits of their menfolk and they began - like 'the numerous fair ones' at the Painter v. Oliver fight in 1820 - to be conspicuous at some of the more fashionable pugilistic matches. A much more regular outlet for the ladies' sporting inclinations had, though, already come into vogue with the rapid spread of archery clubs and meetings. For both sexes the sporting opportunities were growing, with cricket on the upturn in popularity and rowing and sailing regattas now both regular and numerous. The prospects for pugilism were not favourable and the consequences soon began to show in the lack of fincancial backing and the lowering of stakes. A £1000 match was now as likely to be made between pedestrians as between pugilists. The financing of the prize-ring shifted gradually into other hands, and the excitement of gaming, with the hope of profit, gave way to the search for sheer material gain, at whatever cost to scruples.

All of this conspired to make the story of pugilism in the 1820s one of steady decline, but it was a decline punctuated by periodic hopes that the slide had been halted when some notable and evidently fair fight managed to hold back the curtain of descending gloom for a few months. At the beginning of the decade the standards of the past were upheld not only by the continuing presence of 'Gentleman' Jackson but also, in the ring itself, by the stout and estimable Herefordian, Tom Spring, who remained, in his long association with the sport, as blameless as any man of the age could be, 'never losing a friend, except by hand of death'.[7] After beating in turn Ned Painter,

Jack Carter, Ben Burns and Tom Oliver by 1821, there could be little question that Spring was the legitimate heir to the crown of Tom Cribb; Cribb had already become the young man's close friend. The only doubts were about Spring's basic niceness, unwillingness to punish an opponent unnecessarily, and failure to produce a decisive knock-out blow, all of which tended to make his fights last longer than they might have done. In skill, ringcraft, strength and stamina he clearly stood head and shoulders above his contemporaries, so much so that it smacked somewhat of presumption for the contest in that year between Bill Neat and Thomas Hickman (named 'The Gas Man', from his Black Country origins) to be billed as 'for the championship'. The championship was indisputably settled on Spring when he beat the winner of that bout, Neat, at Andover in 1823.

Tom Spring's great challenges, like those faced by Johnson and Cribb, came from outside England. His two fiercest battles were his defences against the Irishman, Jack Langan, as strong and brave a man as he was himself and only a shade less skilled. The first fight, on Worcester racecourse, had elements reminiscent of Cribb's first tough encounter with Molyneux, with home advantage being decisive in securing victory. The enormous crowd proved uncontrollable, the fighters eventually being hemmed into a few square yards, and the ring was always likely to be disrupted completely if the visitor showed signs of supremacy. Without any unfairness on his own part, Spring did eventually turn out victorious when Josh Hudson gave in on behalf of the semi-conscious Langan after seventy-seven rounds and two hours and twenty-nine minutes. The return fight at Chichester was a much more orderly affair, with the boxers operating on a raised wooden stage over another seventy-six punishing rounds. Here both fighters had an equal chance to show their capabilities (though Langan had been disadvantaged by two days' hard coach travel before the venue was finally settled) and Spring eventually wore his man down. The Irishman was determined not to give in. Several times he was brought almost senseless to the scratch in spite of pleas from supporters and opponents alike for him to give in. In the end, a few light blows from Spring were enough to take him off his legs and remove all hope of coming up to his mark again. His great courage was applauded by all. For Tom Spring it meant dreadfully swollen and contused knuckles - 'I never saw such bad hands in any battle', reported one of his backers[8] - a badly bruised body from falls on the wooden planks, which came hard on a fighter brought up on the turf, and winnings from his last three fights totalling £1000. For Langan, it meant a hero's reputation on both sides of the Irish Sea, and a public house in Liverpool where there was always shelter for any of his stranded countrymen.

The Worcester fight apart, all Spring's contests were well ordered affairs. So was the meeting between Neat and Hickman, on Hungerford Downs, near Newbury. There Jackson's management ensured that all 25,000 spectators had a good view, £150,000 was said to be involved in bets and a sporting crowd urged Hickman to give in once defeat was inevitable. Earlier the same year (1821) Hickman had scored a victory over George Cooper on Harpenden Common, where again it was Jackson who played a leading role in keeping both the fight and the large crowd under reasonable control. There were good matches, too, between the 'lightweights', the men who fought at around ten stone and under. Jack 'The Nonpareil' Randall, one of the most skilled of all the bareknuckle fighters and Ned Turner, a left-hand boxer, difficult to attack, were both at the end of their careers (and both died soon afterwards in their early thirties), but Dick Curtis made his debut in 1820 and proved an attractive and popular fighter over most of the decade, only held back by the scarcity of suitable opponents for one of his size, at 5 ft 6 in. and 9 st.

Peter Crawley, who had cut an impressive figure at the coronation, was, as befitted one who had been sworn in as an extra constable for the 1818 Westminster election, another of the small band of pugilists of the day to keep themselves clear of calumny. He held the championship very briefly, beating Spring's successor, Jem Ward, at Royston Heath in January 1827 and immediately announcing his retirement, so that Ward reclaimed the title at once. By this time, the occurrence of a fair fight without cheating or wrangling had become a surprise. Both men fought well, the result was unexpected as most of the money was on Ward, but there could be no faking of this outcome with Ward unconscious for several hours, his pulse weak, from Crawley's knock-out blow to his face. By a bitter irony, the fight which might have restored much of pugilism's reputation ended even more tragically. It was fought on the Northamptonshire border on 2 June 1830, between Simon Byrne and Sandy M'Kay, effectively a decider for the right to challenge Ward. National pride was once more at stake. Captain Barclay, whose training methods had done so much for Tom Cribb twenty years before, had prepared his countryman for the fight, while the Irish turned out in large numbers to support Byrne. There was something of the old style about the meeting. M'Kay was backed by 'swells of the first water', Byrne by 'gentlemen of rank and respectability', and the two of them set to honestly. Byrne was soon getting the upper hand with his cautious in-and-out fighting, dropping on his knee to avoid punishment while inflicting a great deal on his opponent. By the forty-seventh round M'Kay was obviously a beaten man. His face was reduced to a pulp and a blow to the throat finally put him down. When 'time' was called, he was taken to the scratch by his seconds but fell like a log to the ground once they let go of him. He was bled at once and carried to a nearby inn, where he died at 9 p.m. the next night. Any hope of restoring pugilism to its former social stature died with him.

The decline in the sport had been wholesale during the previous dozen years. No aspect of its organisation or practice, from the arranging of matches to the settling of bets after fights, remained free of taint. A sympathetic observer was, by 1822, warning that whenever 'the spirit of manly combat' gives way to greed and 'the art of boxing is made a trade of', there will be constant 'inducements to unfairness and trick'.[9] This was only one of the many criticisms of pugilism's corruption and decline in the sporting press of the day, culminating in the *Sporting Magazine*'s own renunciation of the ring after a particularly disastrous fight in 1831 - 'Comment is uncalled for: but if a final ''knock-down blow'' were wanting for the Ring, nothing could have been more effectual than this, ''the last fight on the list''!'

This was a case where the stakeholder supported a grotesquely unfair verdict on a chaotic fight and immediately handed the stakes to the 'winner', without giving any chance of appeal. It was the culmination of many problems arising over stake money. Bill Neat's inability to raise the £100 to back his challenge of Tom Cribb can be put down to sentiment as none of the sportsmen wanted to see the 40-year-old go into the ring again, but it soon became lack of confidence that made money hard to raise. Jem Ward, for instance, defended his title infrequently because he would not fight for the money that was available. Disputes over stake money - of the sort which disillusioned John Jackson - became more frequent, as did the practice of forfeiting the stake to save wagers, a process which became more tempting as stakes fell in value. This was the case when Sampson's backers withdrew him from his engagement with Josh Hudson in 1824, just as the two were about to enter the ring, claiming that the fight was fixed and that there would be no payout if their man won. The real reason was that they did not fancy the odds at which their bets had been made and sought to salvage them. The calling-off of Barney Aaron's fight with Dick Curtis in the same year was a simpler matter - the stakes were forfeit when it was found that Curtis could not be bought off! Even if the stakes survived until the fight itself, they were not always safe as there was at least one instance of the stake money being stolen during the turmoil of being moved from site to site. (This was at the abortive Bishop Sharpe v. 'Gipsy' Cooper fight, moved from Dartford to Blackheath and still prevented by magistrates. £200 disappeared!)

The choice of venue and the distribution of the gate money also became frequent bones of contention. In rural areas, in the Home Counties and sometimes beyond, farmers could be persuaded to allow one of their fields to be used for a small fee and a share of the gate money. The agreement, though, was easier to reach than to apply. The 'legitimate' collectors of the entrance money were always likely to be displaced, as at the Martin v. Burns fight, by 'certain desperate followers of the ring', who in this case levied a charge of 2s. 6d. on each carriage. There was always likely, too, to be dissatisfaction from the old pugilists if the farmer set up his own wagons round the ring as grandstands, this being traditionally one of their own perks. At the other end of the scale, some provincial tradesmen became prepared actually to pay notable pugilists to bring their fights into their town, bringing with them extra trade. Worcester, for instance, outbid Warwick (which only offered £40) for the first Spring v. Langan fight, while Chichester paid £200, half to each man, for the second fight to take place near the town. The two Brown v. Sampson contests were riddled with commercialism over the venues - Brown paid £65 for the choice of site for the first contest, opting to have it near his native Bridgnorth; but Ludlow's bid of £50 for the second was turned down by Sampson, who insisted on not less that £50 for himself. He likewise rejected a £35 share of the £50 and the stakeholder, Mr Beardsworth, of whom more will be heard later, announced that he would decide the place himself, this being by no means the only issue which he decided in the fight.

Such financial negotiations were more or less public. The real damage was done by the bribery of boxers to throw fights. Although there were occasional suspicions of a 'hocus' by means of doped drink (according to Pierce Egan, Randall thought that such an attempt had been made on him before his victory over Martin),[10] much the most frequent way to fix fights was through bribery. It was a practice which became endemic and it gave particular offence because it extended to the sport's highest levels. The list of known fixed matches is considerable, and includes such notable fights as Stockman v. Cavanagh, Martin v. Burns and Reid v. Sharp (where Cribb as stakeholder returned the stakes in disgust). There were other attempts which came to nothing - Roche, a noted west-country wrestler, thought to try his hand in the prize-ring, being assured that his opponent, Ned Neale, had been bought. Neale had indeed been offered no less than £700 to lose, but he had taken the advice of Cribb and Spring. He accepted an £8 advance and surprised Roche by giving him a tough fight and a final knock-out, his only real danger coming from being thrown physically by the wrestler. There were doubtless other instances where the corruption was successfully hidden.

The saddest outcome for honest supporters of pugilism was that the championship itself seemed to have become contaminated when Jem Ward was allowed to fight, and beat, Tom Cannon for the title which Spring had laid down. Ward's first major encounter, with Abbot, had been one of the most blatant of all the thrown fights. Ward, who by his own later admission was given £100 to lose, was clearly the stronger and superior man, and had great difficulty in losing. In fact, he could not do so convincingly. 'Hit me!' he kept urging Abbot as they closed, and in desperation, lest Abbot should give in, he feigned to swoon on his second's knee after the twenty-second round. His subsequent recovery after Abbot was declared the winner was as remarkable as his collapse - he ran nimbly from the site, leaping a fence on the way! He did confess his faults at an investigation and the magnanimous Tom Cribb urged his youth and ignorance in excuse of his behaviour. Many, though, could not stomach him as champion. Their suspicions, quietened by Ward's straightforward defence of the title against Peter Crawley, were then confirmed by the fiasco of his proposed fight with Simon Byrne in 1829. There was, first of all, the long haggling over terms, which was becoming customary. The fighters accepted £50 each to take the fight to Leicester, where it was to be held behind the brick walls of the cricket ground. The crowd gathered, paying 3s. 0d. each for entrance and 5s. 0d. for a place on one of the wagons that had been brought in the night before to form the outer circle. Belatedly, the local magistrates then intervened, and confusion ensued over the search for another site. Race memories suggested Thistleton Gap, where Tom Cribb had his second victory over Molyneux, but then it was realised that the magistrates' jurisdiction only extended to the borough boundary and so a ring was formed just outside it. Then came the shock announcement that Ward did not intend to fight, claiming that he was ill. His motives for not fighting remain cloudy, with *Bell's Life in London* and the *Sporting Magazine* giving different but equally obscure explanations. What is certain is that illness was not the reason and financial considerations were; Ward had got himself caught up in a conflict of interests between his backers and other friends who had bet on the fight, and there was a £500 bribe somewhere in the background. Two years later, when he eventually met Byrne near Stratford-upon-Avon, Ward won so convincingly that it was hard to envisage how he could ever have succeeded in feigning defeat, and not the least of the exasperation caused by his double dealing came from the conviction that he was a good enough performer to have taken and held the championship without it.

Within the ring, there were few weaknesses in Ward's armoury. He fought carefully, concentrating on repeated blows to the face rather than to the body, and he was equally skilled in defending himself. He usually fought men heavier than his own 12½ st, avoided grappling and wrestling if he could and relied much on his footwork and ringcraft. His departure from his usual cautious and calculating approach when he met Peter Crawley seems to have stemmed from underestimating his much improved opponent and, most of all, from a determination to prove that he was fighting honestly. Certainly the contemporary accounts are hawklike in their search for signs that he was throwing the fight, and all agree that he fought straight, if misguidedly, by persisting in carrying the attack to the heavier man with the longer reach. His Stratford fight with Byrne was his last. After it he followed the usual route into licensed victualling, but the remarkable feature of his long later life (he lived until 1880) was his emergence as an amateur painter whose work, particularly seascapes, graced provincial exhibitions and received favourable notice. Only the most cynical critics would see his artistic talent as yet another aspect of the fictional creativity which had marked his early ring career!

Ward's Leicester escapade, headlined at the time as a 'HOAX ON THE FANCY', proved a serious setback to the most significant of several attempts to halt the decline in pugilistic standards. This was the establishment of the Fair Play Club in 1828. The club's immediate concerns were the good order of fights themselves and behaviour in and around the ring, which had slipped almost as far as the levels of honesty in pugilistic arrangements had. Breaking the ring by spectators, always an occasional gambit to save bets, had become almost a habit, extending sometimes (as at Hudson v. Cannon in 1824) as far as actually cutting the ropes. Seconds were interfering increasingly often in fights, some striking the odd blow on their man's behalf as Bill Richmond once did, and a general melee in the ring involving principals, seconds and spectators was not uncommon. Not surprisingly, the rules of the fighting itself also came to be interpreted more loosely. The unreliability of the result of appeals to any higher authority meant that much was allowed to pass that in earlier days would have meant disqualification - head-butting, hitting a man who was down on one knee, falling on an opponent with knees in his throat or groin and even the equivalent of rugby tackles and blows to the genitals - always described with circumspect reticence in the journals of the day.

As long as Jackson was in charge of affairs, he did his best to lay down the law at individual fights, and some referees only undertook the office on assurances of proper conduct, from seconds in particular. Such steps, though, had only a temporary effect. For years before it was formally dissolved in December 1825, the old Pugilistic Club had lost its force. The Corinthians of the ring, the racy sportsmen on whom so much depended, had their basic concepts of propriety and these were finally offended by the events surrounding the proposed fight between Reuben Martin and 'Young Gas'. The latter admitted being offered £200 to throw the fight, Martin's wife had taken out warrants against both boxers and Martin had had Belcher, the stakeholder, arrested. It was symptomatic of the changing nature of the pugilistic world that when the Fair Play Club was set up two years later, it was ex-fighters and not gentlemen supporters who took the lead. Cribb took a major role and Spring was appointed treasurer. Some well-ordered fights followed, and the club was soon following its predecessor by having its own ropes and stakes, marked with its initials. Almost immediately, though, any revived confidence in the sport was dissipated by Ward's actions at Leicester, and although it was still being reported in 1830 that the club 'is very strict and uncompromising in the observance of its rules', the sting was in the tail - 'if fighting was the fashion, [it] would be serviceable to the cause in many points of view'.[11]

It was not, of course, 'the fashion'. It was being harried by the law more persistently than it ever had been. Even if local justices were prepared to be tolerant they could often not resist pressures from serious-minded citizens. Some still pursued their duty with great courage, like the magistrate who stepped in during the sixty-ninth round of the fight between Ned Neal and Bob Baldwin, only to be ignored by crowd and fighters alike. Not to be put off, he seized one of the seconds and, with that surprising deference in an illegal sport to all other aspects of the law,'it was found impossible to proceed without a departure from every feeling of respect towards"the authorities that be" '. When pugilists did come before the courts, the consequences could be severe if the Crown managed to secure a conviction. After a minor fight between Davis and Winkworth on Hampstead Heath in 1829, the defeated Winkworth walked away from the scene but died the same afternoon. The Old Bailey judge gave Davis a year's imprisonment for manslaughter and Winkworth's second and his bottle-holder were both sentenced to transportation for life for not stopping the fight. Juries, though, were reluctant to convict in prize-fighting cases and Byrne, for instance, was discharged after M'Kay's tragic death. First of all, it proved difficult to find witnesses to swear that Byrne was actually the man fighting, and then physicians convinced the jury that the dead man's injuries might have been received as he was carried upstairs in the inn after the fight.

Provincial magistrates in the midland shires and borough authorities, new to large-scale prize-fights, were initially inclined to turn a blind eye, and this was a factor in the change of geographical balance in the sport, the heavy emphasis moving away from London and the south-east. The first provincial centre to emerge was Norwich, proud of being the regional capital of East Anglia. By 1819 it was attracting a crowd of 10,000 to see Belasco fight Barlee. It was a fashionable social occasion, attracting many ladies as well as men to the hillside overlooking the ring, 'some of them very dashing and many more of respectable appearance, to be spectatresses of bloody noses and cross-buttocks'. Notwithstanding the patronising tones of London journalists, Norwich soon boasted its own Pugilistic Club, which put up a purse of 100 guineas for Painter to fight Oliver. It was another grand occasion, with more than 1000 carriages, 30,000 said to be present, £50 gate money, £80 from grandstand charges and ladies again numerous, who 'seemed to feel with much animation'. Norwich took Ned Painter to heart and he took over the Anchor public house, spending the rest of his life in the city, but Norwich faded from the pugilistic scene after a few brief years.

Other provincial bases were even less permanent, as they were almost bound to be, given the state of the law. For a short time, Warwick, which housed the Hudson v. Cannon fight in 1824, appeared almost to have legalised the sport on its own account. In that sporting city, where the church bells always greeted the start of race week and the Sabbatarians were incensed that the accompanying fair began on the Sunday evening, the justices even allowed twenty-five of the constables to be on duty at the racecourse for the fight. The stage was set up in front of the grandstand, to which 1000 paid the 10s. entrance fee, while the fighters used the jockeys' changing rooms under the stand. 'Thus', said the contemporary report, 'the fun was in some degree legalized'. Worcester, too, whose race meeting was estimated by the police to attract some 200 assorted thieves, with the magistrates in continuous session, was prepared to lend its racecourse for the Spring v. Langan fight, while the course at Lichfield attracted an 'immense' crowd for Jem Burns and Pat Magee in 1826. The local opposition aroused by these events, though, meant that they were unlikely to be repeated. When the Ward v. Cannon fight was taken to Warwick for a repeat of the previous year's event, the mayor, reluctantly and under pressure, ordered that it should be held outside the borough or he would become known as the 'fighting mayor'!

The influence already being exerted by the sober minded, the humanitarians and the employers was soon to be institutionalised by the changes in local government organisation, and the great racecourse fights of the 1820s would then belong only to history. The changes that were to persist into succeeding decades were those which had been having their effect on the sport ever since Tom Cribb's retirement, changes in its social and economic structure and in its ethical expectations. The other great change was already being more than hinted at - the end of the monopoly, and even of the predominance, of the London Prize-Ring. The sport would continue, the number of fights would even grow and the number of annual spectators would go on increasing for many years to come, but it would be a different sport and one largely neglected hitherto by the historians of sport and of society.

9. 'The Pugilistick Club' - hardly a flattering commentry on pugilistic gatherings, and symptomatic of the difficulties in the way of producing an authoritative ruling body for the sport.

9

Fists in the Twilight

The event of the season for fight followers in 1842 was the contest between William Perry, 'The Tipton Slasher', and the giant American, Charles Freeman. The day of the fight, Tuesday 6 December, began with hopes high in anticipation of a good day's sport. A large crowd met at Shoreditch Station to take the 7.30 a.m. train into the country on the Eastern Counties Railway, not yet two years old. No doubt they were happy with the thought that 'there is no railway in the world where more attention is paid to the comfort of the passengers'.[1] It was, alas, to be their only comfort of the day. The resort to the new technology of the railway by the sportsmen was matched by the resort to the new bureaucracy of a professional police force by their opponents. It was past 4 p.m., after much evasion and challenge, when the fight finally got under way - too late on that dull and misty December day for most to see much from the start. After an hour and a half of inconclusive boxing in the enveloping gloom, even the referee, sitting at the ropes, announced that he could not see the action and he put an end to the sport. But it was not the end of the spectators' pains and troubles. They had to find their way back to the railway in the fog and blackness of the night, struggling over heavy fields, tangling with hedges and thickets, falling, if they were lucky, into ditches and, if they were not, into the canal. Sodden and cold, when they did stumble upon the railway, they found that only the late-night train was still to run. It was past midnight when they reached the London terminus and much later when they at last closed their own doors behind them.

It was an experience which typifed the early Victorian prize-ring. Even the phrase itself sits uncomfortably. Victorian Britain and the prize-ring were implacably at odds with each other, according to the canons of a society which saw itself as serious, industrious, respectable and religious. All the old sports inherited from what seemed a barbarous and primitive past were charged with time-wasting, licence, disorder and disrepute. There was some awareness of working-class leisure needs, but little consensus or realism about how these needs might properly be met. The 'Rational Recreation' sought by progressives could embrace everything from Robert Owen's fiddler for workers' country dancing to 'revived' athletic festivals (such as the Tillside Border Games) and such 'striking instances of refinement' as the substitution, at Engton, in Staffordshire, of the Easter bull-baiting by a performance of the *Messiah*![2] Feasts, fairs, traditional games, race weeks - all were under attack. Some, like horse-racing, had powerful enough support to defend themselves, and indeed to rid themselves of their worst abuses. Others went to the wall. Pugilism could muster a few convincing or reputable defences. The arguments in its favour were old and familiar - that it taught fair play, allowed the open settlement of disputes, avoided dagger-fighting and brawling, prevented long-standing rancours and feuds, and prompted emulation of honest combat in spectators. The most respected forum in which these claims had been aired was Jeremy Bentham's Society for Mutual Improvement, which had debated whether magistrates should be censured or praised for their laxity towards prize-fights. Here, in April 1820, the moral claims for pugilism were pushed to their utmost. The sport's chief proponent (referred to for reasons other than mere modesty, as 'Mr M') waxed lyrical over pugilists as 'actors on the stage of valour', and 'playing a glorious part':

There is something fair and *honourable* in an appeal to pugilistic strength and science. It is done openly, not in secret; it is in the presence of umpires to see justice done; no foul blow must be struck; a man is not to be struck when he is falling; he is helped up and time is given him to recover, and when he allows himself to be pronounced vanquished, his person is secure against all further violence.

Mr M concludes, extravagantly, by commending 'the triumphs of boxing' for 'the principles of honour, justice, and humanity, it never fails to produce and support'.[3]

Later defences were inclined to be either more cautious or more choleric. The safeguard against revolution provided by boxing was argued - it imposes a 'most valuable restraint upon the ebullition of rage and the thirst for revenge among the lower orders - teaching them to preserve their tempers and self-possession under suffering'.[4] Its value as a military training ground was pointed out, but this argument gradually lost its force as memories of Waterloo faded and the long years of peace stretched forward to the Crimea. Finally, there was the exasperated call to the editor of *Bell's Life in London* in September 1843 from 'A Yorkshireman' referring to proposals for a national gymnasium and touching on the eternal conflict between what folk need and what they want:

It appears operas, and the execution, in a legal sense, of Shakespeare, are insufficient to draw remunerating audiences to Drury-lane and Covent garden. What say you, Mr Bell, to a jolly good old-fashioned English mill?

That the prize-ring was perceived as old-fashioned was a major part of the problem. This was an age which increasingly took pride in its progress and its modernity. It was an age for crusades - against cruelty to animals, child labour, excessive gambling and Sunday desecration (one of the few offences against decency from which pugilism always remained remarkably free). Evangelical clerics drummed up powerful allies to bring moral reform to the land, and, indeed, at the very time of the Perry v. Freeman fight there was a vigorous campaign against pugilism, one of its leaders being the Revd Joshua Cantley, curate of Broughton, Bedfordshire. This brave saver of souls was so offended by the mounting of the Adams v. Cain fight in his county that he first tried to arrest Nick Adams, having no magisterial authority to do so, and then cut the ropes of the ring itself. Only the timely arrival of a magistrate and his constable and a prompt reading of the Riot Act saved the dedicated cleric from a worse manhandling than he had already suffered.

Apologists for pugilism had always countered charges of disorder by pointing out that the demands of magistrates were regularly acceded to by the boxers and their followers. This readiness to 'move on', coupled with a realistic attitude by the authorities, who had seldom sought to interfere with large boxing crowds once a fight had started, meant that physical clashes were rare. However, it only needed a somewhat keener zeal from the local law enforcers and a deterioration in the control of boxing crowds for this fragile balance to be disturbed. Charges of cruelty were met by the argument that the fighters performed willingly and that the blows given and taken were more lurid in description than they were in fact, another half-truth that failed to carry conviction with the critics. The truth was that the high social and moral claims sometimes made for pugilism had never been easy to sustain even in the sport's best days. They were becoming virtually impossible to uphold now.

Although Jem Ward had largely rehabilitated himself, it was hard to forget that here was a champion who had begun his career in flagrant dishonesty. By the 1830s, 'fair play' had become a debased phrase which meant stretching the rules as far as they would go, while 'honour' if it entered into fights at all, was wholly subservient to contentions over the level of the stake money. Fights between professional boxers to settle personal rivalries were rare and generally ridiculous; they were the meanderings of old men whose real ring days were past. Typical occasions were James Burke taking on Tom Castles, fellow guide to the Haymarket vice dens and freelance minder, and Ben Caunt taking a family quarrel with Nat Langham into the ring. The economics of prize-fighting had long been the ruling factor, but at least the gestures had been there in the challenge and the reply, and the fairness with which a man either won or lost had seemed to be important both to the enthusiasts and to the boxer himself. Now, the old stand-up fight was becoming a rarity and the once rare verdict of disqualification became the commonest means of bringing major fights to an end.

The confused state of the championship for most of the years between the retirement of Jem Ward and the advent of Tom Sayers was no help. Pugilism had to exist without undoubted heroes between Spring and Sayers - and it existed meanly. In the first place, Jem Ward's retirement from active fighting was almost as unsatisfactory as his beginnings. By 1833, when James 'The Deaf'un' Burke had disposed of all other challengers, Ward claimed to have retired. He had written to say so to *Bell's Life in London* in June 1832. When Burke declared himself champion, though, Ward objected. He offered to fight, but wanted £200 a side. These were high stakes at a time when the money in the sport was at a premium and it took Burke two years to find this level of backing. Immediately, Ward raised his demands. Every time Burke was within reach of the stake money, Ward went higher - to £300 and eventually to £500. The leading spirits of the sport, amateurs and pugilists, decided at Tom Spring's anniversary dinner in January 1835 that the champion must always accept a challenge of £200 a side, and that if Ward did not do so Burke was to be declared champion. Burke held the title, without defending it, until he was beaten by William Thompson 'Bendigo' in 1839, in a fight where the farce almost matched the boxing. Burke had been ruptured ten years earlier. Amazingly, the injury and the surgery had only kept him out of the ring for a few weeks, and afterwards he had always worn a truss, even in the ring. Later, he badly hurt his right knee while out boating and could never rely upon its soundness. In the championship fight, Bendigo objected to Burke's rupture belt, which he had to remove. His knee was heavily bandaged and his strength and fitness had been dissipated by the companions upon whom he had to rely for his stake money. It was a sorry end for a simple-minded man, whose vices had been learned from others. He accused a Bendigo of butting then himself butted Bendigo on the ropes, taking the inevitable disqualification as preferable to the defeat that was staring him in the face. The most illustrious presence at this farrago was the 60-year-old John Jackson, in Burke's corner.

Having come to the title largely on the back of his opponent's injuries and unfitness, Bendigo then proceeded to incapacitate himself for over two years with a serious knee injury, incurred as he was returning from watching a steeplechase and demonstrating, with somersaults, how he could steeplechase himself! It was thought that he would be crippled for life, and would never be in a state to defend the championship. The contenders were not impressive. The large and lumbering Ben Caunt was matched with Nick Ward, whose specious claims were based on family reputation - he was Jem's brother - and a suspicious victory over 'The Deaf'un' in his decline. Ward was, technically, one of the best boxers of the day, reared in the old classical tradition, but he was no fighting man. After some success against Caunt in the early rounds of their championship fight (in May 1841), Ward began to feel the weight of Ben's hefty, if erratic, punching and went to ground as soon as possible in every round. Self-preservation went hand in hand with the hope, in this case forlorn, that Caunt's well-known hot temper would provoke him into a foul blow as his opponent was on his knees. Caunt held the title for four years before his old antagonist and fellow Nottinghamshire man, Bendigo, reappeared as challenger. Caunt was 33 years old and Bendigo, 36. It was their third encounter, each having won one of the previous fights on a disqualification. This third contest was no im-provement, with Bendigo 'slipping' down every time he delivered a blow. The crowd was chaotic and threatening, with sticks flying everywhere. The pressure may even have influenced that old stalwart, Squire Osbaldeston, the reluctant referee, who decided eventually that Caunt had fallen without a blow, though this had been Bendigo's tactic throughout. It was a long contest, with little regular stand-up fighting and, according to reports, 'far exceeded in enormity' anything seen in the past thirty years.

Bendigo was the only fighter of the age to defend his title, although his fight with Tom Paddock in June 1850 hardly justifies the credit of being a defence. Bendigo was clearly overmatched in terms of age, weight and strength, and his tactic was to rouse Paddock's well-known temper by constantly falling. This succeeded when he was on the ropes and the lower rope let him down. He was struck with his hand up and obviously grounded. But Bendigo was clearly at the end of his career. It was the turn of 'The Tipton Slasher' to claim the belt and although he lost to Harry Broome, he immediately declared himself still champion when Broome announced his retirement. At length, 'The Tipton Slasher', then ageing - he was approaching his fortieth year - was tempted by a challenge of £400 a side and the championship belt from the young middleweight, Tom Sayer, who had carried all before him in a meteoric career. They met on the Isle of Grain on 16 June 1857. The lighter man systematically wore down his game but ponderous opponent and the country had, at last, a real champion once again.

It had been, at what should have been the sport's highest levels, a twenty-five-year-long story of prevarication, deception and manipulation and sometimes of downright cheating. It had become a case of more talking than doing, with the promises of fights to come always more numerous and more glowing than the fights that actually came off. Within the ring, matters were as bad as they were outside it. Nostalgia for boxing's former days was a constant theme - for Tom Spring, who dealt his blows 'with an ease and mockery of effort, a gracefulness and pleasure that must have been doubly galling', and in whom never before 'were strength, elegance and intrepidity so happily blended in one individual'; and for Tom Belcher, who reappeared in the ring in 1842, after fourteen years' absence, to spar at Dick Curtis's benefit, and, 'by the beauty of his position, and quickness and neatness of his stops and hits, reminded us of what were indeed the palmy days of the Ring'.[5] The present-day fighters showed up poorly by comparison. Ben Caunt might be the champion, but he 'evinced a sad ignorance of the art', showed up badly when he sparred with Tom Spring, and relied only on pluck and strength, 'anything but a well-scienced man, he hits at random and has no idea of self-defence'.[6] Bendigo was held to be 'not a fair stand-up fighter', and it took years to graft even the elements of boxing style on to 'The Tipton Slasher's' charging rushes. Clean blows, given or parried, became a rarity, with whole fights passing without any single punch worthy of a fall. The 'pulling, hauling, squeezing, and hugging' that passed for heavyweight fighting 'would have been accounted as a disgrace to all but pitmen, navvies, and provincial "roughs"',[7] which says more about the directions that boxing was taking than the writer intended. 'Tumble-down fighting' became the fashion, however precisely the New Rules of the London Prize-Ring might debar falling without a blow. The boxers became adept at slipping and stumbling at the first opportunity. Rounds became shorter and shorter as a result. True wrestling throws became less used, especially after the first few rounds of a fight; once one man had established his superiority in throwing, the other usually decided to keep out of distance, resorting to the quick 'in, out, and down' tactic.

The New Rules of 1838 were an attempt, one of several, to bring a greater order and acceptability to the sport. They coincided with the death of 'Brighton Bill' in a fight with Owen Swift, a much publicised tragedy which resulted in the Home Office adding its pressures to those of the reformers by way of urging local authorities to put down prize-fighting. The claim made for the New Rules was they they were 'more manly and humane'. What they resulted in, in practice, was greatly increased scope for dispute and disagreement. Whereas Broughton's rules, insofar as they were concerned with ring practice and not with gambling, had confined themselves to a simple protection against foul blows and being struck when down, the new code tried to cover all eventualities, from the length of the spikes in a fighter's shoes to the prohibition 'of hard substances, such as stones or sticks, or a resin in the hand during the battle'. Fouls included not only falling without a blow (but a man was allowed to slip down in a maul to avoid punishment), but also butting, kneeing and hugging against the ropes. Once a boxer's knee was on the ground, whether at close quarters or at a distance, he was 'down', and this gave legitimacy to what became almost the standard fashion of ending fights - going down quickly on the knee to tempt an opponent into a foul blow, or for a beaten man, deliberately hitting a crouching man as a less painful and less decisive way of accepting defeat. Broughton's two umpires remained, but whereas he had seen them as appealing to a third party only in the case of disagreement, the New Rules accepted the inevitability of dispute and prescribed a referee, confining his role, though, to settling matters referred to him by the umpires. With fight crowds becoming less and less restrained, the rules of combat becoming more legalistic and fighters and their promoters becoming ever more devious, the role of referee became an increasingly thankless one, and few took it upon themselves with anything but the most real reluctance.

New rules for the conduct of matches had been one of the objectives of Tom Spring's Fair Play Club when it was set up in 1828. However, it took more than enough effort for the club to survive and to bring some order and honesty back into the ring. Lacking influential support, its continuing existence was a struggle. It was still trying to infuse new life into boxing in 1832, consigning its new ropes and stakes to Tom Oliver. Three years later it was not under the auspices of the club, but out of discussions at Tom Spring's annual dinner, that the ultimatum was sent to Jem Ward to defend his title or surrender it - a circumstance that Ward to quick to seize upon, retorting that they had no authority for such a pronouncement. The struggle for order and organisation had always been difficult for an outlawed sport, and it was made all the more so by the changing moral and social attitudes which deprived it of most of the upper-class support it had once enjoyed. Although, in the early 1830s, the amateur 'Philanthropics' who met at Jem Burns'in Soho still provided financial aid to pugilists (they distributed £100 in 1832),[8] the boxers were learning that they had to rely more and more on their own efforts and initiatives. The eventual - and remarkable - outcome was the Pugilistic Benevolent Association, which came into being, after months of discussion, in December 1852. It was part friendly society, part closed-shop trade union and part sporting governing body, although in this last capacity it originally confined itself to the maintenance of good order on the ground. It formalised the long-standing system of mutual support that had always characterised pugilism by taking over the organisation of sparring benefits and requiring its members to perform in them to order. It restricted membership to fighters who had fought in the London ring and for stakes of more than £40, and to gentleman supporters who became honorary members on subscribing £2 'or upwards'. The committee would nominate one member to handle the sale of tickets for any inner ring at a fight, and the proceeds of the ticket sales would pay the fees of the ring-keepers, who would be chosen by ballot on the eve of the contest.

Both the New Rules and the Pugilistic Benevolent Association were attempts to bring boxing more into tune with the times. If, by its very nature, the sport could not meet the humane expectations of the day, nor by its very illegality, satisfy the canons of the new respectability, it might none the less be able to benefit from new modes of organisation being set up by society at large. As a sport, too, it could look to new technologies and hope, in particular, to exploit new modes of travel. What pugilism had to face, though, was more than just a change in attitude, a stiffening of opposition towards prize-fighting; it had also to face a much more efficient system of translating those restrictive attitudes into effective action. The often free-and-easy days of local administration - as far as pugilism was concerned - came to an end with the passing of the Municipal Reform Act of 1835. Control of local government, especially in the towns and cities, passed firmly into the hands of those very middle classes whose opposition to sports such as pugilism was most intense. They were given, too, the means to implement their policies much more surely through the establishment of professional police forces. The act authorised the setting up of police forces in boroughs (following the example of the Metropolitan Police, founded in 1829). Counties were given the same power in 1839, and by 1856 every local authority had to have its own force.

The new forces of law and order did not eradicate pugilism, as many had hoped, but they did drive it further underground and prompt it to new stratagems to avoid interference. London pugilists were soon feeling the strength of the new opposition within months of the founding of the Metropolitan Police. When Gow and Burke and their followers arrived at Woolwich in September 1830, they found Superintendent Miller and his men there to greet them, with rowing boats at the ready for the inevitable transfer to the Essex shore. Over there, the superintendent was reinforced by the Essex magistrates, and the only hope of a fight seemed to lie in a hurried return to Middlesex. Then the word was of a warrant to arrest the fighters, who resorted to the game's oldest gambit - the veteran Jack Carter took over Burke's conspicuous hat, cloak and kerchief and drove off smartly with two constables in pursuit, warrants in hand. The ring party, meanwhile, made off in the opposite direction, and the fight - a quick win for Burke - took place at Temple Mills.[9] Superintendent Miller was understandably furious when his constables turned up proudly with Carter, whom he immediately recognised as the wrong man.

The police had their lessons to learn, but as they became more efficient and knowing, an ever larger proportion of intended fights was prevented; those involving large country excursions were particularly vulnerable to police action. How, then, did pugilism survive at all, given the well-organised forces now ranged against it? Why, indeed, did it prove possible to mount the growing number of recorded fights, when it would seem more likely that an actual reduction would result? The experience of other campaigns for good order and sobriety provides much of the answer. The Victorian Sunday settled itself with comparative ease in to the middle-class suburbs and the country towns. It had a much longer task to hem in the licence and noise of the rougher areas of large towns and cities where there was a half century of attrition before the victory of Sabbatarianism was confirmed. So it was with pugilism. There were acknowledged no-go areas for the police forces, and if they did not interfere too openly with the respectable classes fights continued to be winked at. The police were there in some numbers, for instance, at the riotous encounter between the East-Ender, Joe Roe, and Harry Broome, near Greenhithe in 1845. There were over 1000 intensely partisan spectators, more blows were struck outside the ring than in it (though the men fought as well as the crowd would let them) and the outer ring was soon broken; then the ropes and stakes of the ring itself were trampled down, the referee, Tom Spring, quitted the ring and the fight was abandoned. Little wonder that the police contented themselves with noting the names of the principal participants in the event. By the 1850s, regular large-scale pugilism had become confined to a relatively few sites, notably on the southern shores of the Thames and around Birmingham, although there were few places, particularly in the growing industrial areas, which did not manage an occasional successful evasion of police vigilance. Police caution was understandable. Crowds could no longer be relied upon to be as complaisant as they had usually proved in the past, and there could be ugly scenes once they had been allowed to assemble. Tom Paddock's second fight against Harry Poulson in 1851 was mounted at Belper in the teeth of the declared opposition of the magistrates of Nottinghamshire, Derbyshire and Leicestershire alike. It attracted a dubious crowd, the 'roughs predominant as partisans', according to the report, and the magistrates who tried to intervene were violently resisted, one of the JPs being badly beaten up. It took another posse of police from the Derby Borough Force to restore the situation and arrest the two fighters, who were later sent down for ten months' hard labour.

The concept of an organised force to keep order was one which the ring itself sought to copy through the Pugilistic Benevolent Association. Their appointed officers were to have their own clearly distinguishing badges with 'Ring Constable PBA' on them and they alone would keep the ring. The analogy with the police was pushed even further, with Ned Adams as 'inspector' of a pugilistic force of twelve 'constables' for the Paddock v. Jones fight in 1854. Order was indeed better kept during the few years in which this system operated - and that was a factor in drawing back some gentry support to the ring - but it did not long survive the retirement of its moving spirit, Vincent Dowling, the renowned editor of *Bell's Life in London* for many years. The readiness of the ring to exploit new possibilities was also evidenced by its prompt resort to new forms of transport; the age of increased police harassment also proved to be the age of greater speed and mobility for boxing crowds, by way of river steamers and railway.

Getting to the fight had always been something of an adventure, often even a hazardous one. The journey back could be even trickier, with a host of coaches and wagons jostling along at different speeds, frequently in the darkness and on unreliable roads. The coming of steam opened up new horizons. The whole party could be transported to a site which could remain unknown to all but a very few. There were hopes, too, that the crowd could be controlled, and for the promoters there was the expectation of profit from the sale of tickets. Both rail and river were resorted to at much the same time, around 1840. They seemed to promise answers to the twin problems of more effective official policing and the growing unruliness of boxing crowds. It soon became apparent, though, that these new modes of transport also had their limitations and risks.

Sometimes there were mistaken alarms, as in one of the earliest 'railway fights', when Ward and Bailey took the train from Nine Elms Station on the newly-opened Southampton line in October 1839. The pugilists were amazed to find a number of Surrey magistrates entering one of the first-class carriages. Their relief was enormous when the justices alighted at Kingston-upon-Thames - the pugilists had chosen a quarter sessions day for their encounter! In these early days, the pugilists and their followers rode on the ordinary time-tabled trains, but this could give rise to problems. The railway schedules were inflexible, and if a fight was prevented it was hard to move to an alternative site, especially as all the passengers found themselves suddenly reduced to walking once they had left the train. For James Burke's fight against Nick Ward, for instance, there was a comfortable journey down the Birmingham line to Wolverton; but once they arrived the spectators found only two chaises for hire and only a few more available at nearby Stony Stratford (which a few years before had been a thriving posting town on the Birmingham road, but had now slipped into rural quiet). The hoped-for arena in Buckinghamshire, some four miles distant, was then ruled out by mounted constables, and so a trek had to be made into Oxfordshire. It was a cold and wet September morning; little wonder that 'the be-bogged pedestrian railed with bitter inveteracy against the railroads which had subjected them to such unforeseen difficulties, by causing a dearth of the ordinary modes of "civilised conveyance" '.[10]

The answer was the special excursion train. It dawned upon the fighting men that if Mr Thomas Cook could charter a train for his temperance excursions, as he had just begun to do, they might well manage to do the same for boxing matches. William Perry's fight with Tass Parker in December 1843, involving a steamer trip down the Thames to Dartford Marshes, was interrupted by the law, and the search for a safer means of completing the engagement led to discussions with the manager of the Brighton line and the engagement of a special train with tickets at half a guinea each, 'the departure and return being arranged . . . so as not to interfere with the order and regularity of the traffic at the London Bridge terminus'. All went well, and a pattern was set that held until boxing excursions were barred by law in 1868. The favourite railway was the Eastern Counties, from its original terminus at Shoreditch, before the building of Liverpool Street Station, into the broad acres of Norfolk and Suffolk. The Great Western was also hospitable, though its record for finding safe venues was less reliable, while the managements of some of the other companies resolutely set their faces against providing boxers with facilities, so that, for instance, the whole area south-east of London soon became closed to their 'specials'. One advantage of the exclusive train was its relative flexibility. This enabled the Perry v. Paddock fight to take place in December 1850 in spite of police intervention in Wiltshire and Hampshire, the intended venues. The train pulled up in a cutting outside Woking on the return journey, the crowd swarmed out and scrambled up the bank, and the pugilists fought it out on the familiar ground of Woking Common. Another advantage was that the supporters could be well (and profitably) victualled from the commissariat coach, unless the pressure of the crowd at the departure station prevented them from stocking up, as happened when Broome fought Paddock. The new telegraph, still closely associated with the railways, was a mixed blessing. It meant that the result could be reported rapidly and threatened to put the homing pigeons out of business, but it also meant that the Metropolitan Police could telegraph their colleagues in the counties to warn of any excursions heading in their direction. For this particular Broome v. Paddock fight the warning was ineffectual as the managers took an unusual and unexpected route towards Ipswich instead of making for one of the usual inland sites.

The rival to the railway was the river steamer, which could be chartered to go down the Thames to find a suitable location on either the Kent or Essex shores of the estuary. One of the earliest ventures on to the river was arranged at short notice to complete the Perry v. Freeman fight, which had been overtaken by darkness at the first attempt. It proved hard to find an early date free in the boxing calendar and so it was agreed to join forces with John 'Bungaree' Gorrick and James M'Ginty, who had a match in the offing, and to hire two river steamers for a double bill down river. Spring and Broome controlled the sale of tickets, but immediately one of the difficulties of the steamer excursion cropped up. The tickets sold well, but wind of the arrangements spread abroad and the official steamers headed out from London Bridge followed by a whole fleet of small craft of every shape and size. The skippers of the coal-tugs always had their ears cocked for the whisper of a fighting trip and offered the East-Enders the chance to tag along, in the grime, perhaps, but at vastly cheaper rates. This was a factor in the disorderliness to which river fights were prone. Sometimes the competition with the official boat was more organised, prompted by suspicions of profiteering. Johnny Broome was always - not without justification - mistrusted and his entrepreneurial successes were not a little envied. For his brother's fight with Roe in 1845, there was not only the usual tug-boat company, but also somewhat more acceptable alternative accommodation in the shape of the steamer *Lord Nelson*, offering the trip at less than half price. The bargain hunters lost their advantage when the *Lord Nelson* ran aground under London Bridge and they were left stranded! The same antagonism towards Broome resulted in a considerable boycott of his chartered boat, the favoured *Nymph*, for the bout between Sparkes and Langan in May 1847. Not only was there the customary bevy of 'cheapsiders' on the coal-tugs, but also many of the regular boxing enthusiasts had chosen to make the trip down to Gravesend by the regular ferry rather than buy Broome's expensive tickets. Not to be outdone, the *Nymph* sailed serenely downstream and then, off Gravesend, turned sharply and headed back at speed up river. The select band of ticket-holders made for Nine Elms Station and took the train to Woking, and the fight took place on the common before not more than a hundred spectators. Even the pigeon fanciers, it was said, had been left behind and denied the opportunity for sharp wagering that river trips still afforded them.

There were other problems associated with river trips which were never wholly solved. Landing could be difficult, if not dangerous, where there was no available jetty. Another difficulty was that the boat was always more fully laden on its return than it was on the outward journey, when the tickets were sold. Another, for the passengers, was the tendency of the organisers to be interested only in their own man's fight so that the transport departed once that was over, irrespective of any additional attractions. For instance, after Tom Paddock had beaten Aaron Jones in July 1854, *The Waterman No. 7* immediately upped anchor and made for home. Many stayed to watch a second fight, between Spooner and Donovan, to the subsequent profit of the Gravesend Railway. The other possibility was the sort of adverse weather which prevented *The Queen of the Thames* from arriving at London Bridge before midnight after the Orme v. Langham fight, having had to steam against both a fierce head wind and an ebbing tide. With all these hazards, however, the steamer trip remained popular and convenient. The ship could often anchor adjacent to where the ring was to be set up, an advantage seldom enjoyed by the railway, and its deck-chairs could be manhandled ashore to provide seating for those prepared to pay for it.

The increasing exploitation of the new technologies of the age was a sign that pugilism was perhaps after all, in spite of the dubious sporting quality of most of its fare, emerging from its twilight. Among the other signs was a revival of interest among some of the middle- and upper-class supporters who had been largely lost to the ring for the past twenty years. They looked, generally speaking, to a revival of the sport that their fathers had described to them. Few acknowledged that, in the intervening years, pugilism had undergone such drastic changes that it could never be the same again. Patrons from the middle classes might possibly return, but it could never be their sport again, nor could it be just a London sport. Pugilism had gone both to the people and into the regions. The typical star was no longer a Bristol butcher or a Thames waterman. He was more likely to be a midlander from the country's new industrial heartland.

10. The Lowndes Arms, one of the very few remaining London public houses with prize-fighting associations. Just off the King's Road, it was built in 1825 as the development of Belgravia began, and Alex Reid was its landlord in the 1830s.

10

The Tale of the Tipton Slasher

The cathedral still presides benignly over the summer sports of the city of Worcester. Pitchcroft, with its racecourse, lies on one side of the River Severn, and the County Cricket Ground lies on the other. The cadences of the Black Country are still heard there as visitors flock in to what was for many of them, under the old boundaries, their county town. In July 1856, the cricket ground was still part of the cathedral's water-meadows, but the racecourse had been attracting its sporting crowds for over a century and not for horse-racing alone. For many of the older inhabitants, their most vivid memory was of that January day in 1824 when 30,000 people had flocked to see Spring fight Langan, and men had climbed the masts of the moored river boats to have a view of the combat. Now, by contrast, the sun shone, the ground was dry and the new constabulary was there in force to keep the pickpockets at bay. There was time for three of the stall-holders to get together to strike up a bargain.

There were three big men, all touching six feet or more. One, the oldest of the three, had the suspicion of a limp, though he moved nimbly for a man of his size. He was nearing 40 and the irregularity of his features was not helped by missing teeth, which made even his most amiable smile appear as a grotesque grin. He was certainly no figure of fun to the two younger men, the one heavy-fleshed and talkative and the other tall, powerful and sparing of speech. They were well-known figures in the sporting world, particularly in their native West Midlands, and fathers pointed them out to their sons. They were the leading fighting men of the day, certainly so in the view of these racegoers who would not bring that young slip of a lad from Brighton, Tom Sayers, into their reckoning. Harry Broome, growing more corpulent all the while now, had held the championship but had not defended it. Birmingham-born, he lived, all too well, at his brother Johnny's Rising Sun, just off Piccadilly, in London's West End. The towering Tom Paddock came from Redditch, in the north of the county. He had been as near to the title as could be for the past ten years and had fought all the front-rank boxers. The third man, the improbable blend of the ungainly and the athletic, was no less than the present claimant to the championship. Born William Perry, he was known to the whole world as 'The Tipton Slasher' or just 'the Slasher' - or, increasingly these days, as 'Old Tipton'.

The three knew each other well. They had all been matched together in the past, and the talk between Broome and The Slasher was animated. There was constant speculation about whether Perry would ever fight again at his age, and Broome was sounding him out, on behalf of Paddock, a rough-hewn character whose fists were more fluent than his tongue. Perry was willing. Two £5 notes were produced on the spot as an earnest of serious intent. The total stakes would be £200 a side, and they would meet at Alex Keene's Three Tuns in Soho the following Tuesday to draw up the articles and settle the details of the match.

Like so many others, this fight never actually came off. Harry Broome, having originally made the match on behalf of Paddock, later announced himself as The Slasher's backer and trainer and then, after £80 of the stakes were down on each side, Paddock had to announce that through 'want of friends' and his own racing loses he could raise no more. In more straightforward times, this might have been taken at face value. Given the pugilistic morality of the day, there is the distinct possibility that Paddock was deliberately led into the match in the expectation that if Broome changed sides, he and Perry would be able to pick up whatever was on the table by way of stake money. Perry himself had long experience of the difficulties of securing backing - and almost as long experience of the deviousness of the Broomes.

When William Perry had first made his way to London as a teenager in the early 1830s, the older Broome brother, Johnny, was still an active pugilist and Harry was a mere boy. There was no such magnet for aspiring Brummagem pugilists as the Rising Sun was later to become, and the Black Country lad found work labouring, near the river. He had much to put up with. His odd knock-kneed gait invited taunts, which he answered with his fists. He quickly won himself a local reputation in the Battersea Fields and around Chelsea as a game fighter, with the inevitable consequence that he was drawn to Alex Reid's tavern, the Lowndes Arms off the King's Road, a long-standing resort of ring enthusiasts. Here Alex, the old 'Chelsea Snob', gave his regular Tuesday-night sparring exhibitions. It was here that arrangements were made for the young navvy to meet Barney Dogherty, inescapably Irish, to decide who should wear the local laurels. Perry was backed by a knowing butcher, Dogherty by his fellow countrymen, and it was a formal affair, the men being supported in their corners by established pugilists. However, even such small-scale encounters were proving hard to mount anywhere near the centre of London, and young Perry had the first of his many evasive excursions to avoid the law. Wimbledon Common, the intended battleground, was soon ruled out, the police having spotted an early movement of would-be supporters in that direction. An actual start was made a couple of miles away at Mortlake, and Perry took all the seven rounds that were fought there before the police came on the scene. There was a brisk walk a mile eastwards - with the older followers sighing for the comfortable days of Molesey Hurst and Coombe Wood - only to find that Barnes Common was also barred. After that it was back over Putney Bridge and almost back 'home' to Lechmere Common, near the King's Road, where the fight was eventually completed. The outcome was never in doubt. Perry proved to be a hard hitter who punished his man severely from the start. What most surprised the onlookers, though, was his smartness on his feet, his dodging this way and that to avoid the few blows his opponent managed to launch. While he impressed, some compared him unfavourably (and unfairly, for a beginner) with Alex Reid at his best. At least in the 'Chelsea Snob's' young days such a beginning would have ensured support and further progress to more fights. As it was, Perry became frustrated at the absence of opponents. For weeks he turned up dutifully at Alex Reid's on Tuesday nights, but no one came forward to meet his challenge. Disillusioned, he made his way back to Tipton.

He was looking for another start, and the fighting hardware country gave him the opportunity. His sparring, when a group of Birmingham boxers exhibited at Tipton, led to a match with one of them, the experienced Ben Spilsbury. Perry had to look to a local supporter for the £10 stake, but that was the end of his troubles so far as this encounter was concerned. Spilsbury started optimistically until he felt the force of Perry's right whenever he came in - his fierce, swinging blows meant that from now on he was known as The Slasher. The fight, which ended when Spilsbury quitted the ring after nineteen rounds, took place in 1836 on what was becoming a favourite pugilistic occasion in industrial areas, Boxing Day. In November of the next year Perry was matched with another local hero, Jem Scunner, from Gornal in the tough heart of the Black Country, the stakes rising now to £25 a side. Scunner was a big, aggressive fighter, a six-footer of over 13 st., more than Perry's equal in stature. The pattern of the Spilsbury fight repeated itself - rushing attacks at first from Scunner, then an attempt to fight at a distance, the encounter ending within the hour, after he had been hit or thrown down in a half dozen successive rounds. The one ominous feature of the fight was the allegation of fouling against The Slasher, for falling without a blow. His dodging style, and possibly his faulty leg, meant that he did perhaps slip more than most; it was not a practice which his London experience had done anthing to discourage, and it would dog his future career.

The Slasher's seconds were both nationally-known pugilists, Tass Parker of West Bromwich and Tom Preston of Birmingham, who were to meet each other within a few months for the then princely stakes of £200 a side. Emulating the London practice, there was a crowded benefit night for the victors at The Slasher's headquarters, the Fountain Inn, at Tipton. Johnny Broome, meanwhile, was comfortably married and settled as a prosperous tavern-keeper in the capital. Always alert to pugilistic happenings on his native heath, he had noted The Slasher's achievements, but three years passed before he saw an opportunity that appealed to his devious mind. Burke was tied up first with Bendigo and then with Nick Ward. Bendigo went down with injury and Caunt had decamped to America, and Broome saw no profit in dealing with lesser fry. Eventually, with Burke claiming the championship, Broome saw his chance - The Slasher would take up Burke's challenge and a fight was arranged for August 1842. The patrons of the Rising Sun were ready with their backing, until a bemused Perry suddenly found that Broome had opted out and forfeited the £15 already deposited. It was a further lesson in contemporary ring affairs, where the exchange of actual blows in the ring was a very occasional and minimal part of the whole business.

Johnny Broome had, in fact, been siezed of a notion that promised greater profit than a doubtful encounter between his raw, wild-hitting novice and the strong, skilled and tried 'Deaf' Burke, even if he was now well past his best. What Broome eyed with envy was the success that Ben Caunt was enjoying exhibiting with the gigantic American, Charles Freeman, whom he had brought back across the Atlantic. Freeman, 7 ft. tall and 20 st. in weight, had no ambitions to become a prize-fighter, and his 'sparring' with Caunt, which was packing the theatres and assembly halls, was little more than a caricature of boxing. However, some theatre managers indulged in the most more than a caricature of boxing. However, some theatre managers indulged in the most extravagant publicity, even proclaiming the innocent Freeman as 'Champion of the World', ready to meet any challenge. It was not a chance that Broome would let slip. With equal theatricality he threw down a challenge on behalf of an unnamed 'novice', the stakes to be £100 a side. Freeman was prevailed upon to accept, and the usual long string of preliminary meetings to build up the stake money took place - eight further engagements, at Johnny Broome's, Johnny Walker's, Jem Burns's and Tom Spring's. It was a process which allowed more time for the often difficult task of building up the stake money, extended the excitement and the publicity and brought some welcome business to the sporting publicans.

Both fighters went into serious training. Freeman's regime included walking twenty to thirty miles a day, which, by reducing his excess weight, only served to make his Herculean figure the more imposing. Its symmetry, despite its enormous size, was much admired. Widespread interest was aroused by the coming contest and the debate on the relationships between size and strength extended into serious medicine, with an eminent surgeon subjecting both men to a series of tests on lung capacity, respiration, pulse rate and muscular power. In terms of strength for weight, his vote was solidly for Perry, though he was quick to add that many other elements could intervene in an actual fight.[1]

The one intervention that could be predicted with some confidence was from the police, themselves a recent innovation as far as the county authorities were concerned. Another was the use of the railway for transport to the fight. While it was not the first contest to make use of the new locomotion - Nick Ward had used it against Jem Bailey and Ben Caunt in the two previous years - it was probably the earliest to resort to what was destined to become the prize-ring's favourite company, the Eastern Counties Railway. The special excursion train, hired by fight organisers, lay in the future, and the supposedly confidential arrangement was that all should embark on the scheduled 9.30 a.m. train to Sawbridgeworth, twenty-seven miles down the line. Unfortunately for those seeking to keep matters quiet, not only had the circus-like trappings of the contest spread the enthusiasm more widely than usual, but also there were still fight followers tied to their travelling habits of the past. There was such a bevy of wagons and coaches on the road the night before that the authorities had clear warning of the general direction of events.

For all its many generations of avoiding the law, the ring had not yet accommodated itself to the existence of organised police forces in the counties. It was no longer just a case of avoiding a couple of magistrates, backed up by two or three part-time constables (calling out the yeomanry had been an exceptional event) as now even the shires were setting up their permanent uniformed forces, which they were empowered to do in 1839 and required to do from 1856. The early county forces were particularly anxious to show that, even if they were not yet mandatory, they were efficient and necessary. Thus, when the heroes of the day and their attendant host spilled from the train at Sawbridgeworth, there was the local superintendent of police, a magistrate at his shoulder, to greet them. Immuned to such hindrances, though they had never happened before at a railway station, the leaders took the road towards the next county, Essex. The law intercepted them again. The superintendent was empowered to prevent hem in Essex as well as in Hertfordshire. Where to now? Cambridgeshire would have been a possibility, but it was too far for the rail travellers, now reduced to the ranks of pedestrians. They would take that other frequent recourse and 'try back', that is, return in the direction of the capital in the often fulfilled hope of finding somewhere quiet on the way. However, once the motley procession had apparently begun to beat the retreat, the forces of law and order returned to their camp fires satisfied with their victory - and the fight began in the very field near Sawbridge-worth intended in the first place!

By now, though, it was past 4 p.m. on a dull and darkening December day. The pugilists fought for nearly an hour and a half, as the darkness and fog closed in on them. The crowd broke the outer ring and swarmed round the ropes. The fighters became pale, shadowy figures, even from the ringside. Neither had suffered much damage and both were keen to reach a result, but the referee called a halt, saying that he could see too little to be able to pronounce on any appeal made to him. The spectators were in as much danger as the boxers had been when it came to finding their way back to the railway. In the unrelieved blackness, they stumbled into ditches, some fell into the canal, and many took hours to cover the short mile to the station. On arrival they found that all but the late train had had departed and that it did not arrive in London until midnight.

The second attempt to settle the issue was even less successful. Captain Robinson, newly-appointed superintendent of the Essex police, was determined not to be taken in as his Hertfordshire colleague had been. He made it clear that he regarded his own reputation and his post to be at stake, that his authority extended over all the neighbouring counties and that he was prepared to dog the wandering cavalcade until nightfall if need be. He put the word around that if the crowd did not disperse, he would have warrants enforced on the principal actors. Tom Spring still dominated the scene, with old Tom Oliver now filling John Jackson's former role as Commissary, in charge of the official ropes, stakes and other accoutrements of the Prize Ring. The bold captain added insult to injury by calling on the two of them to assist him in the discharge of his duty. There was nothing for it but to go home. The fight was eventually concluded on 20 December, a fortnight after it began. The Scot, M'Ginty, was due to meet the Australian, 'Bungaree', that day, and the leaders got together to hire the *River Thames* for a double bill. Tickets were tightly controlled and in spite of the trail of other craft which built up behind the steamer, the fights were held on the marshes below Gravesend, without interruption.[2]

From the start, it had been an odd contest in pugilistic terms, an exercise for the curious as to how a fighter could tackle an opponent over a foot taller and with commensurate advantages in reach and weight. The Slasher's answer was to dash in and out quickly, to dodge, to try to avoid Freeman's bear-like hugs and shattering throws and to go down on his knees at the first opportunity, blow or no blow. He did this with such regularity and readiness that the 108 rounds of the whole fight took less than two hours. There could be all manner of excuses for The Slasher's mode of fighting - the grass was slippery, there was no other way to tackle such a giant and (by his own account) the recoil from his own punches on that massive frame caused him to lose his balance! None of the excuses would serve, however, once the two umpires at last applied to the referee for a verdict. He immediately pronounced The Slasher's latest fall to be unjustified and 'foul', and the fight was over.

Although he had lost the fight, Perry had made himself a national reputation as the man who braved the American colossus for almost two hours and came out of it relatively unscathed. It might not have been either a polished performance or a dignified one, but at least he lived to tell the tale. He showed great hardiness, nimbleness and courage, though this 'unknown novice' was still without any boxing skills apart from the craft and cunning which he had picked up from those around him. To go down at will, to mock and taunt his opponent, to drive him into his own corner, exposing him to the jibes and threats of the roughneck support he attracted - these were, apparently the extent of the professional lessons which Perry had learned. He seemed unable to fend off Freeman's blows, while his own attacks were of the wildest, relying for the most part on a swinging right hand. Freeman, by contrast, was a revelation. He had quickly picked up some of the rudiments of orthodox boxing and but for the poor timing of his blows would soon have had his opponent floored. As it was, he always caught The Slasher on the retreat, never landing with full force, and he earned widespread approbation, but no material advantage, by never deliberately landing his own massive body on top of Perry's when he threw him.

There was the same contrast in the behaviour of the two men at the handing over of the stakes at Spring's inn, The Castle. Freeman accepted his money with an impressive speech that was both fluent and modest, while The Slasher's response to the few pounds raised by a collection for him was confined to rubbing the side of his nose and a couple of grunts! His promoters, though, could see other pickings to be made, and Johnny Broome organised an extensive round of 'benefits' and exhibitions, particularly in the industrial towns and cities, where The Slasher's somewhat basic talents had their strongest appeal. Freeman returned to the stage and the circus, only to die of lung disease within three years; Perry's party were quick to ascribe that to the battering he had received in their fight, no matter what the medical evidence said. Meanwhile, though the motive for The Slasher's countrywide touring was strictly commercial, the constant sparring with the Broomes and preparations for a fight which was prevented by the imprisonment of his opponent served to improve The Slasher's technique. (The proposed encounter was against William Renwick of Liverpool, to be fought on Tyneside at £50 a side in August 1843, but Renwick was arrested at his training quarters a couple of days before the engagement.) His new-found skills took the opposition by surprise at his next encounter, against his second of former years, Tass Parker.

That favourite vessel of the prize-ring, the Woolwich steamer *Nymph*, was hired for the occasion. A large crowd mustered on Dartford marshes, but in spite of the number of 'amateurs' present, it was the old performer, Peter Crawley, who was prevailed upon to assume the increasingly troublesome mantle of referee. The fight itself, before it was mercifully interrupted by the Kent constabulary, turned out to be a tedious replay of Perry v. Freeman, without the David and Goliath appeal, and with the falling all being done this time by The Slasher's opponent. Parker had started confidently, The Slasher held back, parrying the attacks when they came

11. William Perry, The Tipton Slasher.

and landing heavily with his own right. Parker realised that he was facing a new Perry, immediately retreated, kept out of distance and fell at the slightest opportunity. Like many fighters of the day, he considered that loss on a foul was less damaging to the reputation and a good deal less painful than fighting on to exhaustion. The resumption of the alleged 'battle' was delayed until the end of February by an injury to Perry's hand, and doubtless to allow time for the most lucrative arrangements possible to be made. Recently there had been a number of specially arranged excursion trains for fights, so a quiet word with the manager of the Brighton line resulted in a special from London Bridge, then the London terminus. Johnny Broome and Jem Parker (the brother of Tass) were happy to dispense the tickets, at 10s. 6d. each.

The resumed fight fulfilled every promise of farce that the beginnings had held. Peter Crawley had stood down as referee after the Dartford charade, and Parker's party spent an hour rejecting all suggestions for a new judge. Only when the stakeholder announced that he would give the stakes to Perry unless Parker agreed to one of the many suggestions was it decided that there would be just the two umpires and no third arbiter. Given Parker's intended plan of action, this was all to his advantage. The travesty of a contest lasted for almost an hour. Parker went down at the merest gesture and The Slasher, exasperated, rushed in wildly. Many of the gentry had left in disgust by the time that even Parker's referee had to agree that he had fallen deliberately, and so the fight went to The Slasher. In a supreme triumph of hope over experience, arrangements were immediately begun for a rematch. These were almost as wearisome as the fighting had been; it at last took place, after two and a half years, on Lindrick Common, Nottinghamshire.

The stakes were high - £200 a side - and, against all the odds, it proved a worthy contest. The Slasher fought with a fierce control and Parker made a brave showing before collapsing in the twenty-third round, after taking much punishment. There was something of the old flavour about this fight, a northern edition of the Regency ring. The gentry might be thinner on the ground, most of them Yorkshire racing men, and the crowd might be predominantly local miners, but good order prevailed under Squire Edison, whose acceptance of the role of referee was received with acclamation. The Manchester Commissary marked his ground and set up his ropes with all the ceremony and authority that old Bill Gibbons had displayed in the past. From it William Perry emerged as a serious contender for the confused championship.

This Nottinghamshire fight took place in August 1846. The year before, Bendigo had beaten Caunt, almost inevitably on a foul - as usual, he fell without being struck. It was an indecisive fight with an unsatisfactory and hotly-disputed ending. Bendigo could not carry the title with any great conviction and the search was on to find a clear contender. At the drawing up of the articles for the Bendigo v. Caunt fight, Perry had put down £10 to meet the eventual winner, though given his record at that time, before his battering of Tass Parker, this was just marking a claim rather than serious matchmaking. In the event, after the Parker fight, it was Ben Caunt whom The Slasher challenged, as likely as not because Caunt appeared to have had enough of fighting, the publicity would be useful and the risks of an actual contest were likely to be avoided. Caunt did express his willingness to meet The Slasher - but only for the impossible stakes of £500. Johnny Broome continued to advertise his man, presenting a belt to Perry as a presumptuous symbol of his right to the title, whereupon Caunt called the bluff by lowering his demands to £200 a side. While this delighted The Slasher, who was keen now to show his worth against the best, it did not suit Johnny Boome's book, and it was Johnny who, through his rich clientele at the Rising Sun, held Perry by the purse-strings. He had his eye already on another up-and-coming lad from the West Midlands, Tom Paddock.

It was, indeed, a bad time for someone in The Slasher's position, on the very brink of the championship. The five years between 1845 and 1850 were notable for the absence of fights between the big men. 'Deaf' Burke had died in 1845, aged 35, having regarded himself as being in contention almost to the end. Bendigo had his tenuous hold on the title and was reluctant to put it at risk. Neither he nor Ben Caunt had very strong motives for fighting - both were in their thirties and there were easier pickings from tours and exhibitions. The high stakes that might have tempted them were just not forthcoming, with interest from the monied classes at his lowest ebb. Recent fights had hardly justified anything else. Too many of them had been mere parodies of what the old school expected from the traditional 'fair, stand-up fight'. Most were neither. The increasing problems of evading both the police who sought to prevent fights and roughs who sought to disrupt them were strong deterrents to the widening range of the population that saw itself as respectable and law-abiding. Only Tom Paddock was active, fighting his way up to title contention himself, as another of Broome's 'unknown novices'.

The Slasher could do little but sit on the sidelines during these years when he was in his prime. His frame, never puny, had filled out impressively. Topping 6 ft, he usually had the advantage in size and weight over his opponent - there were no more Freeman-like giants. Years of wielding the shovel had built up his shoulders and biceps and, from the waist upwards, he was a fine figure of a heavyweight. His slightly crooked leg spoiled the symmetry of his appearance, but it was of little practical hindrance in the ring. His rough features, creased early in life so that he always looked older than his years. became all the more fearsome as the number of gaps in his teeth grew. For all his threatening demeanour, he remained a rough and relatively naïve Black Country lad, more receptive to lessons in the dodges of the prize-ring than to learning its more subtle skills. Parrying blows, waiting and counter-punching never became ingrained boxing habits with him, and the old primitive Slasher was always likely to emerge, but he was beginning to learn and to learn more than just ringcraft. He was firmly rooted in his native Tipton, his own tavern, The Champion, in Spon Lane, Tipton. He was a familiar figure at the many local prize-fights, making the early acquaintance of Tom Paddock when he seconded 'Nobby' Clarke against him at Coleshill in 1846.

But these fallow years did not suit him. Being a local hero had its small glories, and he was always assured of a vociferous following, but he had the ambition for much more. He was ready to break away from the Broomes, who had shackled his fighting career as much as they had promoted it. Then his problems were hardly eased by the appearance of another big fighting black, who had the temerity to call himself 'William

Perry', so further muddying the already confused waters of contemporary pugilism. The threat was serious, but shortlived. The new Perry, after beating the well-reputed Bill Burton with consummate ease, was convicted of forging American currency and required, in consequence, to pursue the rest of his boxing career in Australia. Even when the chance of a fight did come up, in 1849, The Slasher's ill-luck continued to dog him. He had to forfeit, on account of illness, to Con Parker, another brother of his old opponent, whom he would, to judge from their records, have beaten convincingly. His next chance of a fight, with the thriving Tom Paddock, was apparently scotched by his own backers, who managed to contrive a 'draw' with Paddock's people and secure the return of the stakes.

However, this proved to be only a delay. The Slasher broke free from his old associates when new backers appeared. The articles for the Paddock fight were revived and Perry found himself in new company. He moved to Liverpool to train under Levi Eckersley, with Jem Ward in the background, and Tom Spring's The Castle became his London base. Under these veterans he was able to breathe in the last few gasps of the old classical pugilistic world. The fight with Paddock, though, had too much of the new pugilism about it - a railway excursion that proved just as difficult and circuitous as the excursions by coach had often been, the consequent late start so that the fight was an eerie affair in the moonlight and the almost obligatory ending with Paddock striking a violent foul blow after a round was ended. At least for The Slasher the encounter was a satisfactory one. He was healthy, fit and strong, and he used his power and experience to demonstrate to young Paddock that the rushing tactics he had used against the light and ageing Bendigo were of no avail here. Paddock was terribly punished about the face, putting the eventual winner beyond doubt, foul or no foul.

Perry was at the peak of his career. He once again made a loud claim to the championship. When Bendigo would not take up a specific challenge - at 40, he at last admitted that his fistic days were over - Perry threw the challenge open to all, for £100 or £200 at will. The answer eventually came from a surprising quarter. Johnny Broome put forward yet another of his 'unknowns', who turned out to be none other that The Slasher's old sparring partner from the touring days, Broome's younger brother, Harry. The Slasher completed another provincial tour before going into training again with Jem Ward, while at the London end young Spring had to take over from his dying father. For a championship fight it aroused little interest in the capital and scarcely 100 passengers turned up to catch the special train, the only representatives of the old school being Tom Oliver and Peter Crawley. The latter was at length agreed upon as referee - with some reluctance on the part of Perry because it was felt (without justification) that he was likely to favour the Broomes. It was a much harder fight than The Slasher had expected from his knowledge of Harry. The skills were expected, but not the confidence and aggression, and especially not the strength of his wrestling which repeatedly had the heavier man on the turf. Matters stood about equal when the usual unsatisfactory ending came about. The Slasher landed a blow as Broome fell to the ground. Impartial observers agreed that it was foul but accepted that it was a mistake and unintentional, doubting whether it could have been held back once Broome started to go down. The Slasher's supporters were furious, vociferous and violent. He himself was in a high temper and accused Peter Crawley of bias. The sight of the venerable and portly Peter struggling out of his coat to take on Perry himself to answer for the insult to his honour brought some bitter humour back to the scene and Perry was ushered away in high dudgeon, still loudly proclaiming himself to be the champion.

Harry Broome, prematurely overweight, retired to his victualling interests and Perry's claim had validity. Certainly, no one sought to face him, and he reaped generous donations by way of lost deposits when fighters or their backers had second thoughts - £25 from Harry Broome when the rematch fell through, £70 from Aaron Jones in July 1856 and £80 from Tom Paddock a few months later. The first signs of decline, though, had been there in the fight with Broome. Some of the agility had gone and the swinging blows did not come with quite the same speed and power. The continued waning of Perry's abilities was finally and clinically exposed by Tom Sayers on 16 June 1857, and The Slasher's reign, troubled, intermittent and seldom certain, was at last over.

Tom Sayers represented the new hope for pugilism; he was the personable sportsman who might perhaps make a new appeal to those classes who were just beginning to feel less ashamed of leisure and less ashamed of enjoying themselves in worthy pursuits. William Perry had epitomised an era when, of all sporting pursuits, pugilism had proved itself the least respectable. Horse-racing had had its serious troubles, plumbing its worst depths in the 1844 Derby, when two 4-year-olds were smuggled into the race, one horse ran under another's name, the favourite lost its chance by fouling and the jockey on another fancied horse pulled back because he had backed another runner. But horse-racing had its Lord George Bentinck and later Admiral Rous to pull things together at Newmarket, it had active civic interest as at York and Doncaster, and it had numerous country gentry continuing to be involved in local meetings the length of the country. Pedestrianism, too, was plagued by fraud and double-dealing, but it had always been a predominantly plebian sport, not settling yet into formalised athletic events and still floundering in a rapidly dating mix of gaming and exhibitionism. There were some glimmering signs that pedestrianism might reshape itself into new forms with standardised events, but in pugilism there was no sign of progress at all, only regression.

In Perry's last fight, as in his early encounter with Jem Scunner just twenty years before, his old Black Country colleague and opponent, Tass Parker, was there in his corner. At the end, there was nothing for it but to return to Tipton, to bask in the fame of having been the champion and to join an admiring visitor in a glass of spirits across his bar. He lived on, like most champions in this most physically punishing of sports, to past his sixtieth birthday. He was born when pugilism was still within easy reach of its best days. By the time he died, in 1881, it was within sight of its new beginnings with legalised boxing. It was not his fault, only his misfortune, to have been part of the sport at a time when dubious commerce had replaced honest speculation, when winning was at a premium over fairness and none but the hardest bitten could survive for long.

11

To the Provinces and the People

The Tipton Slasher's career spanned what have often been acknowledged as the least glorious years in modern British sport. As the country gave slow and often painful birth to an industrialised and urbanised society, its traditional sports found their old social frameworks shaken. A potential mass spectatorship - perceived usually as a 'problem' - began to search for sporting entertainment, while a new seriousness of purpose drew many of sport's old upper-class sponsors into weightier concerns. Even at Newmarket, the First Spring Meeting of 1831 saw attendances reduced by three quarters 'in consequence of the Reform Bill before the House of Commons'.[1] (When the bill reached the Upper House, though, at least two enterprising lords agreed that, since they would each have voted on opposite sides, they might just as well go racing!) The dilution of patronage had resulted in the dilution of authority and control. Even in horse-racing, where the aristocratic hold remained firmest, there were numerous scandals over switched horses, scratched favourites and bribed jockeys. Elsewhere, sharp practice, fraud and brutality were often more apparent than honesty, manliness and fair play. Of all the sports, pedestrianism adapted itself best to the new climate, having less to lose than most by the waning of upper-class support. In spite of its ingrained reputation for fixed matches, well over a thousand athletic contests a year were being advertised by 1856. Pedestrianism exploited the new sporting audiences in the industrial areas and was the first sport to see the potential of the free Saturday afternoon, while cricket responded to the new mood through its professional touring sides, starting with William Clarke's All-England XI in 1846.

The tribulations which the changing world of the 1830s and 1840s brought to pugilism have already been made abundantly clear. The other side of the coin, however, is that there was growth in all directions - in the number and frequency of fights, in the spread of fight locations over the whole country, in the number of fighters and spectators taken as a whole, and even in the finances of the sport. Although the stakes for big individual fights had been generally reduced, there were more varied opportunities than ever before to supplement these with other income. In one of the greatest years of the earlier age, 1805, when Henry Pearce and Jem Belcher were in their prime and Cribb and Gully were the coming men, there were still only some twenty or so fights which achieved national notice. Between 1830 and 1840 the number of publicised contests increased remarkably. *Bell's Life in London*'s annual Chronology of the Ring lists about thirty fights a year during the early 1830s. By 1842 the number was ninety, and by the following year it was 128, quite apart from the 'many minor fights, not in the P.R., of which we have no record'. The fight figures do fluctuate, but the overall picture is one of continuing growth into the late 1860s; 1867, for instance, saw over 150 contests in the United Kingdom as well as many reported from overseas, mostly from Australia and the United States. It could, of course, all have been a result of having more reporters and not more fights, though this could never be more than a partial explanation. The detail of pugilistic reports shows much more conscious organisation of the sport at the popular levels than had been the case in the past. No longer did an anonymous navvy have a set-to with an equally anonymous coachman or costermonger on the edge of town; instead there was a copying of the great fights, building up the stake money by stages at selected local hostelries - even though the stakes might not amount to more than £5 a side in the end. The existence of a sporting press was certainly a force in the promotion of all the sports it covered, both creating and feeding interest. The rightly celebrated editor of *Bell's Life in London*, Vincent George Dowling, was in no doubt about his paper's influence, claiming that it was responsible for the popularity of cricket and for its extension over the country. He told the House of Lords' Select Committee on Gaming in 1844 that players wanted to have their feats recorded, that this 'created a Desire to still more extend their Exertions and their Fame', and that as proof of the success of his journal, it was now receiving 1500 letters a week as against 200 'in former times'.[2]

What was true of cricket was doubtless equally true of boxing, which *Bell's Life in London* covered extensively, often through Dowling himself and later through Henry Downes Miles. Fights were reported in round-by-round detail, running to over 3000 words for major events. There was also the gossip of the ring, the challenges and negotiations, the sparring classes and exhibitions and the 'matches to come'. Pugilistic matters would often occupy one of the vast pink broadsheet pages. As the number of fights increased, the geographical emphasis of the prize-ring changed. Even by the early 1830s the old pattern of matches, either in outer London locations, within daily excursion distance, or associated with major race meetings, had been broken. There were no longer regular venues such as Coombe Wood and Molesey Hurst, and few places housed more than the occasional single fight. Moreover, over a third of the fights were taking place in the growing industrial areas. Typically, by 1838, a single issue of *Bell's Life in London* (8 March) was notifying future contests at Birmingham, Bradford, Belper, Sheffield and Walsall, and by the 1840s over half the matches had moved to the Midlands and North. Within a few years over half the growing number of recorded contests were taking place far away from London and the South-East, in a wide scatter of locations, particularly in the Manchester, Liverpool and Cheshire area and around Birming- ham and Derby.

As a result of more effective policing, the venues became more restricted in the 1850s, but this was compensated for by the reappearance of virtually regular fixtures at two sites in particular - for London contests, the Kentish marshes, near Dartford; and for the West Midlands, Water Orton, near Birmingham. The policy of giving priority to the suppression of those disorders which took place on the doorsteps of the respectable could leave such relatively isolated sites to the pugilists and their spectators for years, in spite of such complaints as that from a correspondent to *The Times* (7 January 1853) over the 2000 or so who came down the Thames by steamer every

Tuesday ('the very scum and refuse') and who left no room for decent citizens on the North Kent Railway, especially in view of the unlit hazards of the Blackheath Tunnel. The justices' unconvincing response was that they could not prosecute without a deposition from the owner of the land.

The changed geography of pugilism was accompanied by changed organisation and a reorientation of the sport's class structure, though neither was as cut and dried as to produce a simple picture. The 'organisation' of pugilism had seldom, for the obvious reason of its illegality, been very precise. The nearest it had come to a national governing body had been in its Regency days with the Pugilistic Club. Tom Spring's Fair Play Club had never achieved the authority it needed to deal with the sport's problems in the late 1820s, and the Pugilistic Benevolent Association did not begin to concern itself at all with the championship until the later 1850s. Pugilism was not, of course, alone in lacking a formal ruling body - the concept itself was alien to the times - but in the Jockey Club and the Marylebone Cricket Club the two other major sports had their well-established institutions as arbiters, designedly or not. The organisation of pugilism, whether or not a formal body was currently in existence, had centred indisputedly on London until the later 1820s. Its headquarters was the sporting public houses: for many years Tom Spring's The Castle in Holborn was unequivocally the centre; and less universally recognised, there were Alex Reid's Lowndes Arms, Jem Burns's Rising Sun in the late 1840s (where he was succeeded by Johnny Broome) and Alex Keene's Three Tuns in Soho in the 1850s. The physical symbols of the sport's formal organisation were more tangible - the official stakes and ropes of the prize-ring. The Fair Play Club was still active enough in 1832 to purchase a new set and give them into the care of Tom Oliver, who had taken over from Bill Gibbons in 1828 and who remained in charge of the commissary until well into the 1850s. The significance of the ropes and the stakes was that they gave official recognition to fights and were acknowledged as so doing - an impromptu battle between Nick Ward and 'Sambo' Sutton, arising out of a dispute, was put off for a few hours until the evening so that the Pugilistic Club ropes could be got hold of, no member of the Ward family being prepared to waste his substance on unofficial fighting.

There had been short-lived provincial organising bodies in the past, at Bristol and at Norwich (where in the heyday of Ned Painter, whom they adopted, there was the Norwich Pugilistic Club). In the 1790s, Birmingham sportsmen had sufficient cohesion to assemble their five-man challenge to London,[3] but regionally-based pugilism on a scale which posed a threat to the hegemony of London only began to emerge around 1830, when the national ring was at one of its lowest ebbs. Jem Ward had taken a hostelry in Liverpool, and that city was soon being identified as 'the metropolis of milling', as one report described it after the Bendigo v. Looney contest. It had been fought within the new blue ropes and stakes proudly marked 'LPR' for the Liverpool Prize-Ring, which had already mounted fights not just locally but as far afield as Gateshead (such as 'Young Molyneux' v. Bill Fisher),[4] Doncaster (the second Bendigo v. Caunt fight)[5] and the Midlands. Liverpool faded, in face of the rise of the Manchester and Birmingham rings, which were responsible for many important matches in the 1840s and 1850s. The Manchester commissary, for instance, handled

The Tipton Slasher's second fight with Tass Parker on Lindrick Common in Nottinghamshire, while the Birmingham Prize-Ring as well as organising the most regular programme of local events, was responsible for Tom Paddock's first major encounter, against the ageing Elijah Parsons. The existence of regional organisations, formal or informal, was recognised in the sporting press, under such fluctuating regional groupings as the Norwich Circuit, the Birmingham School, the Liverpool and Manchester Circuit, the London District and the Hardware Circuit, while other fights were organised at centres which do not appear to have developed any very permanent organisation. Nottingham, for instance, the native place of Bendigo and Ben Caunt's county town, never became an organisational centre for the sport though Paddock's second fight against Harry Poulsen, another Nottingham man, was based in that city and all the deposits were made there. The tempestuous experience of that fight, with the local magistrate suffering a serious beating, was not conducive to seeking a repetition.

The history of the provincial ring in this period remains to be written. Certainly the distinctions between the provincial circuits and the London Prize-Ring were important, most of all in the eyes of Londoners, who were reluctant to see their monopoly of the sport's management slipping away. Even in 1828 the Midlands press was boasting that 'The London Fancy must blush at the *Brums* taking the lead in so important a match' as Tom Brown v. Phil Sampson, while the intense jealousy aroused by Johnny Broome's devious management of pugilist affairs was heightened by the fact that he had made his Rising Sun public house virtually a Birmingham legation in the heart of the metropolis. Where a match was made outside the capital, even if the deposits were all made in London, boxing folk there were quick to point out that it was not 'a London match'. On the other hand, the return fight between Poulsen and Paddock, after their chaotic meeting at Belper, was made in the London Prize-Ring and was managed in conspicuously high style, with a well-appointed first-class saloon coach on the Eastern Counties special train to provide ample supplies of food and drink for the moneyed followers.

Provincial tours had always been a useful source of income (and pubilicity) for successful fighters. They now loomed even larger as actual bouts became harder to negotiate and the audiences for exhibitions grew larger and larger in the growing industrial centres. Manchester, Liverpool, Bradford, Leeds, Newcastle - these were the staple venues in any sporting tour, but no town of any size was without at least an occasional visit from one of the country's greater or lesser pugilistic heroes. Nor were benefits any longer confined to London. If a fight was arranged in one of the regional circuits there was the chance of three bites at the cherry - one near the location of the contest, one at the regional headquarters and possibly one on the fighter's return to London or to his own home base. Even wider horizons also began to beckon, with Burke becoming the first champion to take his talents across both the English Channel and the Atlantic Ocean in search of crowds and challenges. Looking though, for the time being, at the domestic scene alone, it is not surprising that the provinces loomed larger than London and the South-East as they were now the areas producing the notable fighters. Bristol's sun had set long before, and the fighting men of the 1830s and 1840s were virtually all from the Midlands - Bendigo and Caunt from Nottinghamshire, Nat Langham from Leicestershire and a whole group from the West Midlands, led by William Perry and Tom Paddock and including the two Broomes, Tass Parker, Preston and Elijah Parsons. In the same period, between the championships of Burke and Sayers, the captial city and the Home Counties could hardly muster a worthy fist between them - Harry Orme was a brave and skilful East-Ender, but he suffered from being too light successfully to take on the big men; Nick Ward was London born but Liverpool based and hardly the stuff of heroes; while Joe Roe had little claim beyond his courageous challenge to Harry Broome. It was a happy coincidence that when London interest in the ring began to revive, it had a rising star from the South-East, Tom Sayers from Brighton, on which to centre.

The domination of regional accents in the 1830s and 1840s was not a phenomenon confined only to pugilism. The Midlands and the North knew comparative prosperity as competition from industry forced landlords to pay their labourers at higher rates than the rural workers in the South could command. The leisure industry inevitably gravitated to where it could be best supported, and all sport was opening up new territory. The balance of power in cricket was changing with the appearance of strong provincial teams, especially Nottinghamshire. The long-standing turf attractions of Doncaster became so potent that Newmarket's First October Meeting was now regularly denuded of owners and backers, while the corporation at York was investing heavily in the local racecourse so as to match its county rival. It was more, too, than a simple change in geography or even economics. The social structure was changing and with it the aspirations of the various elements in society. Of all the sports, pugilism was the one most at risk in face of the new social expectations.

The general disposition of the aristocracy and gentry to give a more serious tone to their lives and to ration their sporting activities (or keep them more discreet) hit the prize-ring particularly hard. An illegal sport had the least claim of all to decorum, and the sport itself did little to aid its own cause. The presence or absence of Corinthians - gentlemen sportsmen - was a regular preoccupation of fight reports. Where they did turn out, much was made of it. At the resumed Perry v. Freeman fight in December 1842, the steamer passengers included 'a Scotch marquis, two or three scions of the peerage, a sprinkle of military men, a veteran 'salt', hunting and varsity men, doctors, barristers and sundry sporting clubmen'.[6] Three years earlier, the aristocracy was said to have made up 'no inconsiderable proportion' of the 15,000 crowd at Burke's fight with Bendigo, but in general between 1830 and 1850 the interest of the traditional upper classes was at a low ebb. Significant signs of this desertion lie in the great difficulty which fighters faced in raising even the modest stakes they were now often reduced to. There was seldom a single patron with an open purse. Usually it was a matter of gathering the money by a whole series of instalments, often with an ex-pugilist acting as the manager of the negotiations and also investing his own money. Again, there was the sight of a professional fighter acting as referee, a role which such an eminence as 'Gentleman' Jackson did not see as proper for him. An old stager like Squire Osbaldeston could occasionally be persuaded to act, and Dowling himself took on some of the most difficult fights, but it was often a matter of persuading Tom Spring, Peter Crawley or even old Tom Oliver to take on what was becoming an increasingly difficult task and one that could become physically dangerous as crowds grew more and more unruly.

Even where the upper classes remained, their participation in the sport was much more reticent and subdued than it had been in the past. For one thing, they could no longer be confident that they would escape publicity and prosecution if the law intervened in a fight, as Lord Chetwynd found when the Revd Joshua Cantley exercised his clerical wrath on the bout between Nick Adams and Dick Cain in 1841. Crusading evangelicals were not prepared to bow to either rank or station, and the noble Viscount found himself arraigned alongside sundry pugilists, a solicitor and a well-respected innkeeper who was there only to keep an eye on his post-horses. Although the legal proceedings eventually fizzled out, they took over a year to do so as Chetwynd, without consulting the other defendants, had the case moved by writ to the Queen's Bench. What was clear was that there could be no assurance for the quality that they would any longer be allowed to fade quietly out of sight if the police interfered with prize-fights. The fact that the police also progressively confined fights to less and less salubrious locations only served further to limit the attractions of pugilism to all but the least fastidious. Promoters were well aware of this when they seized the new opportunities presented by the river steamers and the railway. Attempts were soon being made to attract a more selective clientele by a combination of high prices for transport and added secrecy. The railway achieved this better than the river steamers as the 'official' boat was usually trailed down the Thames by a whole host of miscellaneous craft carrying the 'cheapsiders' who had got wind of the time and place of departure. By the late 1850s even the organisers were bowing to the inevitable and sometimes hiring out their own two vessels, one for first-class passengers, and one for second, as at the veterans' match between Caunt and Langham. Trains were easier to keep exclusive once the idea caught on of hiring special excursion ones, and were made all the more so if they consisted solely of first- and second-class coaches. For the Bendigo v. Paddock match in June 1850, for instance, the fares for first and second class were £2 and £1 respectively, expensive enough to deter those used to following down river for a shilling or two. Another occasional gambit was an early morning start, tried for the Brassey v. Caunt fight in 1840, which catered for the racing classes gathered at Newmarket. The men were supposed to be in the ring between 6 and 8 a.m. 'to shut out a numerous class to whom early rising and long trots of an autumnal morning are not agreeable'.[7] In the event, word had got round the University of Cambridge, the fighters were not ready before 9 a.m., and there was a crowd of between 2000 and 3000 which was treated to an hour and a half's evasive fighting in the pouring rain and mud before Brassey was eventually worn down by the bigger man.

Such noble patronage as remained with the sport during its most depressed years often added little to its reputation. James Burke was 'taken up' by a group of young bloods later in his career, but had to pay dearly for their staking of his fights. They demanded his company on their late-night roisterings through the darker dens of London's West End, even taking him to Paris, and they generally brought his health so far down with high living and hard spirits that he began to fail as a fighter and died at the age of 35. The withdrawal of the traditional upper-class patronage did indeed leave the sport wide open to opportunists of every sort. George Borrow blamed the Jews for the corruption that became rife. The attitudes of others were more sweeping, with one disillusioned follower seeing around him, in the last days of the Fives Court, only:

12. With the advent of railway excursions to prize-fights, quiet country stations such as this could suddenly find themselves overrun by a trainload of raucous fight followers. This is Shrivenham, on the Great Western Railway, where the bout between Harry Broome and Ben Terry took place in 1846, shortly after this print was made.

the rouged and villainous countenance of the brothel-bully, the saloon girls' fancy-man, or the wary and well-dressed figure of the swell pickpocket. These, with a few dirty-looking mechanics and butchers at a hob-a-nob, compose the present audience, if it may be so called.[8]

Another commentator, four years later, was more damning still of the sport's leading lights - a vast number of these *miscreants* ... are keepers of brothels of the lowest description, and trade in infantile impurities or unhallowed desires'.[9] Even when there was still money in the sport, it was seldom unsullied. The notorious Beardsworth, made wealthy by his Birmingham Repository and other business ventures, skated on the very edge of honesty both on the turf and in the ring. He was the stakeholder at the two fights between Brown and Sampson and was responsible for handing the money over to Sampson after the crowd had effectively forced his opponent out of the ring in the second of them, the disgraceful affair at Doncaster in June 1830. Beardsworth won the St Leger that year with the oppositely named Birmingham, but he also found himself in court - sued successfully by Brown for the return of the Doncaster stake money - and barred from his Warwick winnings because he was in arrears for both stakes and forfeits at Warwick and Winchester. Never a happy settler of accounts, he found that his horse Ludlow was seized by Brown's attorney at Chester races as it was about to enter the Palatine Stakes. Brown got his money and the horse won the race! Incidents such as these, and John Gully's election to the House of Commons, prompted traditionalists to ask who were the gentry now.

Watching sport has always been a triumph of hope over experience. Will the team manage to score two goals in the last five minutes to save the match, hit a six off the last ball or get a home run with the bases loaded at the bottom of the ninth? In the longer term, will this match, or this season, be better than the last several have been? Corruption has to be blatant and long-standing, and alternatives have to be available, before mass interest in a sport disappears. Pedestrianism, with all its ready susceptibility to fraudulent odds and fixed matches, was drawing its crowds with great regularity throughout this period. Similarly, pugilism flourished, but in a new social context. It had always had a plebian following, tagging along to fights in the wake of the carriage trade. What was happening was that this element came near to dominating the whole ring scene, at just the time when divisions within the working classes themselves were growing more pronounced. It was noted by a correspondent to *Bell's Life in London* in 1832 (he was commenting on Mr Spencer Perceval's proposal for a fast day in the light of the cholera epidemic):

> The sober and industrious workmen of all classes will, we are sure, be careful how they mingle with those who are dissolute and idle, and who form, probably, the larger half of all the assemblage of the populace that we ever have in the metropolis. This difference of habits constitutes one great line of separation, and will ever prevent a cordial union between the careful and the negligent classes.

Boxing crowds did not always consist of these 'negligent' classes. There was the old-fashioned good order when Caunt lost to Nick Ward on a foul on an idyllic early spring morning near Stratford-upon-Avon in May 1841, before a muster of sporting gentry, hunting men and local enthusiasts. There was the 'perfect crowd' of pitmen at Perry v. Parker on Lindrick Common, Nottinghamshire, in 1846, and the 'excellent' gathering of yeomen and farm labourers for Nat Langham's fight with George Gutteridge in the Lincolnshire countryside a few weeks earlier. But these were all one-off exercises, not dominated by the habitual fight supporters. It was they, particularly those from the two great urban masses of the capital and the second city, who could make themselves free of labour on Tuesdays at will, and who invariably outnumbered the 'careful' classes at most fights of any consequence.

There was, of course, no easy division that could be made. The 'sober and industrious' would often have their occasional lapses into the dubious pleasures of the turf, the pedestrian match or the ring, and it was Bendigo's 'respectable' brother who was said to have caused the law to prevent one of his fights. It was, though, the everyday behaviour of the roughest parts of the city that came to dominate many prize-fights, making them dangerous for fighters, bystanders and, especially, referees. The crowds were a problem for the organisers, who would welcome them if they could profit from their presence but too often found them a non-paying embarrassment, putting the business of great risk of attracting the attentions of the law.

The economics of the sport had radically altered with the withdrawal of the former wealthy patronage, and the old pugilists who had previously acted only as floor managers now found themselves more often than not in charge of the whole proceedings, alongside interested innkeepers and others. No longer were there rich pickings to be had out of the high stakes which matches of any pretensions used to attract. Stake money running to three figures became a rarity. In 1834, for example, there was only one contest worth more than £50 to the winner (when 'Young Dutch Sam' took on Tom

Gaynor, at £300 to £200) and the great majority of matches were made for £10 or less. There was some recovery in the 1840s and 1850s, but over 90 per cent of all recorded contests were still for £25 or less, and it was a good year if there were more than two or three matches with stakes running into three figures. Even these lower sums were hard to muster and were always posted by instalments, though this was not unwelcome to the sporting publicans who rivalled each other for nomination of their inn as one of the houses where deposits were to be made. That assured a good night's business, and the current financial state of pugilism meant that keen eyes were alway being cast around for the chance of another sovereign or two.

Yet another incidental source of income had been lost to promoters by the disappearance of tradesmen prepared to pay to attract major fights to their area - most, indeed, would now be prepared to pay to keep them away. A rare case of inducement to attract a fight was the £25 paid by a St Albans innkeeper to bring the tragic Burke v. Byrne fight to No Mans Land; this was the fight in which Byrne received fatal injuries. A notoriously tight-fisted backer, as Ben Caunt was known to be, could still, however, make a little from the choice of site - for Langham's fight against Gutteridge he accepted £7 from the other side in exchange for the naming of the venue! Once the steamer excursion and the special train became common modes of transport for the bigger fights, the financial pressures eased a little as the transport could usually turn in a profit, although there were exceptions if a promoter like Johnny Broome was thought to be pitching his charges too high.[10] The methods used by the boxing fraternity to meet the sport's financial crisis all had their roots in the past, but they were now pursued with even greater energy, with a greater sense of show business and, if necessary, by devious means.

Benefits for the fighter, especially in the week following a big fight, had long provided a useful supplement to his income and for a time they continued to do so. The old sparring places, the Fives Court and the Tennis Court, had gone, but there were newer and more commodious premises on hand such as the Westminster Baths and the Bloomsbury Assembly Rooms, and benefits could still attract large crowds. At the benefit to see the giant Freeman, £178 was taken at the door. However, after the early 1840s large-scale benefits fell out of fashion. High hiring charges, the reluctance of landlords and the speculative nature of the audience all played their part in the decline, although a major reason was also the growing reluctance of pugilists to exhibit their skills on each others' behalf. The later benefits tended to be supported only by 'the humbler outsiders of the Ring'. Ben Caunt, for example, failed to show up as promised for Burke's benefit, and this unreliability was tackled in the rules of the Pugilistic Benevolent Association with their strong insistence that members were to turn up without fail to benefits organised by the association. The association, though, having re-established the benefit as a source of pugilistic income, proceeded to overdo matters, sometimes mounting two in a single week.

The incidental profits from the sport, like those from the ring itself, tended to become much more diffused. Instead of the single grand occasion, there were a large number of smaller meetings of enthusiasts, in the provinces as often as in London. The handing over of the stake money after a fight - at least in the decreasing number of cases where the result was not in dispute - was always an occasion, celebrated at one of the pugilistic public houses and usually accompanied by a collection for the loser. This could be a 'handsome' sum. In Harry Broome's case, for instance, after his close defeat by Paddock, it amounted to nearly £100. The railway journey back to town was another occasion for a collection for the worthily defeated - Tom Sayers received over £50 from such a whip-round after his only defeat, at the hands of Nat Langham in 1853.

The new modes of transport also gave rise to new methods of charging spectators. In the past, while it had seldom been possible to levy an entrance fee on all spectators, carriages had been charged for the privilege of forming an outer ring and the pugilists had their own hired wagons which served as profitable grand-stands. The attentions of the law now meant that all fights were hurried affairs and there was little hope of finding a site that could be sufficiently enclosed so as to make an entrance charge from everybody possible. Without their own carriages, the better-off spectators could only be attracted to fights if they were assured of a reasonable view - they were going to be much less comfortable than they had been in the past anyway, squatting or even lying on damp grass - another factor, inciden-tally, in reducing their enthusiasm and their numbers. The answer was to try to form a secure inner ring and to limit entrance to it to holders of privilege tickets which were on sale before the fight. The advantage to the promoters was obvious. There was no longer the difficult collection of fees in the turmoil of the fight itself and the danger of much of it finding its way into unauthorised pockets. They had their cash in advance. The problems, and in this period there inevitably were problems where money in the sport was concerned, were transferred to the paying spectators. For how long and how effectively they would be protected within their inner ring was always a matter of great speculation. Sometimes they might find their privilege tickets not accepted at all, as Londoners found when the Nottinghamshire heavies refused to recognise any but their own tickets at Bendigo's fight with Caunt in 1845.

Even fewer pugilists than in the past could, in all these circumstances, hope to leave the ring as wealthy men. On the other hand, many more were able to achieve comfortable futures as landlords of public houses, exploiting their reputations and continuing their pugilistic interests. Miles's taking image that 'your successful pugilist is a publican in chrysalis, as sure as a caddis shall become a May-fly in due season', was never more apposite than now. Public houses up and down the country had become thriving centres of the sport. As the sport had gone to the people, so its axis had moved firmly into the people's centre of entertainment and leisure. Signing articles, making deposits on stake money, weighing-in where this was called for, handing over the stakes, exhibitions, boxing instruction and even musical evenings with pugilists present were all vivid occasions to light up the drabness of early industrial city life. Their extent can be gathered from a single issue of *Bell's Life in London*, in January 1851. In that week alone, deposits for fights were being placed at the Star, Borough (where there was a weigh-in two evenings later); the King's Arms, Holborn; the Queen's Head, Windmill Street; another house of the same name in Mortlake; and, in Birmingham, at the Odd Fellow's Arms, the Oxford Arms, the General Elliott and the Fortune of War. There were a dozen challenges to matches from fighters or their promoters, all of them to be answered at public houses, one in Windsor, the rest in

London, Birmingham or Manchester. The stakes for Hannigan's victory over Fulham were being sent to the Fox Inn, Manchester, where his backers were invited to collect them. Alex Reid, Alfred Walker, Jemmy Shaw, Joe Roe and Tom Maley were all giving daily sparring lessons in their own or others' public houses, where glove exhibitions were being held weekly. Most of them were expressing their willingness to give private tuition in gentlemen's own homes, as was 'Izzy' Lazarus, then on tour in the North, exhibiting at Preston and offering his services at the George Inn. Nor did the attractions stop there. There was ratting every Thursday at Alfred Walker's and Jemmy Shaw's, a 'harmonic evening' presided over by Jack Grant (soon to be one of Sayers's early conquests) at Harry Brunton's The Bell and twice-weekly concerts at Joe Roe's Catherine Wheel, where a grand show of the fancy was regularly expected.

Pugilism may have lost its former place in the established sporting roll of honour, but it was certainly alive and well within the popular culture of the early Victorian city. There its sins and shortcomings detracted little from the excitement, the tension and the entertainment that it offered. Indeed, given the general conditions of their lives, with hardship, poverty and vice never far away, a smack of those failings in a sport was unlikely to prove a deterrent. Even in the smallest provincial town, the boxing booth at the fairground was one of the strongest attractions, with its glimpse of one of the great ones who had sported in the prize-ring. It mattered little to the sport's mass-following that matches took an age to materialise, that there was endless chicanery in all pugilistic affairs and that promoters had much more of an eye to profit than to honour. If the match came off, and if they could get to it, that was all the satisfaction they needed. It might turn out to be a farce, without a genuine blow from start to finish, but there was always next time.

13. Tom Sayers

12

One Last Bright Star

The English cathedrals have looked down with tolerance over the whole panoply of the people's lives from the Middle Ages onwards. They have been witnesses to their pleasures and their pains, their work and their play. Just as the imposing pile of Worcester had presided benignly over the great fist-fight between Spring and Langan, so, soon after midnight on 16 April 1860, the squat pinnacled tower of Southwark, which had seen Shakespeare's Globe come and go, was kept from its slumbers by another extraordinary boxing scene. A great crowd, all of them men, was thronging to London Bridge Station in the crisp early darkness of that April morning. They came from all directions, some in cabs, some in their own carriages, some making their way on foot, an amazing mix of peers and profesional men, soldiers and lawyers, and such workers as could rustle up the sovereigns for the special trains that were shunting into the station. The first of them was full by 3.30 a.m. but had to await the arrival of two principal actors in the unfolding drama. Tom Sayers appeared, and cheers rang through the station as he mounted to his special compartment. A few minutes later, a final small group of passengers hurried on to the platform, the tall central figure muffled, as if to avoid recognition. This was John C. Heenan, challenger for the championship, who had grown used to harassment by the police both in England and back home in the United States. The long train, packed to overflowing, pulled its slow way over the long brick viaducts just before 4.30 a.m., and within the precincts of the cathedral the bones of the Emersons and the Harvards stirred a little, wondering that their descendants' country should have sent back to them such an apparently famous emissary.

They would have marvelled further had they been able to follow the train on its way through New Cross, through Sydenham and on to Croydon, for all along the route, on both sides of the track, the Metropolitan Police, on foot and mounted, were ranged in force, cutlasses at the ready, for all the world as though they were guarding some royal progress. The county forces down both the Dover and the Brighton lines had been mustered to maintain the guard, but then, at Reigate Junction, the train followed by its equally crowded duplicate, surprisingly turned westwards along the Guildford branch, joining the South Western Railway at Basingstoke and finally coming to a halt at Farnborough, just inside the Hampshire border. With luck, they would have two or three hours before the county constabulary, lulled by reports that all had been quiet at their own particular London terminus, Waterloo, could gather in sufficient force to interrupt the business of the day.

There was time, in fact, for over two hours' excellent fisticuffs, reminiscent of the best fights of the old days, until the inevitable stop was put to the proceedings. Such a well-publicised contest could hardly hope to be allowed much more time than that to settle the issue, although even after the police arrived on the scene it was twenty minutes and five rounds later before they struggled to the ringside. Both pugilists had fought gamely and the interference of the law was felt by many to provide a fitting end, neither man deserving to lose. It left both parties able to claim that their fighter was getting the better of things. Heenan had been the more aggressive, flooring Sayers several times, and the Englishman's right arm had been hurt early on in the bout, much reducing its effectiveness. Sayers, on the other hand, with a long career behind him of taking the best blows of heavier men, showed his usual hardness and endurance and was much less marked about the face than his opponent, whose eyes were nearly closing; of the two exhausted fighters he seemed marginally the less weary. Over the following days, there were the usual haggles over a resumption of the contest, but in the end honour was satisfied on all sides by the awarding of similar championship belts to each of the two men. These, and a half-share in the profits of over £1000 from the railway excursions, were proper reward for their efforts, but, as far as Sayers was concerned, the British public was not going to let it rest at that. A public subscription for their hero quickly topped the £3000 mark, major contributions coming from the Stock Exchange and the City and from members of both Houses of Parliament. The capital was invested by trustees for his children, with Tom to receive the interest during his lifetime - but only on the condition that he never entered the prize-ring again.

It was a highly symbolic qualification, a signal that an epoch in sport was due to come to its end, and an assurance that its final conqueror would not spend his fading years as the punch-bag for lesser men. Tom Sayers had, after all, caught the nation's imagination as no pugilist had done since the days of Cribb and Spring. Set against the lumbering maulers of the day, who often seemed as dedicated to avoiding fighting as to facing up to each other, he shone as a brave and skilful boxer who fought nearly all his fights against heavier men and displayed always the greatest tenacity and stamina. He had arrived at Camden Town from his native Brighton to work as a bricklayer on the North Western Railway, to become, first of all, a hero for the boxing enthusiasts of the London area, who had for so long seen the tattered laurels of their sport carried off by midlanders. By the Heenan fight, though, he was acknowledged by all the land as its sole champion against the American contender.

Sayers's career was remarkable, not least for its intensity. Between 1849 and 1860 he appeared in the prize-ring no fewer than sixteen times, all of them victories apart from one early defeat by the experienced Nat Langham and his draw with Heenan. After an initial £5 fight with Abe Crouch, which he won in thirteen minutes, Sayers came up against the problem that dogged the progress of many middleweights - that of finding opponents of his own size. Eventually he was matched with Dan Collins, well known in London sparring quarters, and the two fought a contest which, as a result of two police interventions, started in October 1850 and was not concluded until April of the next year. Financially it brought Sayers very little. There was 'little profit in three trainings and three fights for one stake', but Sayers's improvement between the first and last instalments of the fight, and his general demeanour, won him many friends and supporters. Opponents, though, were still no easier to find and it was over a year before he faced the popular Jack Grant, who had beaten most of the best men below championship level, including Alec Keene, and entered the ring as the clear favourite. It was a fight which added further to Sayers's growing reputation. There was the familiar railway excursion, to Mildenhall in Suffolk, with £100 a side at stake. Sayers, trained and seconded by the famous pedestrian, Bob Fuller, was an impressive picture of fitness when he stripped and entered the ring 'all wire and muscle'. It was an excellent, long fight, taking in sixty-four rounds over one and a half hours. In it Sayers, for the first time, showed to the full those qualities which were to become his hallmark and the bases of his appeal. He was quick on his feet, nimble about the ring, a hard, fast hitter and an intelligent strategist, not struggling for the fall with an opponent who was clearly the stronger. Above all, in this first long fight, he showed his stamina and his apparent indestructibility, his ability to shrug off the hardest blows, which even seemed to mark him less than they did other men. To top it all, he showed his customary even temper, shaking Jack's hand warmly at the end of the fight, an old-fashioned courtesy which disputed conclusions had made a rarity.

It was becoming a feature of Sayers's fights that they were largely free from the contentions, subterfuges and disorders which had become the commonplaces of the prize-ring. This fight 'was conducted throughout in a way to leave nothing to be desired', and his next encounter, with Jack Martin, received even more fulsome encomiums. In a thirty-five-minute struggle, more blows were given and taken than in any of the two-hour fights of recent years, there were no appeals to the referee and not a single breach of fair play, and Sayers several times refrained from hitting his man when he was half-down, which he could legitimately have done. 'A few more such battles', claimed the press, 'would go far to restore the fallen fortunes of the Prize Ring'. After his one defeat by Langham, when he was far from fit, Sayers showed the same openness in making matches as he did in the ring itself - he took on George Sims for a paltry £25 'to keep his hand in', George being unable to raise any more. While it only took five munutes for Sayers to prove that Sims was nowhere near his class, this readiness to make a match at such a low stake clearly distinguished him from most of his contemporaries, who would never fight unless the price was right - and often not even then.

This was in February 1854, a year which was to prove decisive in shaping his future career. He was faced with the old difficulty of finding opponents near his own weight, in spite of having added a pound or two to his original 10 st. His backers began to look at the heavier men, but they were reluctant to make matches for even money, while the heavyweights were loth to put more at stake than they stood to win. As one reporter graphically put it, 'he was too good a horse, and handicapping him was not easy'. Meanwhile Sayers went on provincial tours, exhibiting all over the country and spreading his already considerable reputation, but in the absence of what he considered to be 'real work', he began seriously to contemplate a move to Australia. It was at this point that a match was made which at once caught the boxing public's imagination. His opponent was to be Harry Poulsen, two stones heavier than Sayers and the survivor of three hard fights against Tom Paddock, one of which he had won. Most thought that Sayers was overreaching himself and backing was at first hard to come by. That hurdle overcome ('by the influence of one of the staunchest Corinthians of modern times', whose identity cannot be guessed at) there was a noticeable increase in middle- and upper-class interest in what was happening. As to the fight itself, it took Sayers 109 rounds and over three hours to wear down his rugged opponent, finishing matters off with a knock-out blow to Poulsen's jaw. Sayers had proved that he could live in the ring with the best of the heavyweights. He was looked on in a new light - as a possible contender for the championship itself.

It was a time when interest in pugilism was, irrespective of the doings of Tom Sayers, showing some signs of revival. Bendigo's fight with Tom Paddock in 1850 had been the first for many years to attract a sizeable upper-class audience, encouraged by the provision of first- and second-class coaches only on the special train into Suffolk. It was hardly the sporting performance that most had hoped for. The ageing Bendigo decided that his only hope was to rouse Paddock's temper by his falling tactics, a ploy which was eventually successful, in spite of all the tolerance shown towards Paddock by the referee, Vincent Dowling, who knew well enough what Bengido's game was. The roughs, moreover, had made their own way to the fight and Dowling found himself bludgeoned about the head for his pains. Such experiences made a resurgence more difficult, but they did not prevent it. Considerable impetus came from the turn of events which overtook the Pugilistic Benevolent Association.

The original thrust of the association had been towards furthering the lot of the pugilists themselves and keeping order at important fights, as well as directing the profits from fight management and sparring exhibitions into the hands of the fighters' own association. Any 'noblemen and gentlemen, patrons of manly sport', who chose to become honorary members were given no more than an equal say in the association's management. They had five seats on the committee, and there were five seats for the pugilists, the treasurer completing the membership.[1] It was soon clear, though, that this early experiment in pro-am control was not working effectively. There was, for instance, an over-zealous enthusiasm for sparring exhibitions among the pugilists who, as always, saw these as a more comfortable road to the sovereigns than ring-fighting. They were putting on more than the market could stand, and even glove-fighting was likely to irritate the law if it took on too high a profile. The gentlemen members of the committee met alone in April 1855 and called a general meeting for a fortnight later, to improve the 'present aspect' of the prize-ring. At the general meeting, the pugilists surrendered their share in the administration and it was agreed that 'in future the whole management of the Association shall be confided to a select committee of gentlemen'.[2]

The pugilists were soon giving encouraging demonstrations of their ability to make attendance at fights a less hazardous enterprise. Their twelve 'ring constables' controlled the crowd efficiently at Paddock's fight with Aaron Jones, regulating entry to the inner ring and protecting the ticket-holders. Meanwhile, the 'select committee of gentlemen' sought to rescue the championship from the slough of doubt and dispute in which it had languished for so many years. They raised subscriptions for a new belt (the previous one had 'gone astray' during the contentions between Caunt, Bendigo and

Perry) and laid down conditions for the championship similar to those which had been proposed at Spring's anniversary dinner some twenty years before, except that this time they also looked to the security of the belt itself! The champion had to meet any challenge with stakes of £200 or more within six months, the belt to be surrendered at the last instalment of the stakes. If the champion held the belt for three years, it was to become his own property; and the winner had to lodge securities that he would abide by these rules before receiving the belt.

Not only was public interest aroused by the prospect of a new, clear champion, but even the sleeping giants of the ring began to bestir themselves. Apart from the honour and pride of the title, the championship belt would be a wonderful talisman to parade around the provinces, a sure guarantee of well-paying audiences in the exhibition halls. Broome, Paddock and Aaron Jones all challenged The Tipton Slasher. It took two years to clear the field and find an undisputed rival to the old champion. Paddock easily disposed of Broome, but then a familiar tale of forfeited deposits, injuries and difficulties in raising stakes finally left Aaron Jones fighting Tom Sayers for the privilege. Great secrecy surrounded the fight. Only those at the Pugilistic Benevolent Association benefit on the eve of the fight knew of the arrangements and the 130 spectators who took the special train from the new Fenchurch Street Station consisted largely of gentry supporters. There were no 'roughs' or 'other noisy demonstrators' and only a handful of pugilists. Three hours of hard fighting ended in darkness and mutual exhaustion. When it resumed three weeks later, Jones made the mistake of allowing Sayers to take the initiative, which Sayers never lost. The way was then open for Sayers to take on The Slasher, a contest which immediately aroused the sort of interest which had marked Perry's early fight with Freeman. This time, it was Sayers who was cast as David and The Slasher as Goliath. Could a boxer who stood under 5ft 9in. and weighed under 11 st. hope to beat one over 6 ft and 14½ st.? Long experience had fostered cynicism - it was a publicity stunt, it wasn't to be taken seriously even if both men did appear to be training, Sayers would forfeit, there would be no fight.

There was. The Slasher's attempt to overwhelm his lighter opponent with wild rushes was dealt with adroitly by Sayers, who feinted, danced and counter-punched his way to the championship. The belt was his, and the country had a popular hero.

As champion, he dealt with two injudicious challenges from Bill Benjamin, who was quite out of his class, and more serious threats from Tom Paddock and from Bob Brettle of Birmingham. By the time he met Brettle, in September 1858, he had his eye firmly fixed on retiring in June 1860, by which time he would have held the belt for three years and it would be his. He did not, in fact, put his championship at stake in the Brettle fight, which was made at odds of £400 to £200, and was spending much of his time touring, sometimes taking two benefits a week in different towns. The Brettle fight brought in further profits. The special train of thirty-six coaches was packed and the Pugilistic Benevolent Association benefited to the extent of £54 10s. from the sale of inner-ring tickets. Sayers fought carefully, obviously not wishing to put himself at unnecessary risk, and won in the seventh round when Brettle had to retire with a badly dislocated arm.

All now seemed to be blue skies, with Sayers the sole unchallenged sun. There were no feasible contenders in sight and he could expect to do the round of exhibitions and benefits as he wished until his official retirement, not that he had ever been a fighter to refuse a match, even at lower stakes than he could legitimately demand. So it was that when challengers began to cross the Atlantic, Sayers responded positively. The result was the fight with John C. Heenan, a meeting which aroused the whole country, drew its support from every social class and proved to be the last great encounter of the English prize-ring.

What lay behind this resurgence of interest in pugilism which gradually swelled up during the 1850s? How deep- seated was it, and what were its prospects of effecting a permanent reformation of the sport? The immediate appeal of the Sayers v. Heenan fight to a broad section of the community is readily explained. Here was a popular English champion - and, therefore, it was taken for granted, the world champion - being challenged by an American in a traditional English sport. It was Cribb v. Molyneux all over again, but this time with new overtones. First of all, the appeal of the fight was wider. Not even that assiduous discoverer of Irishness in the most unlikely boxers, Pierce Egan, had been able to identify any touch of the shamrock in Molyneux, though with sad irony it was in Ireland that his short life ended. Heenan, however, was not only American but also indubitably Irish in his ancestery, which opened up yet another constituency of support for the contest. It became, too, a matter of national concern in more than a narrow boxing sense, not even merely a matter of sport. It raised questions of national pride and national spirit, issues that were to be raised again when England and Australia faced each other on the cricket field. Had John Bull become effete? Did Anglo-Saxon (or Celtic) stock degenerate once it left British shores and the invigorating climate of the home islands?

Beneath all their outward confidence over Tom Sayers, not even the British were confident about the answers to these wider questions. For the moment, though, they had a champion who had carried all before him, who relied on skill, strength and that male virtue coming to be prized almost above all others, 'manliness'. Here was no lumbering mauler of the sort that had dominated the ring for so long, but a clean-cut fighter who did not quibble over stakes, make false matches of raise any doubts at all about his honesty. He was operating, too, in a sport which, for all its inevitable shortcomings, was better organised than it had been for many years. The championship was on a firm basis and attendance at fights had become a less risky and hazardous enterprise than in recent years - at least, the police were not likely to represent more of a threat than one's fellow spectators. Pugilism had once more taken on the appearance of a national sport, with the reassertion of London's primary role in the ordering of its affairs. The Pugilistic Benevolent Association was, significantly, confined to men who had appeared in the London Prize-Ring, and its control was soon firmly in the hands of the ring's more influential followers. Superficially, the omens for the sport could hardly have looked better.

It had suffered more than most from the anti-recreational attitudes that had held their fullest sway in the 1820s and 1830s. These were the decades in which evangelical suspicions extended to all sports and the hedonistic upper and middle classes were in their fullest retreat. The four bills brought before Parliament in the 1830s to 'Promote the Better Observance of Lord's Day', typified the mood at one of its extremes. Given the still limited nature of popular leisure, and for all the half-hearted denials of their promoters, they constituted a frontal attack on sport and recreation by, for instance, having public houses closed to all but travellers and banning 'any pastimes of public indecorum, inconvenience or nuisance'. (Paid attendance at sporting events was already banned under the 1780 Act.) In the eyes of many there was no sport which did not involve such 'indecorum, inconvenience or nuisance', no matter what the day of the week. Pugilism might avoid the wrath of Sabbatarians by sedulously keeping the prize-ring closed on Sundays, but it incited the opposition of all industrial and commercial interests by its irregular invasions into the working week. Its early devotion to St Monday (Monday being the usual day in pre-factory industry for workers to take a holiday) was bad enough, but when it came to settle more and more frequently on Holy Tuesday, that was even worse. Moreover, the lurking fear of violent upheaval from the urban working classes, learned from France in 1789, and to be relearned in 1848 from Europe as a whole, was often reinforced in vivid colours by the behaviour of plebian prize-fight crowds.

Such suspicions, though, had increasingly to live alongside other doubts about the continuing strength of the national character, about its general health and well being. The voice of Lord John Manners (Tory reformer, high churchman and spokesman for aristocratic paternalism) was not the only one linking these doubts to sporting decline:

It has of late years been made frequently a source of complaint that the English people, who of yore were famous all over Europe for their love of manly sports and their sturdy good humour, have year after year been losing that cheerful character.[3]

Tom Sayers was providing one answer to such misgivings, even if it was not that envisaged by the supporters of 'Rational Recreation' or the revivers of old 'country sports'. Pugilism had no part in either movement, but then neither had horse-racing, the still embryonic football or even athletics in any fully recognisable modern form, while cricket still teetered near the edge of respectability in the early 1840s, when Manners was writing. It is hardly too much to suggest that the Crimean War was, in part, started to find out whether the spirit of the masses had been dulled by their work-regulated city lives, whether the nation could be roused.

The wartime mood, from 1853 to 1856, undoubtedly helped the cause of pugilism though not in any direct sense. There was no letting up, as there had been from time to time during the conflict with Napoleon, in police efforts to prevent fights but the attitude towards combat sports had to be somewhat modified, and anxieties over the fitness of the population for military service, aroused by the war, continued through the late 1850s and 1860s, to the general benefit of all physical sports. Again, it is not too fanciful to find a link between the Hyde Park riots of August 1855 and the take-over by the amateurs of the Pugilistic Benevolent Association. While the immediate cause of mass unrest was the stopping of Sunday military band concerts in London's public parks, its roots lay in the growing exasperation of the people with the constant hemming-in of their recreational opportunities. (The Sunday Beer Act of the previous year had put a sharp curb on Sunday drinking by limiting Sunday opening hours to between 12.30 p.m. and 2.30 p.m. and between 6 p.m. and 10 p.m.) The cause of promoting leisure activities rather than preventing them was given further impetus.

There remained the question, though, of what could properly be promoted, by way of sport. The answer was not made any easier by the fact that the social classes had tended over the past decades to go their own separate sporting ways. The rich had their hunting and shooting, yachting and archery. The respectable of all classes - a growing body - were rejecting bull-baiting, street football, cock-fighting, dog-fighting and the like. The few sports where the classes came together, notably cricket and horse-racing (where the actual mix was notional rather then real, for the most part), were celebrated as such. Where did pugilism stand in this divide? During the 1830s and 1840s it had become a predominantly plebian sport, increasingly outside the pale of social acceptability. Could it be rehabilitated? A feature of the pugilistic revival was the attempt to make the sport more exclusive by running only first-class coaches or charging high prices for steamer tickets. Apart from this, there was the effort to secure the same class segregation at fights as had long prevailed at race meetings, where the rich were in their grandstands and the poor on the turf.

A major difficulty was finance. While the upper-class followers were prepared to pay for their own safety and comfort, they were no longer willing to stake large sums to support the prize-ring as such. When Paddock disposed of Harry Broome in 1855 before that 'larger muster of the upper classes' than had been seen for years (it included an Indian prince 'of high rank' and his suite), the betting was, we are told, in tens and twenties of pounds, not in hundreds. Even in the championship fight with Tom Sayers, The Slasher's chief backer was not some sporting gentleman but old Tom Owen, ex-pugilist and publican. Tom was an honest and well-respected man - he was provided with a special seat from which to watch the fight as his creaking joints no longer allowed him to squat on the grass - but it was an indication that investment in the sport was still coming from those who saw it as part of their livelihood, with all the implications for the need for profit that this entailed.

By the 1860s it was becoming clear that much of the country's new sporting life would be built on the foundations of the old. To achieve respected roles in society, cricket and horse-racing were throwing off their old associations with the more disreputable forms of gambling. They were drawing in the crowds, as football, a special case as far as its links with the past were concerned, was soon to do even more dramatically. They were attracting spectators, moreover, who came with changing expectations. The growing popularity of the Oxford and Cambridge Boat Race and the two universities' annual cricket match in the 1850s and 1860s pointed the way - there was true competition between relatively even sides in contests which had been openly and fairly arranged, and which would, by the standards of the day, be fairly resolved. Sporting tastes had been gradually refined. There was a move away from sheer spectacle to clean-cut competition, away from the grinding down of the weaker by the stronger towards the more subtle outcomes of narrow wins or defeats. Significantly, there was not one overwhelming victory by either side in the university cricket matches between 1855 and 1871, nor was there a draw. The running of heats in horse-racing, which made results dependent on stamina, had disappeared from all the major meetings by the middle of the century, while soon the more frequent county cricket matches were being preferred to the wholesale slaughter of local teams by the touring professionals. It was a change in preferences which did not bode well for a sport which had as its essence the wearing down to incapability of the defeated, no matter how long it took.

So, for all the glory attached to Tom Sayers, and for all the excitement that bubbled about the prize-ring in 1860, the long-term prospects for the sport were extremely poor. The possibility of making pugilism legal was never seriously considered, and outside the law any future existence was bound to become more and more shadowy. The condition attached to the hugely successful subscription fund for Tom Sayers after the Heenan fight - that he should never enter the ring again - was a formal farewell, not to the champion alone but to the ring itself. The whole of his career, and particularly this final fight, had been surrounded by an air of nostalgia, a reminder of past ages when men, in memory, fought upright, bravely and honestly. There was always a feeling that the country would not see the like again, that this was the end of a whole sporting tradition and as such was not to be missed.

Events rapidly demonstrated the truth of the matter. Within a few months of the Sayers v. Heenan fight, the veteran Tom Paddock was meeting the enormous Lancashire wrestler, Sam Hurst, for the vacant title, to a total lack of national interest. Pugilism had, virtually overnight, assumed its old mantle of clumsy staleness, to be endured, if at all, by the plebians and the provinces alone. The fading of Tom Sayers himself symbolised the fall of the sport he had graced. Investing his money in American circuses, he was badly advised and had to sell up within twelve months, and the last public sight of him was pathetic to the eyes of those who remembered him in his recent prime. It was at the Heenan v. King fight in 1863, when he was performing one of the traditional courtesies of the sport by acting as second to a former opponent but seemed to be in a daze, unable to help his man at all, his once sturdy frame racked with sickness. The tumultuous crowd that was soon to follow his coffin to Highgate cemetery and had to be beaten back by the police was, fittingly, to be the capital city's last great pugilistic gathering.

13

The First World Sport

Within less than a decade after the Sayers v. Heenan fight, all the leading British pugilists had moved either permanently or temporarily to North America. Aaron Jones had emigrated in the late 1850s - indeed his was the original transatlantic challenge to Sayers, eventually withdrawn to allow Heenan his opportunity. He was followed in 1868 by Joe Wormald and Ned O'Baldwin (the two leading contenders for Jem Mace's title, assuming that he had indeed retired), Bob Brettle (Sayers's last home challenger), Joe Goss and Birmingham's Bill Allen. These last two were unique in having a fight which, to all intents and purposes, began on one side of the Atlantic and finished on the other! Allen pursued Goss to the United States after darkness had forced a drawn end to their harassed encounter in England, where three attempts to pitch the ring had resulted in fewer than two hours of combat.. Then there was the peripatetic Jem Mace himself, sailing nonchalantly between England, Australia and the United States. Only Tom King, conqueror of both Mace and the fading John C. Heenan, stayed contentedly at home, enjoying his domestic peace, growing flowers and putting his brief and impressive boxing career behind him.

There could be no firmer illustration of the prize-ring's new international flavour, and particularly of the movement of its emphasis to the United States. The bareknuckle sport would largely remain there until it came back to its homeland for the final obsequies as the century neared its end. No man now could feel himself to be truly champion without defeating all comers from both sides of the Atlantic. There was no vestige of any international organisation behind the sport. There was no national organisation at all in the United States, and only the very sketchiest and most intermittent one in Britain; yet fighting had become international and the concept of a world championship had begun to take root. Lacking bureaucratic structures, international sport had to begin in an activity where competition arose from challenge and response, where the whole context belonged to a pre-industrial world. The sport itself might be condemned to die with the past which it had outgrown, but before it died it had given to the sporting world the new notion of a universal championship, admittedly conceived of as primarily Anglo-Saxon, in the first instance, but inherently capable of eventual extension to all comers.

For sport to possess an international dimension was certainly no novelty by the middle of the nineteenth century. Leaving aside the British proneness to take home-made sports to all corners of the world, where as yet they usually remained purely expatriate pursuits, there were many more complete examples of organised sport crossing national frontiers. Racehorses were sent from Persia to the Prince Regent.

Squire Osbaldeston, who crops up inevitably in many roles in a story such as this, had imported trotting horses from the United States earlier in the century, and by the 1850s bloodstock was being recognised as a valuable export industry. Part of the opposition to 'cocktail' races, where non-throroughbreds were lightly handicapped when racing against pedigree horses, was the encouragement they gave to unscrupulous owners to disguise the ancestry of their stock and so undermine the valuable trade. Easier travel also meant that English owners were beginning to look to continental race meetings as another source of sport and profit; they offered the added advantage of Sunday racing, much to the disgust of Sabbatarians at home. In tennis, there were international matches, such as Cox's against M M Amadee Charrier of Paris in 1819; pigeon-flying between England and Belgium was established in 1830; and the international yacht races were soon quite common - in 1855, for instance, two English boats were competing against one Dutch, one Belgian, and one French on the Scheldt for a cup presented by the King.[1] Pedestrians from North America had been looking to England to exercise their talents ever since Mr Spillard, from Halifax, Nova Scotia, who was said to have travelled 69,000 miles over the previous twelve years arrived in London in 1796,[2] and Deerfoot had just made a highly successful tour of English running grounds in 1861. In the other direction, cricket professionals had been taken over to the United States as groundsmen and coaches and also to spearhead the local teams' bowling, and the first tours by paid players in organised parties had begun with visits by English players to the United States and Canada in 1859 and to Australia in 1861. International matches between Canada and the United States had started as early as 1844 .

Black Americans had played a significant part in the English prize-ring ever since Richmond's arrival on the pugilistic scene and from well before the establishment of the sport across the Atlantic. From James Burke's 1835 excursion to the United States, with its two contrasting fights, the pace of pugilistic exchange across the oceans had quickened, taking in Australia as well as North America. Ben Caunt had organised a hopeful trip to the United States, looking for challenges but only finding stage performances, and he had brought back the first white American to make a reluctant contribution to the English ring, Charles Freeman. Con Parker had emigrated to the United States in the 1850s, but he had died soon afterwards; John 'Bungaree' Gorrick and William Sparkes had come from Australia to fight in Britain; and the confusingly named William Perry (known as 'Black Perry' to distinguish him from The Tipton Slasher) had come from America, impressively defeated the reputable Bill Burton and then taken his career, at the behest of Her Majesty's judges, to Australia. These were all indications of the fact that the prize-ring was no longer a British monopoly and that the sport had found an independent life in two very distant parts of the world.

What was perhaps remarkable was the lack of impact made by pugilism nearer to its homeland, on the European continent. The early ventures of the Frenchman, Pettit, and the Venetian gondolier into the ring in the mid-eighteenth century[3] had not been encouraging and they had had no successors. The French were given occasional glimpses of the fistic art over the years and several of the ring's professors, such as Jack Adams in the 1830s, did some teaching there, but the usual Gallic attitude towards fist-fighting hovered between bemused curiosity and outright disgust. When Harmer and Fuller (who was to play his part in the sporting histories of both France and the United States) exhibited on a stage at Montmartre races, soon after Waterloo, the Duke of Wellington contributed generously to the collection, but the natives were reputedly more ready with appreciative comment than with silver. Many pugilistic visits to the Continent were, however, prompted not by any missionary zeal but by flight from the attentions of the police at home. After the death of 'Brighton Bill' in his fight with Owen Swift in 1838, Swift and his second, 'The Young Dutch Sam', took refuge in Paris, only to find themselves in further trouble when Swift took on a fight there with Jack Adams. He was surprised to find the French authorities prosecuting him and even sentencing him, in a further hurried absence, to thirteen months' imprisonment and a stiff fine. Across the Channel, where flight was one of the many accustomed routes by which pugilists avoided prosecution, the French action was regarded as somewhat sharp practice, though hardly unexpected from a nation which had never appreciated Anglo-Saxon sports. After all, it was the same with cricket, that other sport which could be 'called purely national', according to a correspondent in 1842, in which no Frenchman would risk his shins, and Latins would turn their backs rather than their bats to 'our swift bowlers'. He rejoiced that there was 'no piracy of this noble game by foreign puddle-blooded curs'.[4] Such jingoistic attitudes did not prevent English pugilists and promoters from availing themselves of the usually tolerant attitude of the continental authorities towards public fist-fighting; by the mid-1860s, one of the occasional means of escaping from police harassment was a steamer trip across the Channel and a ring pitched just outside Calais. It was a fitting burial ground for European fist-fighting with the battles involving Jem Smith, Jake Kilrain, John L. Sullivan, Charlie Mitchell and Frank Slavin, held at Rouen, Chantilly and Bruges between 1887 and 1889.

The Anglo-Saxon communities overseas were more receptive to one of its more rugged sports. America was faced by a pioneering challenge which demanded initiative, individuality and toughness. If its first immigrants, fleeing from religious persecution, were not of the stuff from which ring-fighters were made, the situation changed dramatically with the massive Irish influx of the 1840s. The genesis of Australia's first population inevitably gave it a preponderance of the fighting classes, while its free-wheeling society gave it the atmosphere in which pugilism could thrive. Fist-fighting was there from the First Fleet onwards and though the first recorded Australian fight dates from 1814, it is known that, for instance, Jack O'Donnell, beaten by Caleb Baldwin and Tom Belcher but with a hatful of prize-ring victories to his credit, had been transported there six years before that, still in his prime. It is unlikely that he kept his fists to himself.

Australian pugilism was, from the start, what it had become in Britain, namely, a sport predominantly of the working classes, financed largely by those whose business it was to provide working-class entertainment. Middle-class involvement was discreet and marginal. Again, there were academies in the cities where the athletic could learn the art of self-defence and the merely curious could see sparring exhibitions in gloves. Abraham Davies, transported on a seven-year sentence, operated such an establishment in Sydney in the 1830s, to such appreciation that a benefit for him attracted all the pugilists in the colony and a full gathering of his clientele. For the most part, though, the gentry support for pugilism was subdued, any men of substance often disguising themselves as labourers, the 'better to melt into the crowd'. *Bell's Life in Victoria* said of the typical throng at a big fight that the gentlemen were disguised as toughs and the toughs disguised as gentlemen![5] The sport was never 'respectable' and never reached the gentility which had once allowed English ladies to observe - from their carriages, and at a modest distance - some of the better-organised encounters. On the rare occasions when women were present it was a matter of note, as when they joined their men and flocked from the diggings to see Jim Kelly take on Jonathan Smith at Fiery Creek, Victoria, in December 1854.

By this time the sport was well established and centred, inevitably, on the twin bases of Sydney and Melbourne. From the 1840s Australian matches were being reported in *Bell's Life in London* and before the decade was out at least two Australian fighters, 'Bungaree' and William Sparkes, had made their appearances in the London ring. The former's fight with M'Ginty had provided the opportunity for a double bill - it followed Perry's resumed encounter with Freeman, the American colossus, in a truly international excursion - and although 'Bungaree' lost he acquitted himself well for nearly two hours. He was well received among the large crowd at the handing over of Perry's stake money a few days later. He was no more successful in his battle back in Australia with Bill Davis at Sydney in 1847 but, along with fighters like William Sparkes, he was demonstrating that the Australian ring stood comparison with the British. Sparkes had come to England with a boxing belt and a pedestrian cup as proof of his abilities, and with an impressive home record, including a win over Davis for £100 a side at Liverpool, New South Wales, which had secured him the belt. When Johnny Broome, that indefatigable manipulator of fighters, matched him with Nat Langham, the spectators were surprised at his boxing stance, his left held straight out and his body inclined backwards, a style they knew only from the old boxing prints of the days of Mendoza and Humphries. Once Sparkes was in action, it was clear that he was no novice and had speed and strength; he drew the firstblood and won the first knock-down, in the second round. Eventually he was worn down by the skilled and experienced Langham - the only man, after all, ever to beat Tom Sayers - but he showed 'great game' and was strong on his legs even at the end of the fight.

Back in Australia, Sparkes is recorded as having lost a 'muffler' fight with William Thompson in Sydney at the Tennis Court Inn - one of the many echoes of English pugilism found in the Australian scene. In the first known fight there, at Sydney racecourse in 1814, the combatants had first to run a half-mile race before squaring up to each other, which is distantly reminiscent of pugilism's earliest days in England, when there was always a cudgelling or sword-play prelude. During the most flourishing days of the bareknuckle sport in Australia, the 1850s and early 1860s, the ring took on many of the characteristics of that in Britain. It shared its illegality and was faced by government and police equally determined to prevent prize-fights. It took to the same devices of railway trips and steamer excursions, mounting fights in remote spots as soon after dawn as possible. It was no sport for the tender either in mind or spirit. Getting to the battleground was often arduous and the fights themselves seem to have had a ferocity that had been largely lost in English pugilism where fighters had learned to avoid punishment by losing on fouls if all else failed. To take just one example, Matt Hardy fought Alf McLaren for five minutes short of five hours in July 1863, both of them in the end failing to make the scratch for what would have been the eighty-second round. In the twenty-fifth round Hardy's lip had been split half-way to the nostril, and by the twenty-ninth his face was said to be 'literally chiselled all over', while McLaren fought for four hours on one leg, having dislocated a kneecap early in the struggle!

Like Britain, Australia afforded a better opportunity for black Americans to exploit their fistic skills than their home country did, and fighters like Harry Sallars ('The Happy Nigger') were soon trying their luck there. One of Sallars's opponents, with whom he fought a long and bloody draw, was the remakable 10½ st. Joe Kitche, who won over £2000 in stake money and whose fights had many features familiar to the English prize-ring. There was, for instance the deception worked on the pursuing police when another man took over his clothes and led them off on a false trail, and then there was the boat trip for his fight with Matt Hardy, interrupted by darkness and prevented by police from its planned resumption the next day. Irish fighters gave opportunities for nationalistic appeals and the Melbourne v. Sydney rivalry could always add spice to the proceedings, as in the Kelly v. Smith fight, in which, in what had become all too British a fashion, anticipation was disappointed by a fight low in action and dubious in outcome when Smith suddenly gave in after seventeen rounds. A flourishing sporting press helped to keep pugilism in the news - *Bell's Life in Sydney* and *Bell's Life in Victoria* had their obvious progenitor and, while the respectable newspapers ignored the prize-ring, they and the *Sportsman, Sporting Life*, and *Referee* all reported fights in great detail. *Bell's Life in Victoria* even produced, in 1858, a long and spirited editorial defence of prize-fighting such as English sporting journals had regularly put out in the past - citing its manliness, its value to the national physique and the national spirit and its promotion of military potential and a sense of fair play, and making an appeal that the forces of law and order should find more useful objectives than the prevention of prize-fights.

Australia was to play its part in the final acts of the pugilistic story late in the century, but the sport there suffered a serious setback in July 1867 when up to a dozen people were drowned as the steamers taking followers to the McLaren v. Carstairs fight tried to disembark on a dangerous island beach. The nation was roused. Opposition at once grew stronger and more demanding for suppression, and even the sporting press feared that 'this could be the end of the ailing ring'.[6]

It was certainly a time when fist-fighting was coming under a universal cloud, when few would have predicted even its partial emergence later to perform its last rites. In Britain all influential interest had gone, as had most of the well-known pugilists themselves. New leisure opportunities were opening up for the middle classes and rising standards of living were promoting new sports for the working man to enjoy, given the time and money to avail himself of them. The roughest sector of the urban proletarist was becoming increasingly squeezed and here, the residual home of support for fist-fighting, the unruliness and the inappropriateness of the sport began to stand out all the more sharply by way of contrast with the gentling of all other sporting activities.

The still more fluid society of North America might seem to offer more scope for pugilists, but there, too, society was changing and prize-fighting, never enjoying the comforting ancestry of its former upper-class backing, was beginning to slip from such favour as it had once won. For the time being, though, for the main body of English pugilists, it was the United States that seemed still to promise the rewards that their native country denied them. That other great country of the North American continent, Canada, although a British possession,was largely ignored. Its pugilistic traditions were slim, given the French and Scottish strains in its population. The ring was frowned upon, and such major fights as it housed were the result of escape across the border from the United States to avoid the authorities there. One such was John Morrissey's inconvenient victory over John C. Heenan, the fight which appeared to confuse the challenge to Sayers by an American champion until, by one of those rationalisations dear to the boxing heart, it was decided that as Morrissey was not a native-born American, Heenan was still the right man to take on Sayers. As the only one with backing, he was going to do so anyway!

Apart from such fugitive encounters as this, Canadian pugilism was confined to some intermittent forays in the cities, where the police were always likely to step in and, in the 1860s, in the Pacific West, whence occasional reports of fights found their way into *Bell's Life in London*[7] - a catchweight contest, for instance, for £100 a side between the 11½ st. George Baker and the 15st. George Wilson, near Williams' Creek, British Columbia. This fight, according to the Canadian press, had most of the trappings of the formal ring. Articles were drawn up, deposits were made by stages and the men went into training. The unusual aspect was that, while the *Colonist and Chronicle of Victoria* reported that the men 'will go into training today', the fight was due on 24 October and 'today' was 18 October! The arrangements for this particular match do, however, imply a substantial pugilistic tradition, at least in western Canada, if only by way of a northward drift from the United States, where the emphasis in the sport was moving westwards.

Sparring exhibitions were certainly acceptable and popular in many Canadian cities by the 1880s, but boxing's failure to strike ready chords in the national character was reflected in the eventual slowness of amateur boxing to get off the ground when the gloves were finally put on. Although the Toronto Athletic Club organised its first tournament for the Canadian Amateur Boxing Championships in 1897, it was not until well into the twentieth century that the Canadian Amateur Boxing Association was successfully established.

It was otherwise in the United States. There, from the 1840s onwards, occasional periods of slump apart, pugilism was a thriving sport with many pointers towards the days when that country, through John L. Sullivan, would both lead the bareknuckle world and then inaugurate world professional boxing. The start, though, had been a slow one. The southern states, given the dispositions of their early settlers, were inevitably the first conspicuous cradle of American sport.

Elsewhere, its beginnings, no less important in the long run, were lower in profile, the nearest approach to combat sports coming in the county fairs, where cudgelling sounded distant echoes of English wakes. It was in the South that the gouging style of fighting grew up and even developed into a recognised sport, its participants sharpening and toughening their nails to make them more effective weapons for getting at eyes and ripping off testicles.

It was a style of fighting which persisted in Lancashire through the eighteenth century (and made the rest of the country very wary of Lancashire boxers when they entered the prize-ring) and one in which the real contest only began, rather than ended, when the fighters went to ground. Why it should persist and achieve some formal status in the southern United States is doubtless a reflection of a more sharply divided society, with its great gulf between plantation owner and slave, where respect for life had its sharp gradations and men at the bottom of the pile had little to lose. But it was not a sport that could have long-term interest for the gentry, nor one that they would have been easily able to control, had they wished to do so. Its elements were too primitive, too exposed to the mob. The gulf in society pushed the southern gentry into their own exclusive sports, leading them to create enclosed race-tracks a century before they appeared on the other side of the Atlantic and to look to the honour code of the duel to settle their own personal differences.

American pugilism had to grow on roots other than those which had originally nourished the English ring. Its opportunity came when the social structure of the sport in Britain changed in the 1820s and 1830s and pugilism began to operate in circumstances which suited the New World even better than they did the Old. It assumed a vigorous working-class accent, became even more thoroughly urbanised, ventured into new territories and became enmeshed with the growing range of providers of popular entertainment, with pugilists themselves among its main promoters. It found itself one of the first elements in that entrepreneurial drive which was to transform spectator sport before the nineteenth century had run its course. Its new social context, freed from those traditional aristocratic associations which had little relevance across the Atlantic, was one which the United States could readily identify with.

The states, though, were diverse in their origins and heterogeneous in their ethnic make-up, and pugilism needed time to grow, time to become distinctively American. It had begun to do so by the 1840s, replicating the English ring in its conventions, rituals and trappings, but doing so in its own larger-than-life style. In earlier days, the only press recognition given to boxing was the occasional reference to English prize-fights, by way of tasty snacks for middle-class sportsmen mindful of a distant homeland. Cribb, not Molyneux, had been the leading actor in the few reports of their battles to surface in America. *The New York Times* of 10 July 1823 carried the first full round-by-round report of a local fist-fight, and from then on home-made encounters began to rival English prize-fights for press coverage. It was not an easy growth. The 1820s and 1830s were difficult times for popular sport on both sides of the Atlantic as new forms of leisure activity struggled to emerge in the face of both social and economic pressures. Pugilism in the United States had no marginally respectable past to resort to for justification, and fears of the proletarian mob, associated with prize-fights, were scarcely less real in the settled areas of that country than they were in the United

Kingdom. At the same time, there were more raw regions, where the American version of Victorianism could only operate weakly and gradually (and some with a Catholic or slave-owning heritage where it scarcely operated at all), while policing in general was less effective than in the compact counties of England. Boxing also managed to foster its less disreputable side through academies for the teaching of self-defence and the spread of touring exhibitions of glove-sparring. When the Scot, William Fuller, had fought Molyneux in his youth, his performance was marked by enthusiastic ignorance.[8] By the 1830s he was America's leading authority on boxing, though not, he claimed, intending to introduce prize-fighting to his adopted land. Through his tours and his gymnasium and sparring school in New York, he made a deliberate appeal to the respectable classes, helped by his own gentlemanly demeanour. The general success of touring exhibitions, with ready audiences eager for fist-fighting in any of its forms, was another ambivalent factor in the sport's American growth - on the one hand it raised the level of boxing's popularity, while on the other it tempted pugilists away from the financial and physical risks of the ring itself at the earliest possible stage in their careers, often after only a single fight.

At all events, by 1835, James Burke, the current champion, finding the English scene empty of challenges, had thought it worthwhile to try his hand in America. His backers in the United Kingdom had previously refused to see him risk his title against the Irish champion, O'Rourke, who now happened to be in America. After being well received in New York, Burke made his way to New Orleans, where O'Rourke was based. His vividly contrasting experiences in the fight there with O'Rourke and his later contest with O'Connell, based on New York, underscore the exaggeration to which the young American ring was disposed. The New Orleans fight was a fiasco, with Burke having to flee the ring fearful of his life, pursued by an armed mob. The army was called out and the neighbourhood was not quietened until 2 the next morning. By contrast, his ten-round victory over O'Connell shortly afterwards was staggering in its gentility - a well-organised steamer excursion took some 300 passengers ('and those of a very select kind' - at $3 a ticket!) to Hart Island, where the umpires stopped the fight at the first outburst of cheering and requested, successfully, that 'no ebullition of the feelings of either party should be suffered to take place'. This was not, perhaps, an appeal which would have held much force with the Irish mob in New Orleans, but it was effective here. Burke played the gentlemanly game to the end, giving O'Connell's seconds the chance to retire their helpless fighter rather than punishing him further. It was almost a future vision of the National Sporting Club, with its sepulchral silences during the rounds.

Ben Caunt took his championship belt to the United States some half-dozen years later, only to find no challenger ready for him. The visit, though, was profitable financially, on account of the American entertainment industry's thoroughgoing adoption of boxing as part of its bill of fare. Appearances in the theatre in Pierce Egan's *Tom and Jerry* followed a British pugilistic tradition, as did his exhibitions at Hudson's Sparring Rooms and Pistol Gallery on Broadway, but his bizarre association with the giant Charles Freeman marked a new progression of pugilism into circus - one that was to continue until Tom Sayers lost much of his money in rash investment in that other ring in the early 1860s. The supposed challenge of

Freeman, an amiable and gentle Goliath, was certainly a publicist's kite-flying, the beginnings of a hype which was to carry on over the Atlantic when he went back with Caunt, and culminated in his fight with The Tipton Slasher.

Caunt's visit was a few months too soon to bring him any serious boxing business. His presence undoubtedly helped the rising tide of interest in the sport, much of which centred around the successes of Yankee Sullivan. Born in Cork, Sullivan had emigrated to America in 1838, returning to make something of a reputation in the English ring with his victory over the redoubtable Birmingham fighter, Hammer Lane (who suffered a broken arm early in their fight). Back across the Atlantic, he added to his laurels by beating Vincent Hammond and Tom Secor in bouts which raised fight fever to a high pitch in and around New York. The Secor fight attracted 2000 spectators, carried on five chartered steamers, but by that time Caunt had taken up with Freeman and was soon on his way home.

However flourishing the immediate scene, the contemporary problems of English pugilism were also writ large in America, particularly as far as keeping some sort of order and maintaining a reasonable ring were concerned. 'Yankee' Sullivan and his band of fellow pugilists linked arms to clear the course for the great horse-race challenge for $20,000 a side between the North's Florizel and the South's Fashion in May 1842,[9] but they had no organisation - not even one with such tenuous authority as the Pugilistic Benevolent Association - to aid the running of prize-fights. Racial passions ran high, with Sullivan as the Irish hero. There were spirited urban populations always likely to become turbulent in the unaccustomed excitement of the fight atmosphere, and little steadying influence either in the present or inherited from the past. Fears over the potential anarchy in the sport were reinforced by shock and disgust when McCoy died, choking on his own blood, in a well-publicised fight with Lilley. The courts acted. Lilley fled first to Canada and then to England, while Sullivan was among those convicted as accessories to the manslaughter and was sentenced to two years' imprisonment, reduced after a few months by a pardon from the state governor. Such tragedies as McCoy's death put pugilism into sharp reverse from which it could take years for the sport even partially to recover. The same happened in Britain after the death of 'Brighton Bill' in his fight with Owen Smith and in Australia after the deaths at the MacLaren v. Carstairs match. It happened now in the United States, and it was not until the late 1840s that the American ring could emerge again.

Once the revival did come, it took American pugilism into the centre of the world scene. The thirst for excitement and the relative absence of competing sporting attractions on the large scale gave the prize-ring its opportunity. The great popularity of professional pedestrianism had passed its peak and baseball's first flowering as a major spectator sport lay in the near future. In the 1850s the American ring burst into life, reported prize-fights became much more frequent and the sport spread from coast to coast. New Orleans with its freewheeling leisure inheritance, California with the 'forty-niners, Boston with its burgeoning of Irish immigrants and St Louis, the bustling grand junction of western traffic, all became significant magnets for the growing number of ambitious fighting men. Yankee Sullivan was back in the ring at Harper's Ferry in 1847, easily beating Bob Caunt, whose greatest claim to fame was that he was Ben's brother and whose English career had consisted principally of two defeats, by 'Nobby' Clarke and Bill Burton of Leicester, the latter a victim of 'Black Perry'. It was a prelude to Sullivan's fight with Hyer, the first contest to be widely regarded as for the championship of America, and it had all the echoes of an English championship fight. The fighters enjoyed a six-month build-up of training and sparring exhibitions, they shared the profits from the chartered steamboats and they became national celebrities. Hyer was victorious here, but Sullivan was back again to fight John Morrissey - known as 'Old Smoke' an account of his ferocity both in and out of the ring - a graduate of New York street fighting whose supporters rivalled their man in wildness. George Thompson had deliberately fouled when he fought Morrissey so as to give away the fight and avoid the fury of the mob. Sullivan's skill seemed to be gaining him the upper hand against Morrissey in his turn when the crowd broke up the ring and the contest had to be abandoned. It was Morrissey who later almost confused the issue of Heenan's challenge to Sayers by defeating him in one of his few well-conducted fights, held over the border in Canada.

Morrissey's career encapsulated the strengths and weaknesses of the American ring. It could arouse massive interest, but equally it released wild passions, and as pugilism was an illegal sport there was no means of controlling them. The sport was caught up too in the rough city politics of the day and all in all it was virtually impossible to achieve that sense of separateness from the realities of life which is ideally one element in sport. The problem which exists on the fringes of European soccer crowds in the late twentieth century lay near the heart of American pugilism in the mid-nineteenth century - the fiction that is sport tended to develop into the documentary that constitutes economics and politics. Morrissey gravitated naturally to saloon-keeping, highly successful gambling and, eventually, politics. He became wealthy, built the Saratoga race-track and served two terms in the United States Congress and one in the New York State Senate. If William Fuller was the Jackson of America, Morrissey was certainly its John Gully. Gully, though, found himself in prison for youthful debt only - Morrissey found his way there by shooting two waiters and only political influence got him out.

From the time of the Sayers v. Heenan fight onwards, all the talk was of championships - of America and of the world. From the start, though, the issues were seldom clear-cut. In the absence of governing bodies, there was usually uncertainty about who had the best claim to the American title, while in the twenty years following Mace's retirement, announced in 1866, the British scene was just as confused, with the sport deep in the shadows and the contending claimants of slight distinction. Only with the emergence of Charlie Mitchell in the 1880s was there once more a recognisable British champion. Even by the time of Heenan's second visit to England in 1862 and 1863, there was some vagueness about the status of his fight with Tom King; Tom King was the conqueror of Jem Mace but he had supposedly retired and Mace had reclaimed the belt. Whether the absence of any mention of the championship belt in the articles of the Sayers v. Heenan fight reflects this vagueness is unclear.There had orginally been an implied stipulation by the presenters of the belt that it should not leave the country. The American press boasted that Heenan had gone over to fetch the old belt and to fight Mace, 'the so-called champion', but once in England he claimed that he had come only to appear in a circus troupe. Mace himself was on tour with another circus - yet another example of boxing's growing involvement with the entertainment industry - and so when a fight did take place involving Heenan it was with King. King won an unsatisfying encounter in which it was hard to keep an orderly ring, and there were suspicions of 'hocus' and of the fight having been sold, depending on the viewpoint.

There followed a period during which the biggest fights, whether they involved British or American fighters or both, took place in the United States. First there was the encounter between Joe Goss and Allen in Cincinatti in 1867, claimed spuriously to be for the championship of the World. Goss's credentials consisted of two defeats by Mace and a meaningless draw against him in which there was no action, while Allen had done nothing apart from avoiding defeat by Goss in an unfinished fight! It was a fitting end to such ambitions that Allen should be disqualified for hitting Goss when he was down. The aspirants to the championship in Britain, Joe Wormald and Ned O'Baldwin, having tried unsuccessfully if none too zealously to meet in the London ring, then ventured their luck in the United States, only to find that the police there had become much more sedulous. Three attempts to mount their fight failed. The evergreen Joe Mace did manage to meet and beat Allen in New Orleans in 1870 and was hailed by the *New York Clipper*, with some justification, as 'the unquestioned World's Champion'. In the following year Mace added to the occasional blots on his escutcheon in his two fights with Joe Coburn, in the first of which they shadow-boxed until the militia arrived, clearly having no intention of doing more than pocketing the proceeds.

The malaise by which the sport had been crippled in Britain had followed the pugilists to the United States. Indeed, they had brought too many of their old habits with them, and they found fertile ground in which those habits could grow. As in Britain, pugilism had become confined to the lowest and roughest of the working classes, even to the extent of living on the edge of criminality. Its exponents were subject to constant pressures to throw fights, deposits were always likely to be forfeit, referees could not be relied upon, there could never be any guarantee of a genuine fight and the problem of maintaining order at outdoor prize-fights was never solved. It became an increasingly alien sport, spurned now even by the city bosses who had once looked to the occasional interventions of their pugilistic friends to aid their local causes. There was, too, competition from elsewhere, particularly from the growing attraction of baseball, with its regular provision for regular leisure. The spasmodic events of the ring appeared more and more to belong to the past.

Yet it was in the United States that the curtains closed on prize-fighting for the shortest interval, before the last act was played. By the early 1880s John L. Sullivan had begun his illustrious fighting career, and there was a new audience ready and growing - but wanting something other than the marathon blood-baths of the past. Whereas in Britain there remained a decisive gulf between the new form of combat laid down in the Queensberry Rules and the old bareknuckle fighting, one that was to persist through the decade, in the United States there was a readiness to compromise. The difference is partly explained by a more dynamic, more adaptive society, but generalisations on the need to modernise sport to bring it into closer harmony with modern methods of production are not always the whole answer or even the major part of it. The system of American law and its variations from state to state meant that even slight ameliorations of the old primitive ring rules could result in a reasonable chance of holding fights in closed arenas, hence solving many of the difficulties of crowd control. The United States also had a greater need for boxing - the Briton now had winter sport in the form of Association football to fill his half-day of Saturday leisure. At all events, more Americans from outside the working classes turned their attention to boxing, their interests fostered by the efforts of old pugilists in their sparring schools and in the YMCAs, and the sport itself responded by its readiness to modify the old London Prize-Ring rules, eventually to do so even at the level of the world championship and so bring the bareknuckle days to an end.

John L. Sullivan, from the start, not only distinguished himself in traditional fist-fighting under London Prize-Ring rules but also showed a penchant for four-rounders, in which lightweight gloves were worn. After he had beaten Ryan in a prize-ring contest at Mississippi City in 1882, and got the better of 'Tug' Wilson, the claimant to the British championship, in a four-round glove-fight the same year, his own claims to be world champion were as clear as any fighter's could be, given the fugitive and chancy nature of the bareknuckle sport. The elusive, backing-away style of the English boxers, their emphasis always being on stamina and endurance, infuriated Sullivan, who had always found his numerous glove-fights far more rewarding than his forays into the prize-ring. He would, he said, only defend his title wearing gloves and under the Queensberry Rules.

The pre-eminence of John L. Sullivan, even before it resulted in the ending of pugilism, marked the transfer of the sport's balance of power to the United States, where, in the heavyweight classes at least, it has predominantly remained ever since. As well as becoming a sport which had extended over much of the Anglo-Saxon world, it had become the first to develop the concept of a world championship and the first international sport whose emphasis, if not transatlantic, was certainly henceforth mid-Atlantic. Indeed, the contrast between the old and the new homes of pugilism was nowhere better illustrated than in the two fight reports that appeared side by side in *Bell's Life in London* of 30 June 1885. One was of Sullivan's five-round gate money fight under Queensberry Rules against Jack Burke at Chicago Driving Park, where 12,000 people saw Sullivan win on points. The other was of a prize-fight at Charlton, on the outskirts of London, between two unnamed contenders for £10 a side; there were only about forty people present, and the fight was notable only because it passed off without police interruption.

14

The Last Bareknuckle Days

With the retirement of Tom Sayers the British prize-ring virtually collapsed. The collection for him, well supported in the business houses of the City, was the final contribution of any significant part of the establishment to the old fighting style. His funeral, five years later, underlined the take-over of what was left of pugilism by the roughest edges of society. Amid the riotous rabble that followed the coffin and then threatened to destroy Highgate Cemetery, the only dignity came from Sayers's huge mastiff, sitting bolt upright and alone in the open carriage behind the hearse. The championship disintegrated. Sayers had seen off a whole generation of fighters and there was no space for any new hero. Big fights became harder and harder to mount, especially after the railways, first by disinclination and then by law, ceased to provide special excursions. The sport's organisers - tavern-keepers, bookmakers and money-lenders now, for the most part - had no prospects beyond the wringing of a last harvest of sovereigns from the gullible. For the pugilists there was only connivance in the usually devious schemes of their backers and the hawking of their skills around the world, more often in the circus than in the square ring. Only the last defiant, desperate flourish of the late 1880s remained, and even that had to be made from continental retreats.

The collapse of interest after Sayers's departure from the ring was immediate and wholesale. The meeting of Tom Paddock and Sam Hurst for the vacant championship stirred very few hearts - an ageing veteran on his last legs, whose coarseness and ill temper had never been designed to win friends, against an ungainly northern wrestler with no boxing reputation at all. It was almost irrelevant that Hurst managed to win, with a chance blow, after less than ten minutes. This opened the door to Jem Mace, the last skilled practitioner of the English ring, who in better times might have proved as good a sportsman as he was a boxer. He easily disposed of the much heavier Hurst, whose broken leg now made him look like an enlarged parody of the limping Tipton Slasher of yesteryear. But then Mace's colours were lowered by Tom King, who held out brief hopes of heroism and revived interest, until he had the wisdom to retire into domestic contentment and become a prize-winning flower grower, leaving Mace to claim the championship again.

Jem Mace hailed from one of the early cradles of pugilism, Norfolk, and came to the ring by way of his fairground boxing-booth where he took on all comers. His early career demonstrated both his boxing abilities and his doubtful reliability. Nobody was convinced that Bob Brettle had really knocked him unconscious with a single blow within three minutes in 1858, and suspicions were strengthened by Mace's savagely precise destruction of 'Posh' Price soon afterwards and his complete conquest of Brettle himself two years after their first fight. Once he had gained the championship, and received a salutary lesson from Tom King on how easily it might be lost, Mace and his backers resolved to hold on to the crown for as long as possible with the least possible hazard. Out of a tangle of abortive challenges, real or imagined injuries and touring engagements, the only actual fights to take place over a half dozen years were two against Joe Goss, both won by Mace with relative ease. Even getting Mace into the ring itself did not guarantee a fight - the same two heroes spent over an hour staring at each other when they met at Meopham in Kent in 1866, after which the referee generously declared the encounter 'a draw'. With approaching £1000 from ticket sales to be divided between them, both sides were content enough, but spectator confidence inevitably sank further. At other times, there were Mace's performances with Ginnett's touring circus, other exhibitions and the show-biz farce of his trip to Ireland to meet Joe Coburn and company from the United States for a proposed title fight, Coburn having refused to take him on 'with an English crowd at his back'. He need not have worried. There was never any real prospect of the fight taking place, with both sides looking much more seriously to profit than to pugilism.

Mace claimed to have retired in 1867. It was in tune with the times and with his own early reputation as 'an in-and-out fighter' that some of his most notable fights were still to come, but his disavowal of the title revealed both the poverty of the remaining boxing talent and the inability of promoters to mount successful matches. A series of injuries, forfeits and police actions, involving Goss, Joe Wormald, and Ned O'Baldwin, culminated with O'Baldwin missing the special train from his 'fight' with Wormald in April 1867 - after some 300 would-be spectators had travelled on it at the usual exorbitant prices. It was then that English pugilism moved virtually lock, stock and barrel to the United States, leaving the championship in petty and disputed hands and in the deepest shadow until well into the 1880s. Jem Mace, though, continued to be active. First he was a publican in Melbourne, but it was a bad time for prize-fighting in Australia, just after the drowning tragedy at the MacLaren v. Carstairs match, and soon he was in America, beating Tom Allen for the proclaimed 'Championship of the World'. Never one to leave well alone, he resumed the profitable pantomime that he had begun with Joe Coburn in Ireland some four years before. This time they got as far as mounting two 'fights' for the championship. The first was a repetition of the farcical inactivity of Mace's second fight with Goss, during which they waited for the militia to arrive; the second, in Mississippi, started with some mild fisticuffs (in which Mace may well have been coming off second best) but soon reverted to the endless shadowing, shuffling and staring at each other which made the referee's drawn verdict come almost as a relief.

Under the headline 'American Pugilists in England', a symptom of the degree to which he had become a stranger in his own country, Mace and others were back for a series of benefit shows in 1872. Then he was on the move to Australia once more, where he joined Larry Foley, helping him first in his fighting career and later in training young fighters and promoting glove-boxing under the Queensberry Rules. One of the founders of the National Sporting Club, A. F. Bettinson, had the ingenious theory that, through his association with Foley, Jem Mace passed on the skills and ringcraft of the best British tradition of fighting first ot his Australian pupils - the likes of Peter Jackson, Frank Slavin, Bob Fitzsimmons and others - and then to the United States, since they all finished their careers in America taking the same style with them. In short, the new and highly successful 'American' style of boxing of the turn of the century was none other than old English style writ large.[1] Whether or not this theory is put down to national pride alone, there is little doubt that Jem Mace did preserve, even into his old age, abilities which the English ring had forgotten during its decade of virtual oblivion. When, at 64, he sparred with the world championship contender, Dick Burge, at the National Sporting Club in October 1895, he could still astonish members with his ease of movement, the fluidity of his style and the calculation in his strategy.

While the major link between the old bareknuckle days and modern boxing was undoubtedly that forged by John L. Sullivan, the contribution of Jem Mace to the transition was also significant. No one could have been more thoroughly steeped in the old prize-ring fashions at the start of his career than Mace. He played all the traditional roles - tavern-keeper and part-time pedestrian, running for stakes, seconding and promoting other pugilists - and yet he spent much of his later life accommodating to the new glove sport, assisting in its growth on both sides of the world. Fittingly, one of his last appearances was on the last night of the Coronation Tournament at the National Sporting Club in 1902, when a distant touch of royalty had at last returned to boxing; Mace was there as second to Tom Sharkey, the American.

Sharkey was contesting with his fellow-countryman, Gus Ruhlin, for a £1500 purse and stake money of £500 a side, the sort of money which Mace had rarely seen in his own fighting days. They were indoors, before a highly controlled audience, and the duration of their labours had limits set to it. It had all been so different in the past, and it was the differences which had spelt the end of the old prize-ring. Chaos and corruption had gone hand in hand to bring it down. It had become much more difficult actually to mount matches of any consequence after 1860, when the sport had lost all claims to acceptability, but there had been money still to be made from it. More and more, prize-fighting had come to consist of the unscrupulous fleecing the gullible.

In the final decades of the nineteenth century, sparring exhibitions were a more legitimate means of entertaining the public than prize-fights. They could give some impression of the sport's skills, if little or nothing of its excitements. At the humblest levels, in the travelling fairground booth, there was more than mere sparring on offer for the local worthies who sought to stand up to the resident pugilist for three rounds to earn a sovereign or two and much local glory. Fighters who had made their reputations usually toured in groups of four or five to make a full programme of entertainment possible. Public halls, hotels, swimming baths and even theatres were among their varied venues as they trekked through the provinces. The pugilists' rewards for these wandering endeavours could be very variable, depending both upon their reputations and their organisation, but they were likely to fare, at that time, considerably better than, say, professional cricketers, who could seldom make much more than £5 a week. At the top end of the entertainment scale, as star circus performers giving sparring and fitness displays in that other ring, the best-known pugilists would command the salaries of top-billed theatrical performers - they were the precursors of the general move of spectator sport into its eventual ambit of show business. Heenan toured with Howe and Cushing's and Mace toured with both Pablo Fanque's and Ginett's. King, too, tried his hand with a travelling troupe, but it was not a life that suited him and he was back at his own fireside within a few weeks. The star pugilists had now the air of popular entertainers. Their sparring tours were systematically publicised by their own press agents and public relations men, described by contemporaries, for want of a better word, as 'secretaries'. Significantly, Jem Mace's factotum, at one stage, was Harry Montague, later secretary to Myers' Great American Hippodrome and Circus.

For the older pugilist, there was an honest pound to be made from giving sparring lessons and organising exhibitions. It helped if, as often happened, he was a publican himself, but otherwise he could operate from someone else's tavern. An evening's sparring took place in many public houses at least once a week, while the resident pugilist advertised himself as available to give instruction in self-defence, either there or privately at the would-be pupil's own house. By the 1870s there were many issues of *Bell's Life in London* in which the only mention of pugilism was by way of the twenty or more advertisements from publicans offering instruction or sparring contests, the latter beginning to take on a more competitive air as glove-fighting began to take up elements of the Queensberry Rules. The extent to which this process could be followed in Britain was always limited by the uncertainty of the law - it reached its ultimate in the United States with John L. Sullivan's numerous and highly profitable four-rounders at Madison Square Gardens. Even so, the $100,000 he made in the ring had to be set against the $1 million that came from his theatrical tours and lectures.

In Britain, as the old sport was forced into greater secrecy than ever, the public house became the essential link in the communication system. Business could still thrive on fistic gossip and the deposit night for stake money was still a guarantee of good takings, so much so that these could often compensate for the forfeit of stake money later if the fight failed to come off. Inevitably only the credulous came to believe in the seriousness of any proposed encounter until it actually took place.

While publicans, particularly some of the ex-fighters like Nat Langham, were still the main organisers of prize-fights, they were increasingly joined by others whose interests in the sport were exclusively financial. They were a miscellaneous collection of speculators, often looking no further than the profits to be made from the special excursion tickets to the fight, until that lucrative source was stopped, as far as railway travel was concerned, in 1868. The inactive Mace v. Goss fight was only one of many where there was clearly never any intention of bringing matters to any combative conclusion and the only object was to exploit the spectators. The match between Bob Brettle and Jack Rooke provided one of the more blatant examples - it began on 31 December 1861, and was allegedly for £200 a side and a bet of £300. They sparred for just over an hour before the police arrived. They resumed the next day, when the police came on the scene more promptly (almost certainly having been told of the location by telegram), and they eventually concluded the event three months later, taking an hour and forty minutes to plod through five rounds. They finally agreed a draw after a quarter of an hour without a blow on either side. The bigger the fight, the greater the tendency to side-line the old pugilists and put all the management into non-sporting hands. In Mace's later matches, real or proposed, the only aspects of the organisation which were certain to be efficient were the financial ones.

The facts of pugilism in the 1860s almost defy exaggeration, certainly as far as fights at the national level went. Locally, the sport could draw in a whole mix of characters, honest or otherwise. At Portsmouth - which had become a minor centre of prize-fighting, thanks to the growing presence of the Royal Navy and other services, and where Tom King began his fighting career - those charged with manslaughter after a ring death in 1867 were, respectively, a tithe collector, a lodginghouse-keeper, a captain in the 100th Regiment, a former instructor at the Portsmouth Military Gymnasium and another pugilist.[2] Whoever the moving spirits behind prize-fights were, the disorder which the biggest of them was now causing in London could not long continue. The closed excursion train, with the carefully controlled sale of tickets (marked only 'There and Back') reduced the likelihood of chaos from spectators at the fight itself, should that happen to take place, but transferred the tumult to the London terminus from which the train was to depart. This became common knowledge among the criminal and near-criminal classes as well as among sportsmen. The scenes at Fenchurch Street Station before the fight between Mace and King were typical, with ticket-holders having to fight their way through gangs of roughs to reach the platform. Many were deterred and returned home. Others had their tickets, and more besides, taken from them. Such chaos was becoming less and less aceptable even in the Kentish marshes or on the distant beaches of Essex, let alone in the centre of London. By the time that Parliament stepped in to ban rail excursions to prize-fights, most of the railway companies had already opted out of such hazardous, if profitable, operations. One of the last to do so was the Great Western, which compromised by providing only minimal co-operation with the promoters. When Mace's fight with Goss was prevented at Wootton Bassett, there was no cruising around for an alternative site as in the old days. The train steamed straight back to London. With heavy sarcasm, *The Times* reported, under the heading 'Prizefighting under difficulties' that 'whatever else may be said against the Great Western Railway, they certainly do manage a prize-fighting excursion capitally'. Was there, perhaps, symbolism in the fact that the year which saw the banning of prize-fighting excursions also formally ended what once had been another fruitful source of business for some railway companies, namely public executions (particularly if, as at Bodmin, their sidings afforded a good view of the gallows!)? Prize-fights and public executions alike were acts of violence which belonged to a rapidly receding past.

The attitude of the press, and particularly the sporting press, was decisive. George Bernard Shaw's analysis of the decline of pugilism in his preface to *Cashel Byron's Profession* - that it did not die of villainy but had lived by it, and died of tedium - is too slick to be wholly true, but he is on more certain ground when he goes on to admit that its real collapse came when the sporting press withdrew its participation and support. That section of the press, and *Bell's Life in London* in particular, had not only provided the publicity which fed and fostered interest in the ring throughout the kingdom and beyond, but it had also, in its later days, provided some of those organisational elements which helped pugilism to survive. The editor of *Bell's Life in London* became the regular holder of stake money (as he was also for pedestrian events, holding as much as £15,000 at any one time), he or one of his journalistic colleagues became the most reliable stand-by as referee, and the press maintained some semblance of continuity in the sport in even its darkest and most spasmodic days. The 1860s, though, saw this connection diminish and finally die. Although *Bell's Life in London* was still holding stake money, by 1863 the editor had forbidden any of his staff to officiate at prize-fights, following several painful episodes of attacks from disaffected spectators. It was between 1868 and 1870 that the prize-ring gradually faded from the newpaper's columns. By 1872, the ring section, which had once spread generously over one of those massive pink pages, had been reduced to the occasional brief sub-paragraph under the main heading of 'Boxing, Wrestling, & c', and this was in an ever-thicker newspaper, which was giving virtually full-page coverage to angling and billiards, for instance.

There could be no surer indication of the changes in the nation's sporting habits, or of the prize-ring's total failure to accommodate itself to these changes. Other than in its growing commercialism, it stood quite outside those shifts in leisure preferences which had begun to make themselves apparent from the mid-century onwards. New leisure opportunities and new leisure provision were revolutionising the sporting life of Victorian England and of the English-speaking world in general, and they were creating an environment in which the old human blood sport could not survive. There was, first of all, more free time for most sections of the population. It was, too, regular free time, not the occasional release offered by the old local festivals, the race week or the unofficial worship of St Monday. The economic revival of the 1860s produced a demand for shorter working hours, while the years between 1860 and 1875 saw the peak in the growth of the Saturday half-day holiday. There was free time now for the growing mass of workers engaged in large-scale factory production, as well as for those in trades and crafts where the rhythms of labour had always been largely in their own hands and where four or five hectic days of continuous sweat could win two or three days of release. There was free time for the workers as well as the work-shy, and a quite new and much enlarged clientele to be catered for.

The regularity of the new leisure and its predictability were accompanied also by its firmer definition. There was more of it, but it was subject to tighter time limits. It called for recreation which was itself time limited, which was reliable and which was locally available. Such a closely defined leisure pattern was quite alien to the country's traditional spectator sports inherited from the eighteenth century, and their accommo-dations to it were, for the most part, slow and partial. Horse-racing introduced its new commercial park courses in the 1870s. They were enclosed, charged for admission and were among the few that moved to having racing on Saturday, still the least usual day for meetings until the turn of the century. Racing, though, had never depended for its economic survival on popular support and in any case local meetings were still usually an annual rarity and therefore such interference as they might offer to work patterns could be endured. Cricket became predominantly a

Saturday game at club level from the 1860s, but the first-class fixtures held to their convention of Monday and Thursday starts to three-day games until after the First World War, leaving for Saturday afternoon crowds the unpredictable prospect of an exciting climax, a tame draw or even an early finish and no play at all. The organisational similarities between pugilism and pedestrianism had taken both along much the same paths for much of their earlier history, and the runners, trainers and promoters had nothing to learn from the ring about fixed matches, drugged performers or artificially rigged odds. This was so much so that modern athletics had to make a clean start, distancing itself completely from the old professional sport, which nevertheless continued alongside the new. The difference in legal opportunity between the running-track and the ring began to come through strongly though from the middle of the century - commercial running-grounds were established, the emphasis in the sport moved to the major population centres, particularly to the towns and cities of the Midlands and the North and, most significant of all, meetings began to concentrate heavily on Saturday afternoons and, once they were available, Bank Holidays. No such chance was open to prize-fighting and the sport stuck stubbornly to its old habits of weekday matches. Indeed, the distribution of contests through the week showed virtually no change in the late 1860s from what it had been fifty years earlier, with Tuesday still the most favoured day.

Denied the right to develop its own stadia or to regularise itself, pugilism, an outlaw and fugitive sport, could only pursue its cold and lonely road to oblivion. It had lived for too long outside the pale of respectability for there to be now any hope of gradual amendment. The physical damage of the fist-fight and its easily argued offence against human dignity were sufficient reasons for condemnation. The root cause now, though, for its inevitable total rejection was its indelible association with public disorder, its renegade anarchy, its air of criminality and, finally, its defiance of the strengthening conventions of the emerging sporting world. Economics and social policy may have dictated new time dimensions for sport, but sport could respond successfully because the interests of spectators had changed. They looked now, with greater sophistication, for something beyond the spectacle and sensation which had once satisfied them. They wanted contests with a new emphasis on equal chances, more skill and less dependence on sheer brute force and endurance. They looked for more sensitive means of achieving results than the grinding of the loser - whether it was horse, man or team - down into the ground. As spectators, while they were not yet looking for luxury, they did want safety and security, and readiness to pay an entrance fee began to take priority over financial involvement through gambling. This also coincided with the interests of paid players and promoters, who were looking for regular incomes, not the occasional and unreliable windfall which was all that the actual prize-ring could offer. It was, in the last resort, not the cruelty of prize-fighting which turned popular opinion against it, but rather the sport's total inability to meet any of the new expectations which other activities were learning to satisfy. For the middle and upper classes this was particularly marked; they made their own sports more exclusive and resorted increasingly to the closed club, so freeing themselves of some of the irksome restrictions on public sport, such as those preventing Sunday play.

Sport in general was on course to become not merely respectable but even praiseworthy, a medium for the expression of that favourite Victorian pseudo-virtue, manliness. Only the manly art itself looked like being excluded from the pantheon of sporting worthiness. The success being enjoyed by the instructors in self-defence and the schools of arms was evidence of the amateur demand, while the professionals, weary of the long conflict with the law, sought a means to combine sparring with genuine contest. The taming and tailoring of the ring was overdue.

If the Queensberry Rules, from their appearance in their first form in 1867, had immediately set up an alternative form of boxing, distinct from the old fist-fighting, they would have little part to play in this story. As it was, the impact of the rules was gradual, both in terms of creating a new amateur sport and in terms of changing and eventually ending the old bareknuckle pugilism. The eighth Marquess of Queensberry, whose boxing interests, in tune with the times, took him to both Australia and the United States, probably drew up his rules for glove-fighting with the co-operation of Arthur Chambers, who was to be one of the few English boxers to emerge at international level in the 1870s, when he held the American lightweight championship. The original rules (see Appendix A) appropriated the tempo of the long-standing sparring exhibitions, but they were clearly aimed at establishing a new and amateur sport. With their limitation of fights to three two-minute rounds, plus a fourth if needed for a decision, they were so drastically different from what the prize-ring was accustomed to that they appeared to offer little to fist-fighting.

The rules were designed to do for boxing what the establishment of strict amateur rules was doing for athletics, distancing the new sport from the old professionalism. The new 'sparring cups' for gentlemen amateurs got off to a slow start with only three entries in 1870. *Bell's Life in London* advised on the need for better organisation, clearer instructions on the conditions for entry and holding the cups and better publicity,[3] and within five years the glove sport was well on its way. The original separation into three weights - heavy, middle and light - was further refined in the interests of more equal competition. The Amateur Featherweight Championship was filling the City Gymnasium Club by 1874, the West London Boxing Club was holding monthly meetings and seeking to attract new members by offering cups for novices and Lilley Bridge was mounting its annual meetings for 'the cups in connexion with the Amateur Boxing, Wrestling and Bicycling Championships'.[4]

As a humbler social level, publicans had begun to offer cups for sparring contests, but the ring itself became even further outcast as the revised style of boxing began to gain a foothold. Fist-fights were seen as sorry legacies from the past. It was under the heading of 'Brutal anachronisms' that *The Times* of 18 February 1877 was reporting a prize-fight in the Birmingham area and expressing concern that the police made no appearance and 'seem to have been quite in the dark with regard to occurrence'. The police were now expected both to know and to act. The old conspiracy of silence had been narrowed. After the death of Thomas Callis in a fight with Charles Davis near Long Reach in March 1872, the police made a series of raids on this old venue in the Kentish marshes. It had become virtually impossible to mount fights of consequence any longer. Even an occasional large gathering of would-be spectators was unlikely to bring off a fight successfully - the Birmingham police hounded a crowd of 600 to 700 in 1877, until, after two hours of stalking, the organisers gave up and the crowd dispersed.

The difficulty for those seeking to preserve and revitalise what was left of pugilism was to know what compromises they would have to make to achieve legality. The Queensberry Rules in their first form sanitised the sport they had known out of all recognition, and they were particularly reluctant to surrender the concept of fighting to exhaustion. Various compromises eventually produced the Queensberry Rules of Endurance, the basis of the modern rules of professional boxing and very similar to those later adopted by the National Sporting Club (see Appendix B), with the major exception of a limit on the number of rounds. There was an awkward and uncomfortable period of transition, during which little significant fighting took place. Typical of the confusion was the 'glove fight for £100' held at the Surrey Gardens in Walworth in March 1878, before which the gloves were submitted to Scotland Yard for police approval. There was a poor attendance and the strong-arm attendants hired to keep order were not called upon to perform. The comedy extended to the reporter's account of the fight's conclusion - lacking the language of the new ring, he wrote that the fight was awarded to Harrington 'on account of Rooke being unable to recover in the ten seconds allowed for a man to get up when he has been knocked down'! Later in the same year, though, there were convictions for minor prize-fights, even though the combatants did wear gloves. It was not until boxing was taken under the acceptable wing of the National Sporting Club in the 1890s that its relative freedom from prosecution was established, but by then it was no longer fist-fighting.

The final curtain was effectively drawn across the bareknuckle sport in the late 1880s. A bizarre collection of the aristocratic and the wealthy joined together to form the Pelican Club, whose main aim was the promotion of fist-fighting in their own club premises. Reform of any sort was the last thing that was on the minds of the brash and racy characters who made up the club and its atavistic atmosphere would ring with cries of 'more blood!' if the boxers were tempted to prefer caution and science to violent action. The club signed its own death-warrant by its association with the disgraceful fight between Jem Smith and the Australian Frank Slavin in Bruges in 1889, when a whole crowd of roughs crossed the Channel for the contest, determined to make sure that Smith did not lose (which was exactly what much of the betting was on) and making a fair fight impossible. It was a scene of wholesale disorder, with fists and clubs flying and even knives and revolvers threatening. There was no option but to declare a draw. The brief revival had demonstrated beyond doubt that the days of the old prize-ring were past; even taking contests abroad could no longer guarantee their security or their probity. The Pelican Club closed down and its replacement, the National Sporting Club, was launched under quite different colours - it was middle class and respectable and it mounted highly-controlled contests under strict rules and to an almost unnatural silence during the rounds.

The effective end of pugilism itself came when John L. Sullivan resolved to put his world championship at stake only in a glove-fight under the Queensberry Rules. When he fought James J. Corbett on 7 September 1892 it was in a brightly illuminated arena, before a crowd of 10,000 many of them from the respectable classes and decorating the ringside seats in their formal evening dress. Corbett won. There was a new champion and a different sport.

Appendices

Appendix A

Marquess of Queensberry Rules

1. To be a fair stand-up boxing match in a twenty-four-foot ring, or as near that size as practicable.

2. No wrestling or hugging allowed.

3. The rounds to be of three minutes' duration, and one minute time between rounds.

4. If either man fall, through weakness or otherwise, he must get up unassisted, ten seconds to be allowed him to do so, the other man meanwhile to return to his corner, and when the fallen man is on his legs the round is to be resumed and continued until the three minutes have expired. If one man fails to come to the scratch in the ten seconds allowed, it shall be in the power of the referee to give his award in favour of the other man.

5. A man hanging on the ropes in a helpless state, with his toes off the ground, shall be considered down.

6. No seconds or any other person to be allowed in the ring during the rounds.

7. Should the contest be stopped by any unavoidable interference, the referee to name time and place, as soon as possible, for finishing the contest; so that the match must be won and lost, unless the backers of both men agree to draw the stakes.

8. The gloves to be fair-sized boxing gloves of the best quality, and new.

9. Should a glove burst or come off, it must be replaced to the referee's satisfaction.

10. A man on one knee is considered down, and if struck is entitled to the stakes.

11. No shoes or boots with sprigs allowed.

12. The contest in all other respects to be governed by revised rules of the London Prize-Ring.

Appendix B

National Sporting Club Rules

1. All contests to be decided in a roped ring not less than 14 ft. or more than 20 ft. square.

2. Contestants to box in light boots or shoes (without spikes) or in socks. The gloves to be of a minimum weight of 6 oz. each. Contestants to be medically examined before entering the ring, and to weigh on the day of the contest.

Should bandages be agreed to, the length and material of same to be approved and deposited with Management of the Club at the time of signing articles. The length of the bandage for each or either hand not to exceed 6ft., and width not to exceed 1 in.

3. In all contests the number of rounds shall be specified. No contest shall exceed fifteen rounds, except championships, which shall be limited to twenty rounds. No round shall exceed three minutes in duration. The interval between the rounds shall be one minute.

4. A contestant shall be entitled to the assistance of two seconds, whose names shall be submitted to the Committee for approval. The seconds shall leave the ring when time is called, and shall give no advice or assistance to the contestants during the progress of any round.

5. In all contests a referee and a timekeeper shall be appointed by the Committee. the referee shall award a maximum number of five marks at the end of each round to the better man, and a proportionate number to the other contestant, or, when equal, the maximum number to each.

If a contestant is down, he must get up unassisted within ten seconds; his opponent meanwhile shall retire out of striking distance, and shall not resume boxing until ordered to do so by the referee. A man is to be considered down even when he is on one or both feet, if at the same time any other part of his body is touching the ground, or when in the act of rising.

A contestant failing to continue the contest at the expiration of ten seconds shall not be awarded any marks for that round, and the contest shall then terminate. The referee shall decide all contests in favour of the contestant who obtains the greatest number of marks. If at the conclusion of any round during the contest one of the contestants should attain such a lead on points as to render it an impossibility for his opponent to win or tie, he must then be declared the winner.

Marks shall be awarded for 'attack' - direct, clean hits with the knuckle part of the glove of either hand on any part of the front or sides of the head or body above the belt; 'defence' - guarding, slipping, ducking, or getting away. Where contestants are otherwise equal the majority of marks shall be given to the one that does most of the leading off or who displays the better style.

6. The referee shall have power to disqualify a contestant for any of the following acts: for hitting below the belt, for using the pivot blow, for using the kidney punch, for hitting with the open glove, the inside or butt of the hand, or with the wrist or elbow; for holding, butting, shouldering, intentionally falling without receiving a blow, wrestling or roughing, remaining in a clinch unnecessarily, for not trying, or for any other act which he may deem foul. The referee shall also have power to stop the contest if in his opinion a contestant is outclassed or accidentally disabled.

7. The breaking of any of these rules by a contestant or his seconds shall render such contestant liable to disqualification.

8. A contestant disqualified for any cause whatever shall not be entitled to any prize.

9. The referee shall decide (1) any question not provided for in these rules; (2) the interpretation of any of these rules.

Sources and Bibliography

This section indicates the major sources on which the book is based. Fuller bibliographies are available in, e.g., Paul Magriel, *Bibliography of Boxing: A Chronological Checklist of Books in English published before 1900* (New York, 1948); John Ford, *Prizefighting: The Age of Regency Boximania* (Newton Abbot, 1971); Randy Roberts, *Papa Jack: Jack Johnson and the Era of White Hopes* (New York, 1983).

As suggested in the Introduction, much primary evidence of nineteenth-century popular sport is still relatively unused. This is certainly so with pugilism. There are, for instance, well over 200,000 close-packed columns devoted to the ring in the vast pink pages of *Bell's Life in London and Sporting Chronicle*. All references to major fights after the mid-1820s - that is, after Dowling became editor - owe something to *Bell's* reports, as do important events such as the founding of the Pugilistic Benevolent Association. The rest of the massive bulk of material there could only be sampled, and this must remain the case until there are many more concentrated and limited studies of the sport, or a comprehensive index becomes available. The monthly *Sporting Magazine*, from its beginning in 1792 until it deserted the ring in disgust after 1830, is a more accessible source, in spite of its belated and unreliable indexing. It reported all major fights, and many minor ones, and account has been taken of all the magazine's contributions.

Other journals consulted were *The Times* and its predecessors (frequently), *The Morning Post*, and the *Weekly Dispatch*. Occasionally resort was made to the provincial press, including *Aris's Birmingham Gazette*, *Warwicksire Advertiser*, *Birmingham Journal*, *Worcester Herald*, and *Dorset County Chronicle*, though these tended to follow national reports, and unless a local fighter was involved seldom added much to the standard press sources.

Another important repository of contemporary press reports is Henry Downes Miles' *Pugilistica*, which constitutes the nearest approximation available to a collection of historical documents on the British ring. Its subtitle proclaims it as *The History of British Boxing, containing Lives of the Most Celebrated Pugilists; Full Reports of their Battles from Contemporary Newspapers, with Authentic Portraits, Personal Anecdotes, and Sketches of the Principal Patrons of the Prize Ring, forming a Complete History of the Ring from Fig and Broughton, 1719-40, to the Last Championship Battle between King and Heenan, in December 1863*.

As a history in its own right, Miles' work has many shortcomings. Entirely biographical, it wanders up and down the years. It is coloured by the author's prejudices, particularly his contempt for Pierce Egan, and by his pessimistic view of pugilism in his own day, though there is some justification for both. *Pugilistica* is much less readable and less immediately interesting than, for instance, Fred Henning's *Fights for the Championship* (Licenced Victuallers' Gazette, 1902) which is more extensive than its title would indicate, but is at a further remove from the original sources. Miles' value lies in his open plagiarism, his readiness to use full press reports, usually, from those that have been checked back to the original, with a minimum of editing - unless he happened to be pruning Egan's ornate extravagances. Many of Miles' reports of early fights are virtually identical with those in *Pancratia: or a History of Pugilism* (2nd Edition, London, 1815), published anonymously but almost certainly the work of Bill Oxberry, comic actor, dramatist, theatre manager, tavern landlord and part-time sporting journalist. The J.B. responsible for the introduction to *Pancratia* bears all the hallmarks of Jonathan Badcock who, as *Jon Bee*, produced the *Annals of Sporting and Fancy Gazette* between 1822 and 1828. Captain John Godfrey, *A Treatise upon the Science of Defence* (1747) is the major source for the beginnings of organised pugilism, along with *Recollections of Pugilism and Sketches of the Ring* (1801) by *An Amateur*. As an intriguing apologia, the *Memoirs of the Life of Daniel Mendoza*, ed. Magriel (London, 1951) gives some first-hand insights into the ring in its heyday.

The most prominent pugilistic journalist of the first quarter of the nineteenth century was, of course, Pierce Egan. His *Boxiana* (5 volumes, 1812-29) and *Book of Sports*, a reminiscence, in 1832, are necessary texts, even if they have to be treated with caution to appraise the flights of fancy into which his pre-Dickensian linguistic flourishes frequently led him. He is admirably placed in J.C. Reid, *Bucks and Bruisers: Pierce Egan and Regency England* (London, 1971). B.R.M. Darwin's *John Gully and his Times* (London, 1935) also has interesting material, particularly on Gully's post-prize-fighting career.

For the later history of pugilism Miles had his own eyewitness accounts and those of the remarkable George Vincent Dowling, editor of *Bell's Life* from 1824, who had won early fame as the first man to seize Spencer Perceval's assassin when the Prime Minister was shot in the lobby of the House of Commons. Dowling was one of the most important influences on nineteenth-century popular sport. Personally interested in all the Ring's affairs, he produced many of *Bell's* fight reports himself, published his *Fistiana* in 1840, and continued it annually until his death in 1852, gave influential evidence to parliamentary committees, and was active over many years as sporting organiser, stakeholder, and fight referee.

Other reliable sources for the later bareknuckle days are thin on the ground. Among the more useful is Guy Deghy's well-informed, if somewhat disordered, *Noble and Manly: The History of the National Sporting Club* (London, 1956). More quixotic, and more revealing of attitudes than of facts, is L. Fitz-Bernard, *Fighting Sports* (1921; 1975 edition, Liss, Hampshire). The well-known literary references to boxing belong predominantly to the middle years of the century. Their element of nostalgia prompts a degree of caution in regarding them as reliable sources for other than the excitements of the sport. George Borrow always mixed fact and fantasy, and both he and Thackeray (in, for instance, the Derby Day fight in *Pendennis*) were writing of times some three decades past. The one account with real immediacy is William Hazlitt's superb essay arising from the Neat/Hickman contest - 'The Fight', in the *New Monthly Magazine* of February, 1822.

The recent flowering of boxing history in North America, led by Elliott Gorn's *The Manly Art: Bare-knuckle Prize-fighting in America* (Ithaca, 1986) is replenishing a previously inadequate store which had to rely on Alexander Johnson, *Ten - and Out! The Complete Story of the Prize Ring in America* (3rd edition, New York, 1947), Dale Somers, *The Rise of Sports in New Orleans 1850-1900* (Baton Rouge, 1972) and, more broadly, on J.R. Betts, *America's Sporting Heritage: 1850-1960* (Massachusetts, 1974). Forthcoming works such as Jeffrey Sammons's *Beyond the Ring* and Michael Isenberg's much needed *John L. Sullivan and His America* will doubtless take the American renaissance further. For the Australian Ring, the standard work is now *Lords of the Ring* (Cassell: Australia, 1981) from Peter Gorris. Keith Dunstan's 'The Boxing Passion', in *Sports* (Melbourne, 1975) also proved useful.

It is not possible to list all the material relating to other sports or to the general social background that have contributed, over the years, to this account. Among the contemporary evidence from other sports, the *Racing Calendar*, for instance published annually over the whole period of pugilism's history, provides firm evidence of the interplay of patronage between the racecourse and the Ring. Similar sidelights appear in G.R. Buckley's two volumes of press references, *Fresh Light on Eighteenth-Century Cricket* and *Fresh Light on Pre-Victorian Cricket* (Birmingham, 1935 and 1937). Among the more significant general histories are Harold Perkin, *The Origins of Modern English Society, 1780-1880* (London and Toronto, 1969), Robert W. Malcolmson, *Popular Recreations in English Society 1700-1850* (Cambridge, 1973), James Walvin, *Leisure and Society 1830-1950* (London, 1978), Peter Bailey, *Leisure and Class in Victorian England: Rational Recreation and the Contest for Control* (London, Toronto, and Buffalo, 1978), and Hugh Cunningham, *Leisure in the Industrial Revolution c.1780-c.1880* (London, 1980).

Notes

Abbreviations

The following abbreviations are used in these notes.

Egan Pierce Egan, *Boxiana, or Sketches of Modern Pugilism* (London, 1821)

Ford John Ford, *Prizefighting: the Age of Regency Boximania* (Newton Abbot, 1971)

Henning Fred Henning, *Fights for the Championship* (1902)

Miles Henry Downes Miles, *Pugilistica: the History of British Boxing* (Edinburgh, 1906)

Pancratia Anon. (Bill Oxberry), *Pancratia: or a History of Pugilism* (London, 1811)

Chapter 1: Jack Broughton's Rules

1. Pepys's *Diary*, 5 August 1660.
2. Hylton Cleaver, *A History of Rowing* (London, 1957), 24.
3. See Richard Parkinson (ed.) *The Private Journal and Literary Remains of John Byrom* (Manchester Chetham Society, 1854) I,1, 117.
4. *Pancratia*, 32-4.
5. ibid., 37.
6. Miles, I, 44.
7. There are minor variations of wording in different versions of the rules. This version is from *Pancratia*, 42-3.
8. *Daily Advertiser*, February 1747; in Miles, I, 26.

Chapter 2: Illegal, Immoral and Injurious

1. *Pancratia*, 51-61; Miles, I, 35-6.
2. *Aris's Birmingham Gazette*, 27 August 1787.
3. *Pancratia*, 64, 53.
4. Miles, I, 45-7.
5. ibid., I, 39-40, 51-2.
6. Henning, I, 57.

Chapter 3: A Fashionable Sport

1. *Pancratia*, 71-2; Miles, I, 58.
2. *Pancratia*, 148.
3. ibid., 80-1.

4. *Sporting Magazine*, I, February 1794, 237.
5. ibid., I, March 1793, 369.
6. ibid., III, July 1793, 256.
7. ibid., XLII, March 1821, 283.
8. ibid., II, May 1793, 85.
9. see, e.g., *Daily Advertiser*, 6, 12, 19, 20, 21 and 27 July 1787.
10. *Pancratia*, 76.

Chapter 4: Bristol's Crown and the Geography of Pugilism

1. *Pancratia*, 132.
2. ibid., 116.
3. ibid., 216-7.
4. Miles, I, 170.
5. See above, p.28.
6. Miles, I, 138.

Chapter 5: The Sport and the Law

1 *Pancratia*, 180-1.
2 See p. 36, 50.
3 See above, p. 42.
4 *Pancratia*, 194.
5 *Sporting Magazine*, August 1811, 224-7.
6 ibid., April 1827, 403.

Chapter 6: The Black Challenge and Bill Richmond

1 Miles, I, 289-90.
2 *Pancratia*, 233-4.
3 Miles, I, 246.
4 ibid., I, 90.
5 *Pancratia*, 347-50; Miles, I, 254-5; *Sporting Magazine*, 37, Dec 1810, 97-102, 120-2.
6 *Pancratia*, 364-70.
7 Miles, I, 288.
8 Egan, III, 404.
9 *Sporting Magazine*, 9, February 1822, 246.
10 ibid., 18, June 1826, 187.

Chapter 7: Mr Jackson and Mr Gully

1 Ford, 44 47.
2 ibid., 52.
3 See p. 38.
4 This happended in Turner v. Scroggins, 26 March 1817 (Miles, I, 376).
5 *Sporting Magazine*, 12, July 1823, 192.
6 *Bell's Life in London*, 19 June 1836.
7 See p. 50.
8 Miles, I, 183-9; Henning, I, 310 ff.

9 *Sporting Magazine*, 32, June 1808, 144.
10 Miles, II, 110.
11 ibid., 25, March 1830, 352.
12 *Sporting Magazine*, 9, March 1822, 270.

Chapter 8: The Hollow Crowning

1. *Sporting Magazine*, 5, New Series, December 1819, 127.
2. Miles, II, 388-90.
3. *Sporting Magazine*, 5, New Series, October 1819, 6. The fight is wholly ignored by Henning.
4. ibid., 6, New Series, June 1820, 150.
5. ibid., 5, New Series, June 1819, 103.
6. ibid., 3, New Series, October 1818, 18.
7. Miles, II, 51.
8. Mr Sant; see Miles, II, 43.
9. 'An Observer', in *Sporting Magazine*, 10, New Series, September 1822, 292.
10. Egan, III, 198.
11. *Sporting Magazine*, 1, 2nd Series, July 1830, 191.

Chapter 9: Fists in the Twilight

1 According to Edward Churton, *The Rail Road Book of England* (London, 1851), I, 110.
2 *Sporting Magazine*, 2, April 1793, 57.
3 Egan, III, 583-697.
4 *Sporting Magazine*, 25, December 1829, 95-9.
5 Miles, III, 185.
6 ibid., 59.
7 ibid.
8 *Bell's Life in London*, 30 March 1832.
9 Henning, II, 210.
10 Miles, III, 220.

Chapter 10 The Tale of the Tipton Slasher

1 Mr Hutchinson; see Miles, III, 166.
2 See pp. 101-2.

Chapter 11: To the Provinces and the People

1 *Sporting Magazine*, III, 2nd series, May 1831, 66.
2 House of Lords, *Select Committee on Laws Respecting Gaming* (1844), 89.
3 See p. 38.
4 *Bell's Life in London*, , 29 November 1835.
5 Miles, III, 48.
6 ibid., III, 180.
7 ibid., III, 63.
8 *Sporting Magazine*, I, 2nd series, June 1830, 97.
9 *Bell's Life in London*, 12 December 1834
10 See p. 102.

Chapter 12: One Last Bright Star

1 *Bell's Life in London*, 26 December 1852.
2 ibid., 11 and 25 March 1855.
3 Lord John Manners, *A Plea for National Holy Days*, 2nd edition (London, 1843), 7.

Chapter 13: The First World Sport

1 *Sporting Magazine*, 26, 3rd series, August 1855, 156-8.
2 ibid., 6, January 1796, 197.
3 See pp. 18, 20, 24.
4 *Sporting Magazine*, 25, 2nd series, August 1842, 292.
5 13 June 1867.
6 *Bell's Life in Victoria*, 13 July 1867.
7 *Bell's Life in London*, 5 January 1867.
8 See p. 62-3.
9 *Sporting Magazine*, 25, 2nd series, July 1842, 209.

Chapter 14: The Last Bareknuckle Days

1 Guy Deghy, *Noble and Manly: The History of the National Sporting Club* (London, 1956), 132.
2 *The Times*, 2 September 1867.
3 *Bell's Life in London*, 1 January 1870.
4 *The Times*, 24 March 1877.

Index